Taste of Home's

COOKING FOR ONE OR TWO

BACON-WRAPPED CHICKEN (P. 179)

Taste of Home Books

Editor: Heidi Reuter Lloyd
Food Editor: Janaan Cunningham
Associate Food Editor: Coleen Martin
Cookbook Project and Recipe Editor: Janet Briggs
Art Associates: Lori Arndt, Linda Dzik, Maribeth Greinke, Niki Malmberg
Associate Editors: Julie Schnittka, Jean Steiner, Susan Uphill
Test Kitchen Director: Karen Johnson
Test Kitchen Assistants: Suzanne Kern, Megan Taylor
Food Photography: Rob Hagen, Dan Roberts
Food Stylists: Julie Herzfeldt, Joylyn Jans, Kristin Koepnick
Senior Food Photography Artist: Stephanie Marchese
Food Photography Artist: Julie Ferron
Photo Studio Manager: Anne Schimmel
Graphic Art Associates: Ellen Lloyd, Catherine Fletcher
Chairman and Founder: Roy Reiman
President: Russell Denson

Taste of Home Books
© 2003 Reiman Media Group, Inc.
5400 S. 60th St., Greendale, WI 53129

International Standard Book Number:
0-89821-380-0
Library of Congress Control Number:
2003091380

PICTURED ON FRONT COVER: Greek Chicken Dinner (p. 163), Honey Cashew Green Beans (p. 252) and Frozen Lemon Pie (p. 288).

PICTURED ON BACK COVER: Gingersnap Berry Dessert and Strawberry Truffle Tarts (both recipes on p. 282).

To order additional copies of this book,
write to: *Taste of Home* Books, P.O. Box 908, Greendale, WI 53129. To order with a credit card,
call toll-free 1-800/344-2560 or visit our Web site at **www.reimanpub.com**.

TABLE OF CONTENTS

PAGE 21

PAGE 67

PAGE 271

Taste of Home's
COOKING FOR ONE OR TWO

It's Here! A BIG Cookbook Filled With 506 Small-Size Recipes To Meet Your Needs

IT WAS A BIT of a surprise when we started receiving thank-you notes for publishing recipes for one or two in *Taste of Home*.

It didn't take long for the few notes to become many. Soon after that, a common theme emerged, "Thanks for the great recipes...By the way, have you ever thought of doing a *whole book* of recipes for one or two?"

This cookbook is for all of those people: the empty nesters, the novice cooks trying to master the kitchens in their first apartments, the newlyweds, the senior citizens, and the moms and dads whose families eat in shifts, all wanting different things.

Taste of Home's Cooking for One or Two is filled with 506 tried-and-true recipes that taste delicious and look good, too. It's a collection of the best small-size recipes anywhere.

The majority of recipes come from great cooks across the country who've been serving their specialties to appreciative loved ones for years and were willing to share the recipes. Readers from *Taste of Home, Quick Cooking, Country Woman* and *Light & Tasty* responded to our request to help make this book a reality. We thank them all.

Some of the recipes come from the experienced home economists in our *Taste of Home* Test Kitchen. In fact, these professionals have made and tested *every single dish* in this cookbook to guarantee you'll enjoy tasty results.

Most of the 506 recipes have never before been published. Others are classics from *Taste of Home* and its sister publications that readers have told us are cherished "keepers" they serve time and again.

How the Book Is Organized

Cooking for one or two can be a challenge. The first chapter of this book, Pared-Down Cooking, can help simplify the task.

We offer strategies for meal planning, grocery shopping, setting up your kitchen, downsizing favorite recipes and storing various foods. We also provide sources for small-size bakeware, which can be difficult to locate.

But the best part of this book, truly, is the wide variety of recipes. As you page through, you might find yourself creating a mental list of all the recipes you want to try. You can make roasts, casseroles, cakes and other dishes that are traditionally served in big quantities…all sized just right for one or two.

In general, this book's chapters are organized by course, starting with Breakfast & Brunch and ending with Just Desserts. When we get to main dishes, you'll find chapters arranged by main ingredient: Beef & Ground Beef, Chicken & Turkey, etc.

For those days when you're in a hurry, we offer a whole section of pre-planned menus. This time-saving chapter, Meals for One or Two, begins on page 76. The 20 full menus offer 79 dishes that can be mixed and matched into hundreds of combinations.

At the back of the book are two indexes. The first is a general index, by course, ingredient and cooking method. The general index also includes a listing of all recipes that include nutritional analysis information.

The second index is alphabetical so you can find a favorite recipe again once you've enjoyed it and remember it by name.

Many of the recipes have gorgeous, full-color photos, so you can see what they'll look like before you begin making them. If you weren't hungry when you started looking at this book, things are about to change.

We hope you'll enjoy *Taste of Home's Cooking for One or Two* and the 506 dishes it contains. Thanks for bringing us into your kitchen. Happy small-size cooking. We mean that in a really big way!

PARED-DOWN COOKING

Cooking for one or two is easy
once you know a few basic
guidelines. Turn to this chapter
for help planning and preparing
meals, shopping for groceries,
buying small-size bakeware and
downsizing favorite recipes.

STRAWBERRY TRUFFLE TARTS (P. 282)

PARED-DOWN COOKING BASICS

Cooking for one or two can be a challenge because many recipes make four to six servings or even more. This cookbook offers a variety of choices to create delicious home-cooked meals without lots of leftovers as well as tips to make meal preparation easier.

START AT THE GROCERY STORE

Begin with foods that are the right portion size for 1 or 2 servings. Examples of this are: steaks, chops, chicken pieces, fish fillets and link sausage. Or, select other items that can be divided easily. Separate the amount needed for the current meal. Freeze the remainder in single-serving portions for future meals. Ground meat, shrimp, stew meat, scallops and beef tenderloins fit into this category.

Buy frozen vegetables and fruits in bags so that the amount needed can be easily poured out of the bag. Buy fresh fruit and vegetables by the piece rather than by the bag. Even though the bag might be a better price per unit, it's not a bargain if half the bag spoils before it can be used. Or, buy by the bag and share it with a couple of friends or neighbors.

For small amounts of fresh vegetables, look in the produce section for prepackaged stir-fry vegetable combinations. For example, coleslaw mix makes a good substitute for shredded cabbage. When available, buy the smallest size of canned items. The 3-ounce can of tuna is ideal for a single serving.

PLAN AHEAD

If you're dreaming about a juicy roast, but don't want to buy one because of leftovers, try this. Purchase the smallest roast you can find. Some are available as small as 2 pounds—a pork tenderloin is generally less than a pound. Invite guests over for dinner or plan to use the leftover meat for another meal in a salad, casserole, potpie or sandwich. Also keep a portion for a quick and easy roast dinner later in the week.

SET THE KITCHEN UP RIGHT

Smaller yield recipes require smaller food preparation tools. These appliances are the perfect size for small quantities: mini food processors, toaster ovens, mini coffee makers, countertop grills and electric skillets.

Don't forget about cookware and bakeware. If a saucepan or skillet is too large, too much evaporation could occur, causing sauces to burn and food to dry out. Choose baking dishes that are slightly larger than the volume of the recipe to allow for some bubbling around the edges.

For purchasing information on scaled-down bakeware, see page 10.

ADJUSTING YOUR FAVORITE RECIPES

Select recipes with yields between 4 and 6 servings. Recipes often can be divided proportionally by 2, 3 or 4. Entrees, side dishes, soups, salads, sandwiches, chilis and stews usually lend themselves to proportional downsizing. Desserts and breads can be more challenging.

Recipes that start with small measures of ingredients, such as 1/8 teaspoon, dashes and pinches, can be difficult to adjust for smaller yields. When scaling down seasonings such as herbs, salt, pepper or spices, it's best to round off to the next smallest measure. You can always add more seasonings during cooking or just before serving if needed.

Cooking and baking times may need to be adjusted, too. A good instant-read thermometer is the ideal way to determine the doneness of certain items. Casseroles are usually done when they reach 160°-180°, or they are heated through, bubbly around the edges or browned on top. Some items, such as steaks, chops, fish fillets and chicken pieces, will usually require the same amount of baking time for a small item as a big one, since the thickness of the item, rather than the weight, determines the cooking time.

Here's a handy reference chart for determining the amount of ingredients you'll need.

REDUCING INGREDIENTS		
Original Amount	Half of Recipe	One-Third of Recipe
1 cup	1/2 cup	1/3 cup
3/4 cup	6 tablespoons	1/4 cup
2/3 cup	1/3 cup	3 tablespoons plus 1-1/2 teaspoons*
1/2 cup	1/4 cup	2 tablespoons plus 2 teaspoons
1/3 cup	2 tablespoons plus 2 teaspoons	1 tablespoon plus 2-1/4 teaspoons*
1/4 cup	2 tablespoons	1 tablespoon plus 1 teaspoon
1 tablespoon	1-1/2 teaspoons	1 teaspoon
1 teaspoon	1/2 teaspoon	1/4 teaspoon*
1/2 teaspoon	1/4 teaspoon	1/8 teaspoon*
1/4 teaspoon	1/8 teaspoon	dash*
*amount is rounded down		

HOW WE CALCULATE NUTRITIONAL ANALYSES

When a choice of ingredients is given in a recipe (such as 1/3 cup of sour cream or plain yogurt), the first ingredient listed is generally the one calculated in the Nutritional Analysis.

When a range is given for an ingredient (such as 2 to 3 teaspoons), the first amount was calculated.

Only the amount of marinade that is absorbed during preparation is calculated.

Garnishes listed in recipes are typically included in our calculations.

We sometimes include cooked rice or pasta in the ingredient list but do not calculate it in the Nutritional Analysis. The Nutritional Analysis will state if it was calculated without the rice or pasta.

Cookware and Bakeware That's Sized Right

Scaled-down bakeware and ovenware is being offered by more manufacturers, and as a result, it's becoming easier to find.

For example, Corningware offers Pop-Ins, which are single-serving containers. Pyrex has microwave and oven-safe storage containers in round and rectangular shapes, with sizes starting at 1 cup for round containers. Baker's Secret has a line of minis for single-serving baked goods.

Many of these smaller items can be found in the housewares department of department stores, cookware specialty stores and on the Internet. We've shown a sampling of items that are ideal for the scaled-down recipes in this book.

Here are contacts for specific items, in case you can't find them at a nearby store:

Doughmakers Set of 4 (7-1/2-inch diameter) pizza pans. Available from: www.Metro Kitchen. com, 1726 Taylor Street, Atlanta, GA 30318 1-888/892-9911.

Fox Run 6-1/2-inch pie plates. Available from: www.grandgourmetwi.com, The Grand Gourmet, 18900 W. Bluemound Rd., Brookfield, WI 53045, 1-262/785-5566.

Nordic Ware 6-cup Bundt pan. Available from: www.bundt.com or Nordic Ware, Highway 7 & 100, Minneapolis, MN 55416-2274, 1-800/328-4310.

Wilton 6-inch and springform pans and two-piece single tart pans. Available from: www. wilton.com or Wilton Industries, 2240 W. 75th Street, Woodridge, IL 60517, 1-800/794-5866 (U.S.), 1-800/387-3300 (Canada).

Baker's Advantage Mini Pie Plate. Available from: www.KitchenEtc.com or Kitchen Etc., 32 Industrial Drive, Exeter, NH 03833, 1-800/232-4070 (U.S.), 1-603/773-0020 (Canada).

Calculated Industries KitchenCalc Recipe Scaling Calculator. Available from: www.calculated. com or Calculated Industries, 4840 Hytech Drive, Carson City, NV 89706, 1-800/854-8075.

Two other web sites that carry cookware items which might be of interest are:

www.Cooking.com, 2850 Ocean Park Blvd., Suite 310 Santa Monica, CA 90405, 1-800/663-8810.

www.Cookscorner.com, Cook's Corner, 836 S. Eighth Street, Manitowoc, WI 54220, 1-800/236-2433.

Food Storage Guidelines

Pantry Storage

Check the sell-by or use-by dates on pantry items. Discard items that are past those dates. In the pantry, store opened items tightly closed and place in a cool dry place. Times given in the chart below are for pantry storage of opened items.

Refrigerated Foods

The use-by date on refrigerated items is only for the unopened item. Use the times given in the chart for opened foods. Keep refrigerator temperatures between 34°-40°F. In the refrigerator, store leftovers in covered refrigerator containers or wrap them in plastic wrap or foil. Resealable plastic bags also are great for storage.

Frozen Foods

For the best quality, foods should be frozen in a freezer that can maintain 0°F and is at least two-thirds full.

Cool cooked food quickly before freezing.

Store food in containers that are moisture-proof and vapor-proof, such as foil, freezer bags, freezer wrap and plastic freezer containers. Remove as much air as possible when packaging the food.

Label and date packages before freezing.

Spread out the packages for quicker freezing. Stack them after they are solidly frozen.

Defrost foods in the refrigerator, microwave oven or cold water.

Generally, small items will defrost overnight in the refrigerator. Most items take 1 or 2 days and bulky, large items will take even longer to thaw.

To defrost in a microwave oven, follow the manufacturer's directions.

To defrost in cold water, place food in a water-tight plastic storage bag. Place bag in cold water. Change the water every 30 minutes until the food is thawed.

FOOD STORAGE CHART
The times given are for optimum quality.

Food Item	Opened Item Pantry Storage	Opened Item Refrigerator Temperature 34°-40°	Freezer Temperature 0°
DAIRY			
Butter		1 to 3 months	6 to 9 months
Cheese			
Brie		1 week	6 months
Cottage/ricotta cheese		1 week	not suitable
Cream cheese		2 weeks	not suitable
Cheddar, brick,			
Monterey Jack, Swiss		3 to 4 weeks	6 months
Mozzarella		1 week	6 months
Parmesan/Romano,			
grated		2 months	6 months
Cream			
Ultrapasteurized		1 month	not suitable
Whipping, half-and-half		3 days	2 to 4 months
Eggs			
Whole (in the shell)		4 to 5 weeks	not suitable
Whites, uncooked		2 to 4 days	12 months
Yolks, uncooked		2 to 4 days	12 months

(continued on next page)

FOOD STORAGE CHART

Food Item	Opened Item Pantry Storage	Opened Item Refrigerator Temperature 34°-40°	Freezer Temperature 0°
Milk			
Milk		7 days	3 months
Buttermilk		7 to 14 days	3 months
Evaporated		4 to 5 days	
Sweetened condensed		4 to 5 days	
Margarine		4 to 5 months	12 months
Sour Cream		7 to 21 days	not suitable
Yogurt		7 to 14 days	1 to 2 months
MEATS: Beef, Pork, Lamb			
Fresh			
Chops		3 to 5 days	4 to 6 months
Ground Meat or Stew Meat		1 to 2 days	3 to 4 months
Roasts		3 to 5 days	4 to 12 months
Sausage, fresh		1 to 2 days	1 to 2 months
Steaks		3 to 5 days	6 to 12 months
Leftover cooked meats/			
casseroles		1 to 4 days	2 to 3 months
Process Meats			
Bacon		7 days	1 month
Ham		3 to 5 days	1 to 2 months
Hot Dogs		1 week	1 to 2 months
Luncheon meat		3 to 5 days	1 to 2 months
POULTRY			
Chicken/Turkey			
whole		1 to 2 days	1 year
parts		1 to 2 days	9 months
Leftover, cooked		1 to 4 days	1 to 4 months
FISH & SEAFOOD			
Fillets/Steaks			
Lean fish (cod, sole, halibut,			
orange roughy, flounder)		1 to 2 days	1 year
Fatty fish (catfish, perch,			
salmon, whitefish)		1 to 2 days	2 to 3 months
Scallops/shrimp			
uncooked		1 to 2 days	3 to 6 months
cooked		3 to 4 days	3 months
Leftover, cooked seafood		3 to 4 days	3 to 6 months
FRUITS			
Apples, fresh		1 to 3 weeks	
Berries, fresh		1 to 2 days	12 months
Citrus fruits, fresh		3 to 5 days	not suitable
Cherries, fresh		1 to 2 days	12 months
Juice concentrates			
frozen			12 months
reconstituted		6 days	
Melons, fresh		1 week	not suitable
Peaches, fresh		3 to 5 days	12 months
Pears, fresh		3 to 5 days	12 months
VEGETABLES			
Asparagus		3 to 4 days	8 to 12 months
Broccoli		3 to 5 days	8 to 12 months
Carrots		1 to 2 weeks	8 to 12 months

FOOD STORAGE CHART

Food Item	Opened Item Pantry Storage	Opened Item Refrigerator Temperature 34°-40°	Freezer Temperature 0°
Cauliflower		3 to 5 days	8 to 12 months
Celery		1 to 2 weeks	not suitable
Cucumbers		3 to 5 days	not suitable
Mushrooms		2 to 3 days	not suitable
Onions			
Yellow, red	2 to 3 weeks		
Green		1 to 2 weeks	
Peppers		3 to 5 days	8 to 12 months
Potatoes	1 to 2 months	not suitable	not suitable
Salad Greens			
Head lettuce		5 to 7 days	not suitable
Loose		1 to 2 days	not suitable
Spinach		3 to 5 days	not suitable
Tomatoes	until ripened	2 to 3 days	not suitable
Vegetables, other fresh		1 to 2 days	8 to 12 months
STAPLES			
Baking Powder	18 months		
Baking Soda	18 months		
Canned Goods			
Fish & seafood		2 days	
Fruit		1 week	
Pasta sauces		5 days	
Vegetables		2 to 3 days	
Cereal			
Cook before eating	6 months		
Ready to eat	2 to 3 months		
Cornmeal	12 months		
Cornstarch	18 months		
Flour			
all-purpose	15 months		
whole wheat		6 months	
Herbs/Spices			
herbs	6 months		
ground spices	6 months		
whole spices	1 to 2 years		
Jams & Jelly		12 months	
Ketchup/Chili Sauce		4 to 6 months	
Mayonnaise		2 months	
Mustard		6 to 12 months	
Nuts	3 to 6 months	3 to 6 months	6 to 12 months
Oils			
canola, corn oils	6 months		
olive oil	4 months		
Pies			
custard		2 to 3 days	not suitable
fruit, unbaked			8 months
fruit, baked		4 to 5 days	1 to 2 months
pumpkin		4 to 5 days	2 months
Rice			
brown	1 month	6 months	
white	2 years		
Salad Dressings		3 months	
Shortening	8 months		
Soy Sauce		12 months	
Sugar			
Brown	4 months		
Granulated	2 years		
Worcestershire sauce	12 months		

BREAKFAST & BRUNCH

Get your day off to a great start with the 28 delicious rise-and-shine recipes in this chapter. Choices range from wonderful waffles and omelets to satisfying sandwiches and casseroles.

BACON BREAKFAST SANDWICHES (P. 30)

CRESCENT BRUNCH BAKE (P. 16)
VEGGIE CHEESE OMELET (P. 16)

VEGGIE CHEESE OMELET

(Pictured on page 15)

One stovetop pan and measuring utensils are all you need to make this delicious dish.
The seasonings are heated into the omelet itself to increase the flavor of the filling.
It's a great breakfast or evening meal.
—Jan Collier, Lubbock, Texas

1/4 cup egg substitute
2 tablespoons shredded Parmesan cheese, *divided*
1/8 teaspoon dried oregano
Dash garlic powder and pepper
1/4 cup sliced zucchini
2 tablespoons diced sweet red pepper
1 bacon strip, cooked and crumbled
1/3 cup shredded cheddar cheese

In a bowl, combine egg substitute, 1 table-spoon Parmesan cheese and seasonings. Coat an 8-in. nonstick skillet with nonstick cooking spray and place over medium heat. Pour egg mixture into skillet.

As egg sets, lift edges, letting uncooked portion flow underneath. When the eggs are set, layer zucchini, red pepper, bacon and cheddar cheese on one side; fold omelet in half. Sprinkle top with remaining Parmesan cheese. Remove from the heat; cover and let stand for 3-4 minutes or until cheese is melted. **Yield:** 1 serving.

Nutritional Analysis: One serving (prepared with reduced-fat cheddar cheese) equals 229 calories, 14 g fat (8 g saturated fat), 40 mg cholesterol, 414 mg sodium, 5 g carbohydrate, 1 g fiber, 22 g protein. **Diabetic Exchanges:** 3 lean meat, 1 vegetable, 1 fat.

CRESCENT BRUNCH BAKE

(Pictured on page 15)

My mother used to make this on holiday mornings. It was always a big hit
with our overnight guests.
—Aaron Matthews, Montreat, North Carolina

1/4 pound bulk pork sausage
1 tube (4 ounces) refrigerated crescent rolls
2/3 cup shredded cheddar cheese
2 eggs, lightly beaten
1/4 cup milk
Salt and pepper to taste

Crumble sausage into a skillet; cook over medium heat until no longer pink. Drain. Unroll crescent dough into one long rectangle; seal seams and perforations. Press dough onto the bottom and up the sides of a greased shallow 3-cup baking dish. Trim dough even with edge of dish. Fill with sausage and cheese. In a bowl, combine the eggs, milk, salt and pepper. Pour over cheese. Bake, uncovered, at 425° for 16-20 minutes or until a knife comes out clean. **Yield:** 2 servings.

ORANGE OATMEAL

(Pictured at right)

I like to make this for breakfast because it's quick yet out of the ordinary. The orange flavor adds a little something extra to a weekday breakfast.
—Bernice Haack, Milwaukee, Wisconsin

   1 **cup water**
3/4 **cup orange juice**
1/8 **teaspoon salt**
   1 **cup quick-cooking oats**
1/4 **teaspoon grated orange peel**
   1 **to 2 tablespoons brown sugar**

In a saucepan, bring the water, orange juice and salt to a boil. Stir in oats and cook for 1 minute or until oatmeal reaches desired consistency. Stir in orange peel. Serve with brown sugar. **Yield:** 2 servings.
  Nutritional Analysis: One serving (prepared with 1 tablespoon brown sugar) equals 222 calories, 3 g fat (trace saturated fat), 0 cholesterol, 151 mg sodium, 43 g carbohydrate, 4 g fiber, 7 g protein. **Diabetic Exchanges:** 2 starch, 1 fruit.

EGGS DELMONICO

These creamed eggs on toast get their rich, comforting flavor from a can of cream of mushroom soup mixed with melted cheddar cheese. What a nice way to get the day going!
—Edie Farm, Farmington, New Mexico

   1 **can (10-3/4 ounces) condensed cream of mushroom *or* cream of chicken soup, undiluted**
1/2 **cup shredded cheddar cheese**
   3 **hard-cooked eggs, sliced**
   1 **tablespoon finely chopped pimientos**
Toast *or* English muffins, split and toasted
Paprika *or* minced fresh parsley

In a saucepan, heat soup over medium heat until hot and bubbly. Reduce heat; stir in cheese. Cook and stir until cheese is melted. Fold in eggs and pimientos; cook until heated through. Serve over toast or English muffins. Garnish with paprika or parsley. **Yield:** 2 servings.

BISCUITS AND SAUSAGE GRAVY

(Pictured at left)

This is an old Southern recipe that I've adapted. Maybe you'd like to try it and take a quick "trip" to the South.
—*Sue Baker, Jonesboro, Arkansas*

```
1/4  pound bulk pork sausage
  2  tablespoons butter or margarine
  2 to 3 tablespoons all-purpose flour
1/4  teaspoon salt
1/8  teaspoon pepper
1-1/4 to 1-1/3 cups milk
Warm biscuits
```

In a skillet, cook the sausage over medium heat until no longer pink; drain if necessary. Add butter; heat until melted. Stir in the flour, salt and pepper until blended. Gradually add the milk, stirring constantly. Bring to a boil; cook and stir for 2 minutes or until thickened. Serve over biscuits. **Yield:** 2 servings.

MY HUSBAND'S FAVORITE OMELET

My husband asks me to serve this super-easy omelet at least once a week. As you can imagine, during our more than 40 years of marriage I've made this dish too many times to count!
—*Mary Bitterman, Willow Street, Pennsylvania*

```
  3  eggs
1/2  cup milk
  3  tablespoons finely chopped onion
  3  tablespoons finely chopped celery
  3  tablespoons finely chopped broccoli
  2  tablespoons chopped carrot
  2  tablespoons chopped pimientos
  3  bacon strips, cooked and crumbled
1/2  teaspoon salt
1/4  teaspoon pepper
  1  tablespoon butter or margarine
  4  thin slices process American cheese
```

Beat eggs with milk just until combined. Stir in the vegetables, bacon, salt and pepper. In a medium skillet, melt butter over medium heat; add egg mixture. As eggs set, lift edges, letting uncooked portion flow underneath. When eggs are set, transfer to a warm platter and top with cheese. **Yield:** 1-2 servings.

BLUEBERRY SAUCE

Orange juice, spices and almond extract add spark to this breakfast sauce. You can make it even when blueberries aren't in season, since it calls for blueberry spreadable fruit.
It goes great with French toast, crepes, pancakes or waffles.
—Jean Ficociello, Valley City, Ohio

1 teaspoon cornstarch
Dash ground cloves and cinnamon
2 tablespoons orange juice
1/2 cup 100% blueberry spreadable fruit
1/4 cup butter *or* margarine
1-1/2 teaspoons lemon juice
1/8 teaspoon almond extract

In a saucepan, combine the cornstarch, cloves and cinnamon. Stir in the orange juice until smooth. Add the remaining ingredients. Bring to a boil, stirring constantly. Cook for 1-2 minutes or until a syrup consistency. **Yield:** 3/4 cup.

HAM 'N' EGG POCKETS

(Pictured below)

Our Taste of Home Test Kitchen created this yummy breakfast sandwich using a tube of convenient crescent rolls. One bite will show you why the classic combination of ham and cheese has stood the test of time.

1 egg
2 teaspoons milk
2 teaspoons butter *or* margarine
1 ounce thinly sliced deli ham, chopped
2 tablespoons shredded cheddar cheese
1 tube (4 ounces) refrigerated crescent rolls

In a bowl, combine egg and milk. Melt butter in a small skillet over medium heat. Add egg mixture; cook and stir until completely set. Remove from the heat. Fold in the ham and cheese.

Separate crescent dough into two rectangles. Seal perforations; spoon half of the filling down the center of each rectangle. Fold in ends and sides; pinch to seal. Bake at 375° for 10-14 minutes or until golden brown. **Yield:** 2 servings.

RUSTIC QUICHES

(Pictured at right)

*The first time I made this recipe, I liked it so much that I made another one
the next night. I enjoy it for dinner as well as breakfast.*
—Kari Caven, Post Falls, Idaho

1/2 cup plus 2 tablespoons all-purpose
    flour
1/4 teaspoon salt
  5 tablespoons plus 1-1/2 teaspoons
    shortening
  2 to 3 tablespoons cold water
1/4 cup sliced fresh mushrooms
1-1/2 teaspoons butter *or* margarine
1/3 cup diced fully cooked ham
1/2 cup shredded cheddar cheese
  1 egg, lightly beaten
1/2 cup half-and-half cream

In a bowl, combine flour and salt; cut in the shortening until crumbly. Gradually add water, tossing with a fork until a ball forms. Roll out pastry to fit two 4-1/2-in. tart pans with removable bottoms. Transfer pastry to pans. Trim pastry to 1/2 in. above top of pans; flute edges above edge of pans. Prick bottom and sides of pastry with a fork. Line shell with a double thickness of heavy-duty foil. Bake at 450° for 8 minutes. Remove foil; bake 4-6 minutes longer or until light golden brown. Reduce heat to 375°.

Meanwhile, in a skillet, saute mushrooms in butter until tender. Remove from the heat; add the ham and cheese. Spoon into tart shells. Combine egg and cream. Pour over mushroom mixture. Bake at 375° for 20-25 minutes or until a knife inserted in the center comes out clean. Let stand for 5 minutes before serving. **Yield:** 2 servings.

HUEVOS RANCHEROS

(Pictured at right)

*I started making these for my mom one year when I was home from college.
They're still one of her favorites when I visit. My son likes them, too.*
—Liane Davenport, Greensboro, North Carolina

1 tablespoon butter *or* margarine
4 eggs, lightly beaten
1 cup (4 ounces) shredded cheddar
  cheese
1 small tomato, seeded and chopped
  (about 1/2 cup)
1/4 cup picante sauce
2 flour tortillas (8 inches)
3 tablespoons sour cream
Additional picante sauce

In a skillet, melt butter over medium heat. Add eggs; cook and stir until eggs are completely set. In a bowl, combine the scrambled eggs, cheese, tomato and picante sauce.

Spray one side of 1 tortilla with nonstick cooking spray. Place tortilla greased side down on a griddle. Spoon half the egg mixture on half of the tortilla. Fold over and cook over low for 1-2 minutes on each side or until cheese is melted and tortilla is golden brown. Repeat with remaining tortilla and egg mixture. Cut into wedges and serve with sour cream and additional picante sauce. **Yield:** 2 servings.

RUSTIC QUICHES
HUEVOS RANCHEROS

CINNAMON-APPLE PUFF PASTRY SHELLS

What a wonderful way to get your fruit in the morning!
These apple-stuffed shells come from the Taste of Home Test Kitchen.

2 frozen puff pastry shells
2 medium tart apples, peeled and sliced
2/3 cup plus 1 tablespoon apple juice, divided
3/8 teaspoon ground cinnamon
2 tablespoons brown sugar
1 teaspoon cornstarch
1 tablespoon finely chopped walnuts

Bake pastry shells according to package directions. In a saucepan, combine the apples, 2/3 cup apple juice and cinnamon. Bring to a boil. Reduce heat; simmer, uncovered, until apples are tender. Stir in brown sugar. Combine cornstarch and remaining juice until smooth. Stir into apples. Bring to a boil; cook and stir for 2 minutes or until thickened. Stir in walnuts. Split pastry shells; spoon apple mixture into pastry shells. **Yield:** 2 servings.

WAFFLES FROM SCRATCH

(Pictured at right)

On Saturdays when I was growing up, my mom and I always went shopping, but before we left, she made my favorite lunch, home-made waffles. They were about 8 inches around and prepared in a grill set on top of the stove. Oh, they were so delicious!
—Florence Dean, Towson, Maryland

1-1/2 cups all-purpose flour
1 teaspoon baking powder
1/2 teaspoon salt
2 eggs, *separated*
1 cup milk
1/4 cup butter *or* margarine, melted
Confectioners' sugar and fresh fruit *or* maple syrup

In a bowl, combine the flour, baking powder and salt. Combine the egg yolks, milk and butter; stir into dry ingredients just until moistened. In a small mixing bowl, beat egg whites on medium speed until soft peaks form; gently fold into batter.

Bake in a preheated waffle iron according to manufacturer's directions until golden brown. Top with confectioners' sugar and fruit or serve with syrup. **Yield:** 4 waffles (about 6 inches).

Ham 'n' Egg Breakfast Wrap

(Pictured at right)

We are chicken farmers, so we always have lots of eggs to use up. I came up with this recipe for something different that can be served for breakfast or dinner.
—Kathryn Martin, Quarryville, Pennsylvania

1-1/2 teaspoons butter *or* margarine
1 egg, lightly beaten
2 ounces thinly sliced deli ham, chopped
1 tablespoon chopped green pepper
1 tablespoon chopped onion
1 tablespoon salsa
1 tablespoon sour cream
1 flour tortilla (8 inches), warmed
2 tablespoons shredded cheddar cheese

In a small skillet, melt butter. Add egg; cook and stir over medium heat until completely set. Add the ham, green pepper, onion and salsa; cook until heated through. Spread sour cream over tortilla. Spoon filling over sour cream and sprinkle with cheese. Fold ends and sides over filling and roll up. **Yield:** 1 serving.

TIMELY TIP

Use frozen chopped onions when a recipes calls for a small amount of onion, such as 1 or 2 tablespoons. It saves time and eliminates any leftover onion.

Spiced Date Oatmeal

You can prepare this hearty oatmeal in a hurry. And if you don't have dates available, try substituting raisins. Everyone will love this filling dish.
—Patricia Kaliska, Phillips, Wisconsin

2 cups apple juice
1 cup quick-cooking oats
1/2 cup chopped dates
1/4 teaspoon ground cinnamon
Dash ground nutmeg
Milk
Coconut, optional

In a saucepan, bring apple juice to a boil. Stir in oats; cook 1 minute. Remove from the heat; stir in the dates, cinnamon and nutmeg. Cover and let stand for 5 minutes. Serve with milk and sprinkle with coconut if desired. **Yield:** 2 servings.

BREAKFAST SAUSAGE FRIED RICE

*This is my husband Kevin's favorite recipe. He likes to make it in the morning
for the two of us. It has nice flavor and really fills you up.*
—Tami Thomas, Palmdale, California

1/4 pound bulk pork sausage
1 egg, lightly beaten
3/4 cup cold cooked long grain rice
4 teaspoons soy sauce
1/4 teaspoon minced garlic
Pepper to taste

Crumble sausage into a skillet; cook over medium heat until no longer pink. Remove with a slotted spoon and set aside. In same skillet; cook and stir egg over medium heat until completely set. Stir in the rice, sausage, soy sauce, garlic and pepper. Cook until heated through. **Yield:** 2 servings.

Nutritional Analysis: One serving (prepared with turkey sausage, 1/4 cup egg substitute and reduced-sodium soy sauce) equals 232 calories, 8 g fat (3 g saturated fat), 137 mg cholesterol, 787 mg sodium, 23 g carbohydrate, trace fiber, 15 g protein. **Diabetic Exchanges:** 2 lean meat, 1-1/2 starch.

TIMELY TIP
*Use jarred minced garlic when a recipes calls for a small amount of garlic,
such as 1/4 teaspoon.*

VANILLA FRENCH TOAST

*We discovered this recipe in Mexico. We couldn't figure out what made this French toast so
delicious until we learned the secret was vanilla—one of Mexico's most popular flavorings. Since
then, we've added a touch of vanilla to our waffle and pancake recipes. It makes them all very tasty.*
—Joe and Bobbi Schott, Castroville, Texas

2 eggs
1/2 cup milk
1 tablespoon sugar
1 teaspoon vanilla extract
Pinch salt
6 slices day-old bread
Maple syrup *or* cinnamon-sugar

In a bowl, beat eggs; add the milk, sugar, vanilla and salt. Soak bread for 30 seconds on each side. Cook on a greased hot griddle until golden brown on both sides. Serve with maple syrup or cinnamon-sugar. **Yield:** 2 servings.

CINNAMON PANCAKES

My mom made these pancakes for me when I was growing up, and now I make them for my children. My daughter likes them so much, she says "no" to any other kind.
—Jeanne Silva, Owasso, Oklahoma

1/2 cup plus 2 tablespoons all-purpose
    flour
  2 tablespoons sugar
  1 teaspoon baking powder
1/2 teaspoon ground cinnamon
1/4 teaspoon salt
  1 egg
1/2 cup milk
  1 tablespoon vegetable oil
3/4 teaspoon vanilla extract
Maple syrup

In a bowl, combine the flour, sugar, baking powder, cinnamon and salt. In another bowl, combine the egg, milk, oil and vanilla. Stir into dry ingredients just until combined. In a lightly greased electric skillet, drop batter by 1/4 cupfuls; press lightly to flatten. Fry until golden brown, about 2 minutes on each side. Serve with syrup. **Yield:** 2 servings.

GARLIC CHEESE GRITS

(Pictured at right)

My sorority chapter gathers for a family social every November, and it's a tradition that I bring these grits. The recipe is great for breakfast but also as a side dish for other meals. Here, it's scaled down to serve two.
—Rose Tuttle, Oviedo, Florida

  1 cup water
1/4 cup quick-cooking grits
1/2 cup cubed process cheese
    (Velveeta)
1/4 teaspoon garlic powder
1/4 cup cornflakes, coarsely crushed
  1 to 1-1/2 teaspoons butter *or*
    margarine, melted

In a saucepan, bring water to a boil. Slowly stir in grits. Reduce heat; cook and stir for 4-5 minutes or until thickened. Add cheese and garlic powder; stir until cheese is melted. Pour into a greased 2-cup baking dish.

In a bowl, combine cornflakes and butter; sprinkle over grits. Bake, uncovered, at 350° for 10-15 minutes or until firm and top is lightly toasted. **Yield:** 2 servings.

Nutritional Analysis: One 3/4-cup serving (prepared with reduced-fat process cheese and 1 teaspoon butter) equals 170 calories, 5 g fat (3 g saturated fat), 17 mg cholesterol, 499 mg sodium, 23 g carbohydrate, trace fiber, 8 g protein. **Diabetic Exchanges:** 1-1/2 starch, 1 fat.

CHICKEN SAUSAGE PATTIES

(Pictured at right)

Tart grated apples give these patties a special flavor. To save time in the morning, I make them up the night before I cook and serve them. They're a healthy, welcome addition to Sunday brunch.
—Mary Webb, Longwood, Florida

2 tablespoons chopped onion
3/4 teaspoon plus 2 teaspoons olive *or* canola oil, *divided*
1/2 cup grated peeled tart apple
1 tablespoon minced fresh sage *or* 3/4 teaspoon rubbed sage
1/4 teaspoon salt
1/8 teaspoon pepper
Dash ground cinnamon
1/4 pound ground chicken *or* turkey

In a nonstick skillet, saute onion in 3/4 teaspoon oil until crisp-tender. Add apple; cook until tender, about 5 minutes. Let stand until cool enough to handle. Stir in seasonings. Crumble chicken over apple mixture and mix well. Shape into four 1/2-in.-thick patties.

In a skillet, cook patties in remaining oil over medium heat or until juices run clear. **Yield:** 2 servings.

Nutritional Analysis: One serving (prepared with ground chicken breast) equals 137 calories, 7 g fat (1 g saturated fat), 33 mg cholesterol, 330 mg sodium, 5 g carbohydrate, 1 g fiber, 13 g protein. **Diabetic Exchanges:** 2 lean meat, 1/2 fruit.

NUTTY BUTTERMILK OAT PANCAKES

(Pictured at right)

Friends served these luscious pancakes for breakfast when we were visiting years ago. I begged for the recipe and have been making and enjoying them ever since. They mix up in a snap.
—Joan Hallford, North Richland Hills, Texas

1 cup quick-cooking oats
1-1/4 cups buttermilk
1/2 cup all-purpose flour
1 tablespoon sugar
1 teaspoon baking powder
1/2 teaspoon salt
1/4 teaspoon baking powder
2 tablespoons plus 1-1/2 teaspoons vegetable oil
1 egg, lightly beaten
1/3 cup finely chopped pecans

In a bowl, combine oats and buttermilk; let stand for 5 minutes. In another bowl, combine the flour, sugar, baking powder, salt and baking soda; stir into oat mixture with oil and egg. Fold in pecans. Let stand for 10 minutes. Pour batter by 1/4 cupful onto greased hot griddle. Turn when bubbles form on top; cook until the second side is golden brown. **Yield:** 8 pancakes.

CHICKEN SAUSAGE PATTIES
ORANGE SAUCE (P. 29)
NUTTY BUTTERMILK OAT PANCAKES

CORNED BEEF HASH

(Pictured at left)

This is one of my favorite dishes for brunch. It's hearty and has such great homemade taste. I sometimes serve it with horseradish sauce for a little extra kick.
—Carrie Chaplin, Clendenin, West Virginia

 2 tablespoons vegetable oil
 1 cup diced fully cooked corned beef
 1 cup diced cooked potato
1/4 cup chopped onion
1/4 teaspoon salt
1/8 teaspoon pepper

In a small heavy skillet, heat oil over medium-high heat. Stir in the remaining ingredients. Flatten mixture with a metal spatula. Cover and cook until bottom of potato mixture is crisp. Turn and brown the other side. **Yield:** 2 servings.

CORN BREAD BREAKFAST CASSEROLE

This tasty baked dish starts with a tube of corn bread twists purchased from the refrigerated section of a grocery store. Our Test Kitchen home economists created this hearty casserole.

 1 tube (11-1/2 ounces) refrigerated
     corn bread twists*
1/4 pound bulk pork sausage
 3 eggs
 2 tablespoons half-and-half cream
1/8 teaspoon pepper
Dash salt, optional
1/2 cup Mexican cheese blend *or*
     cheddar cheese
 2 tablespoons chopped green chilies

Unroll and separate corn bread dough along perforations into 16 pieces. Using 10 or 11 pieces, line the bottom and sides of an ungreased shallow 3-cup baking dish. Flatten and press dough pieces together to seal perforations. Bake at 375° for 11-14 minutes or until golden brown.

Meanwhile, crumble sausage into a skillet; cook over medium heat until no longer pink. Drain well and set aside. In a bowl, combine the eggs, cream, pepper and salt if desired. In the same skillet, cook and stir eggs over medium heat until completely set. In a bowl, combine the sausage, scrambled eggs, cheese and chilies. Spoon into prebaked crust. Top with remaining dough. Flatten and press together to cover top; seal edges. Bake 18-22 minutes longer or until top is deep golden brown. Serve immediately. **Yield:** 2 servings.

*Editor's Note: This recipe was tested with Pillsbury refrigerated corn bread twists.

ORANGE SAUCE

(Pictured on page 27)

The cheery color and pleasing flavor of this sauce will help wake you up in the morning.
It's tasty over homemade pancakes or waffles. I find it a refreshing alternative to maple syrup.
—Cloris Wilkison, Kokomo, Indiana

2 tablespoons sugar
1/2 teaspoon cornstarch
1/8 teaspoon grated orange peel
1/3 cup orange juice
1 teaspoon butter *or* margarine

In a small saucepan, combine the sugar, cornstarch and orange peel. Stir in orange juice until smooth. Bring to a boil; cook and stir for 1-2 minutes or until thickened to a syrup consistency. Remove from the heat; whisk in butter. **Yield:** 1/3 cup.

VEGETABLE SCRAMBLED EGGS

(Pictured below)

I like to have friends and family over for a special Sunday brunch,
especially when there's a "big game" on television.
These colorful eggs go perfectly with sausage, toasted English muffins and fresh fruit.
—Marilyn Ipson, Rogers, Arkansas

4 eggs
1/2 cup chopped green pepper
1/4 cup milk
1/4 cup sliced green onions
1/4 to 1/2 teaspoon salt
1/8 teaspoon pepper
Small tomato, chopped and seeded

In a small bowl, beat eggs. Add the green pepper, milk, onions, salt and pepper. Pour into a lightly greased skillet. Cook and stir over medium heat until eggs are nearly set. Add the tomato; cook and stir until heated through. **Yield:** 2 servings.
Nutritional Analysis: One serving (prepared with egg substitute, fat-free milk and 1/4 teaspoon salt) equals 96 calories, trace fat (trace saturated fat), 1 mg cholesterol, 567 mg sodium, 9 g carbohydrate, 2 g fiber, 14 g protein. **Diabetic Exchanges:** 2 vegetables, 1 lean meat.

BACON BREAKFAST SANDWICHES

(Pictured on page 14)

This recipe is a standby when I need to make breakfast in a snap. Our children eat these sandwiches eagerly and agree they're better than any fast-food variety.
—Rose Carol Brown, Park Forest, Illinois

1 tablespoon butter *or* margarine
4 eggs
2 tablespoons snipped chives *or* green onion tops
1 tablespoon water
1/4 teaspoon salt
Dash pepper
2 English muffins, split and toasted
8 bacon strips, cooked and drained
4 slices tomato
4 slices American cheese
Additional chives, optional

Melt butter in a skillet. Beat the eggs, chives, water, salt and pepper; pour into skillet. Cook and stir gently until eggs are set. Top each muffin half with the eggs, bacon, tomato and cheese. Broil for 1-2 minutes or until cheese is melted. Garnish with chives if desired. **Yield:** 2 servings.

BANANA MILK DRINK

(Pictured at right)

When money was short and times were tough, my mother still made this treat for us. We thought it was happiness in a glass. I recall running home from school, hoping to find this delicious drink ready for me. I made it often for my own children, and I still mix it up today...but now I like to call it "nostalgia in a glass".
—Jeanne Brown, Buffalo, New York

1 large ripe banana
1 cup milk
1-1/2 to 2 teaspoons sugar
1/2 teaspoon vanilla extract
Dash ground cinnamon, optional

Place the first four ingredients in a blender; cover and process until smooth. Pour into glasses; sprinkle with cinnamon if desired. Serve immediately. **Yield:** 2 servings.
Nutritional Analysis: One serving (prepared with fat-free milk and 1-1/2 teaspoons sugar) equals 120 calories, trace fat (trace saturated fat), 3 mg cholesterol, 66 mg sodium, 26 g carbohydrate, 2 g fiber, 5 g protein. **Diabetic Exchanges:** 1-1/2 fruit, 1/2 fat-free milk.

PUFFY APPLE OMELET

(Pictured at right)

*With all the eggs our chickens produce,
I could make this omelet every day!
I guess I consider it to be mostly a festive dish,
but you could fix it anytime,
including for a light supper.*
—Melissa Davenport, Campbell, Minnesota

  3 tablespoons all-purpose flour
1/4 teaspoon baking powder
1/8 teaspoon salt, optional
  2 eggs, *separated*
  3 tablespoons milk
  3 tablespoons sugar
  1 tablespoon lemon juice
TOPPING:
  1 large tart apple, thinly sliced
  1 teaspoon sugar
1/4 teaspoon ground cinnamon

In a small bowl, combine flour, baking powder and salt if desired; mix well. Add egg yolks and milk; mix well and set aside. In a small mixing bowl, beat egg whites on medium speed until soft peaks form. Gradually add sugar, 1 tablespoon at a time, beating on high until stiff peaks form. Fold into yolk mixture. Fold in lemon juice.

Pour into a greased 1-1/2-qt. shallow baking dish. Arrange apple slices on top. Combine sugar and cinnamon; sprinkle over top. Bake, uncovered, at 375° for 18- 20 minutes or until a knife inserted near the center comes out clean. Serve immediately. **Yield:** 2 servings.

Nutritional Analysis: One serving (prepared with fat-free milk and without salt) equals 272 calories, 6 g fat (2 g saturated fat), 213 mg cholesterol, 105 mg sodium, 49 g carbohydrate, 3 g fiber, 9 g protein. **Diabetic Exchanges:** 2 fruit, 1 starch, 1 lean meat, 1/2 fat.

CINNAMON-HONEY GRAPEFRUIT

Naturally delicious grapefruit gains even more great flavor in this recipe. I like to prepare this as a light breakfast. But it also makes an appealing addition to your morning meal.
—Mrs. Carson Sadler, Souris, Manitoba

  1 medium grapefruit, halved
  2 teaspoons honey
Dash ground cinnamon

Loosen grapefruit sections. Place grapefruit halves cut side up in an ovenproof pan. Drizzle each grapefruit half with 1 teaspoon honey; sprinkle with cinnamon. Broil 2-3 minutes or until bubbly. Serve warm. **Yield:** 2 servings.

APPETIZERS
& BEVERAGES

For a hearty start to a meal or a midday snack, turn to the 24 mouth-watering appetizers and beverages featured in this chapter. Choices range from palate-pleasing pinwheels to delicious dips and drinks.

GUACAMOLE DIP (P. 47)

HONEY SOY WINGS (P. 34)
SPANAKOPITA TARTS (P. 34)

HONEY SOY WINGS

(Pictured on page 33)

*I'm not sure where I found this recipe, but everyone who tries it agrees it's a
great change of pace from traditional buffalo wings.*
—Meredith Sayre, Monaca, Pennsylvania

6 whole chicken wings
1/4 cup picante sauce
3 tablespoons honey
1 tablespoon Dijon mustard
1 tablespoon vegetable oil
1 tablespoon soy sauce
3/4 teaspoon ground ginger
1/4 teaspoon grated orange peel
1/8 teaspoon hot pepper sauce,
    optional
Celery sticks and blue cheese salad
    dressing, optional

Cut chicken wings into three sections; discard wing tips. In a large resealable plastic bag, combine the picante sauce, honey, mustard, oil, soy sauce, ginger, peel and hot pepper sauce if desired; add wings. Seal bag and turn to coat; refrigerate for 8 hours or overnight.

Drain and discard marinade. Place wings on a foil-lined 15-in. x 10-in. x 1-in. baking pan. Bake, uncovered, at 400° for 15 minutes; turn wings. Bake 18-22 minutes longer, turning every 10 minutes or until chicken juices run clear. Serve with celery sticks and blue cheese salad dressing if desired. **Yield:** 2 servings.

SPANAKOPITA TARTS

(Pictured on page 33)

*A traditional Greek spinach and feta cheese pie is downsized to an appetizer in this handy recipe.
The tarts start with purchased phyllo dough, so they're not only delicious, they're easy, too.*
—Sarah Briggs, Greenfield, Wisconsin

3 tablespoons thinly sliced green
    onions
1-1/2 teaspoons olive *or* vegetable oil
1-1/2 cups torn fresh spinach leaves
1/2 cup crumbled feta cheese
1 to 2 teaspoons dill weed
1 tablespoon minced fresh parsley
7 sheets phyllo dough (about 14
    inch x 9 inch)
3 tablespoons butter *or* margarine,
    melted

In a small skillet, cook onions in oil until tender. Stir in spinach; cook and stir for 2 minutes longer. Cool and squeeze dry. In a bowl, combine the cheese, dill and parsley. Stir in spinach mixture; set aside.

Place one sheet of phyllo dough on a lightly floured surface. Lightly brush with butter. Top with another sheet of phyllo dough; brush with butter. Repeat with remaining dough. Place a 6-oz. custard cup upside down on dough. Cut around custard cup with a small pizza cutter.

Place about 4 teaspoons of cheese mixture in the center of each circle. Bring edges of circle up and around cheese, forming a tart. Brush dough with butter. Place on an ungreased baking sheet. Bake at 350° for 25-30 minutes or until golden brown and spinach mixture is hot. **Yield:** 6 tarts.

PINEAPPLE MANGO SALSA

(Pictured at right)

My husband, Scott, and I make this recipe a lot in the summer when we eat outdoors, but it's also a great flavor burst to liven up the winter. It makes an interesting topper for chicken tacos or other poultry entrees as well.
—Jeanne Wiestling, Minneapolis, Minnesota

1/4 cup diced fresh mango *or* peach
1/4 cup canned pineapple chunks, quartered
1 tablespoon finely chopped red onion
1 teaspoon cider vinegar
3/4 teaspoon minced fresh cilantro *or* parsley
1/8 to 1/4 teaspoon ground ginger
Dash crushed red pepper flakes
Dash salt, optional
Tortilla chips

In a serving bowl, combine the mango, pineapple, red onion, vinegar, cilantro, ginger, pepper flakes and salt if desired. Cover and refrigerate for 1-4 hours. Stir before serving. Serve with tortilla chips. **Yield:** about 1/2 cup.

Nutritional Analysis: One 2-tablespoon serving of salsa (prepared with unsweetened pineapple and calculated without salt or tortilla chips) equals 17 calories, trace fat (trace saturated fat), 0 cholesterol, 2 mg sodium, 4 g carbohydrate, trace fiber, trace protein. **Diabetic Exchange:** Free Food.

ORANGE-SPICED PECANS

Orange juice, cinnamon and cloves give a pleasant taste to these sweet nuts.
A handful or two really hits the spot.
—Nell Hood, New Bern, North Carolina

1-2/3 cups pecan halves
1/3 cup sugar
2 tablespoons orange juice
1 teaspoon ground cinnamon
1/8 teaspoon ground cloves
1/8 teaspoon salt

Place pecans on an ungreased 15-in. x 10-in. x 1-in. baking pan. Bake at 275° for 10 minutes. After 6 minutes, in a small heavy saucepan, combine the sugar, orange juice, cinnamon, cloves and salt. Cook and stir until mixture comes to a boil. Cook and stir 2 minutes longer. Remove from the heat. Stir in warm pecans until evenly coated. Spread in a single layer on a foil-lined 15-in. x 10-in. x 1-in. baking pan. Cool. **Yield:** about 2 cups.

OLD-FASHIONED STRAWBERRY SODA

(Pictured at right)

With just a quick pulse of the blender, you'll have what I call a "refreshing sipper". This recipe makes just enough for my husband and me.
—Ginger Hubbard, Anderson, Missouri

1 cup milk
1/2 cup fresh *or* frozen strawberries
1/2 cup vanilla ice cream, softened
2 tablespoons sugar
2 to 3 drops red food coloring, optional
1 cup ginger ale, chilled

In a blender container, combine the milk, strawberries, ice cream, sugar and food coloring if desired; cover and process until smooth. Pour into two tall glasses. Add chilled ginger ale and serve immediately. **Yield:** 2 servings.

SWEET AND CRUNCHY PARTY MIX

My niece and I came up with this recipe. I've served it at a family Christmas party and as a snack at work. Folks always gobble it up by the handful.
—Diane Simkins, East Greenville, Pennsylvania

2-1/2 cups Rice Chex cereal
1-1/2 cups oyster crackers
1 cup goldfish crackers
3/4 cup salted peanuts *or* cashews
1/3 cup packed brown sugar
1/4 cup butter *or* margarine
1 teaspoon honey
1/8 teaspoon ground cinnamon
1/2 teaspoon vanilla extract

In an ungreased 15-in. x 10-in. x 1-in. baking pan, combine the cereal, crackers and peanuts. In a small heavy saucepan, combine the brown sugar, butter, honey and cinnamon. Cook and stir until butter is dissolved and mixture comes to a boil. Remove from heat; stir in vanilla (mixture will bubble up some). Pour over cereal mixture; toss to coat evenly.

Bake at 325° for 7 minutes; stir. Bake 10-15 minutes longer, stirring every 5 minutes. Cool, stirring several times. **Yield:** about 5 cups.

FRAPPE MOCHA

Using coffee ice cubes adds body to this refreshing drink. What a treat!
—Beverly Coyde, Gasport, New York

1 teaspoon instant coffee granules
1/4 cup boiling water
1 cup milk
4-1/2 teaspoons chocolate syrup
1/2 cup crushed ice

In a small bowl, dissolve coffee granules in water. Pour into ice cube tray; freeze. In a blender, combine the milk, chocolate syrup and ice cubes. Blend until smooth. Add crushed ice; blend. Serve immediately. **Yield:** 2 servings.

PIZZA TURNOVERS

(Pictured below)

Your mouth will start to water when you smell the tantalizing aroma of these little turnovers baking. They were a favorite on our Christmas buffet years ago.
—Janet Crouch, Three Hills, Alberta

3 tablespoons chopped fresh
  mushrooms
2 tablespoons chopped green pepper
2 tablespoons chopped onion
1 tablespoon butter *or* margarine
5 tablespoons tomato paste
2 tablespoons water
1/2 teaspoon dried oregano
1/8 teaspoon garlic powder
1/2 cup shredded mozzarella cheese
1 package (15 ounces) refrigerated
  pie pastry
1 egg, lightly beaten

In a small saucepan, saute the mushrooms, green pepper and onion in butter until tender. Add the tomato paste, water, oregano and garlic powder. Reduce heat to medium-low. Stir in cheese until melted. Remove from the heat.

Cut 3-1/2-in. circles from pie pastry. Place 1 teaspoon filling in the center of each circle. Brush edges of dough with water. Fold each circle in half; seal edges with a fork. Brush the tops with beaten egg. Place the turnovers on a greased baking sheet. Bake at 425° for 12-14 minutes or until golden brown. **Yield:** 14 turnovers.

Editor's Note: Turnovers may be frozen, unbaked, for up to 2 months. Before serving, bake at 425° for 16-18 minutes or until golden brown.

FRESH VEGETABLE SALSA

(Pictured at right)

This salsa is one of my husband's favorites. I can easily double or triple the recipe when we're having family or friends over, and I often do. I also adjust the "heat" setting to suit the tastes of our guests.
—Susan Dahlheimer, Medina, Ohio

1 cup chopped seeded plum
  tomatoes
1/4 cup thinly sliced green onions
2 tablespoons chopped sweet yellow
  pepper
2 tablespoons chopped jalapeno
  pepper*
1-1/2 teaspoons minced fresh cilantro
  or parsley
1/4 teaspoon salt
1/8 teaspoon pepper
Tortilla chips

In a bowl, combine the tomatoes, green onions, yellow pepper, jalapeno pepper, cilantro, salt and pepper. Cover and refrigerate for at least 30 minutes. Serve with chips. **Yield:** about 1 cup.

Nutritional Analysis: One 1/2-cup serving of salsa (calculated without tortilla chips) equals 29 calories, trace fat (trace saturated fat), 0 cholesterol, 305 mg sodium, 6 g carbohydrate, 2 g fiber, 1 g protein. **Diabetic Exchange:** 1 vegetable.

*Editor's Note: When cutting or seeding hot peppers, use rubber or plastic gloves to protect your hands. Avoid touching your face.

TIMELY TIP
*Unused peppers and onions can be chopped, then frozen.
You can use them in stir-fries, soups and casseroles.*

HAM-IT-UP SESAME PINWHEELS

(Pictured at right)

These cute bite-size swirls taste wonderful whether you make them with Swiss cheese or cheddar. They go together quickly and never fail to satisfy.
—Teresa Jarrell, Danville, West Virginia

1 tube (4 ounces) refrigerated
  crescent rolls
2 thin slices deli ham (about 7 inch x
  4 inch)
2 teaspoons prepared mustard
1/2 cup shredded Swiss *or* cheddar
  cheese
1 tablespoon sesame seeds

Unroll dough into two rectangles; seal perforations. Place ham on rectangles. Spread mustard over ham; sprinkle with cheese. Roll up from a short side; pinch seam to seal. Roll in sesame seeds. Cut each roll into 5 slices. Place slices cut side down on an ungreased baking sheet.

Bake at 375° for 10-12 minutes or until golden brown. Immediately remove from baking sheet to a serving plate. Serve warm. **Yield:** 10 appetizers.

Fresh Vegetable Salsa
Ham-It-Up Sesame Pinwheels

TORTILLA PINWHEELS

(Pictured at left)

My sister-in-law is always trying new recipes when we get together. Both the men and women in our family declared this one a winner. Here, the recipe is sized for one.
—Lynda Wagoner, Trinity, North Carolina

> **2 tablespoons shredded cheddar cheese**
> **2 tablespoons cream cheese, softened**
> **2 tablespoons sour cream**
> **1 tablespoon chopped green onion**
> **2 teaspoons chopped green chilies, drained**
> **2 teaspoons chopped ripe olives**

Dash garlic powder

> **1 flour tortilla (8 inches)**
> **1/4 cup salsa**

In a bowl, combine the first seven ingredients until blended. Spread over tortilla. Roll up; wrap in plastic wrap. Refrigerate for 2-3 hours or until firm. Cut into 1-in. slices. Serve with salsa. **Yield:** 1 serving.

PEPPERONI BREAD

The recipe for this quick version of pizza came from my aunt. I've learned over the years that teens love this one.
—Sherry Adams, Mt. Ayr, Iowa

> **1 French *or* Italian sandwich roll (about 4 to 5 inches long)**
> **2 to 3 tablespoons pizza sauce**
> **8 slices pepperoni**
> **1/4 cup shredded mozzarella cheese**

Slice roll in half lengthwise. Place on baking sheet. Spread pizza sauce over each half. Top with pepperoni. Sprinkle with mozzarella cheese. Bake at 350° for 10 minutes or until heated through. Broil 4 in. from the heat for 2 minutes or until cheese is bubbly and golden brown. **Yield:** 2 servings.

Nutritional Analysis: One serving (prepared with 2 tablespoons pizza sauce, turkey pepperoni and part-skim mozzarella cheese) equals 132 calories, 3 g fat (2 g saturated fat), 9 mg cholesterol, 356 mg sodium, 19 g carbohydrate, 1 g fiber, 7 g protein. **Diabetic Exchanges:** 1 starch, 1 lean meat.

SWEET AND SOUR SPREAD

I asked the hostess at a party to share her recipe for Sweet and Sour Spread. She wrote it down on a napkin. It took a while for me to try it because the recipe looked so simple, I thought it wasn't complete. But it's the real thing, and it's really good!
—Joanne Klingel, Stroudsburg, Pennsylvania

1 package (3 ounces) cream cheese, softened
2-1/2 teaspoons prepared horseradish
2 tablespoons apple jelly
2 tablespoons pineapple preserves
1/2 teaspoon ground mustard
1/4 teaspoon black pepper
Assorted crackers

In a mixing bowl, combine cream cheese and horseradish. Spread cream cheese mixture in a 4-in. circle on a serving plate. In a bowl, combine the apple jelly, pineapple preserves, mustard and pepper. Spread over cream cheese. Serve immediately with crackers. **Yield:** 2-4 servings.

PARMESAN POPCORN

(Pictured at right)

This is an old recipe. We've found that once you start eating the popcorn, you won't stop until it's gone. That's why it has the nickname "Nibble Bait".
—Pat Ross, Dearborn, Michigan

4 cups popped popcorn
2 tablespoons grated Parmesan cheese
2 tablespoons butter *or* margarine, melted
1/4 teaspoon paprika
3 drops hot pepper sauce
1/4 teaspoon salt

Place popcorn in an 8-in. square baking dish. Bake at 350° for 5 minutes or until heated through. Combine the Parmesan cheese, butter, paprika and hot pepper sauce. Pour over popcorn; toss to coat. Sprinkle with salt. Serve warm. **Yield:** 1-2 servings.

CRAB AND CREAM CHEESE DIP

Horseradish adds a touch of zip to the crab and onion in this creamy dip.
It goes well with all kinds of crackers.
—Nadine McGehee, Greenville, Mississippi

1 package (3 ounces) cream cheese,
    softened
2 tablespoons mayonnaise
1-1/2 teaspoons thinly sliced green onion
1-1/2 teaspoons diced pimiento, drained
1-1/2 teaspoons Worcestershire sauce
1/2 teaspoon prepared horseradish
1/3 cup crabmeat, drained, flaked and
    cartilage removed
1 tablespoon finely chopped pecans
Assorted crackers

In a mixing bowl, combine cream cheese and mayonnaise. Stir in the green onion, pimiento, Worcestershire sauce and horseradish; mix well. Stir in crab. Place in a 1-cup serving bowl; sprinkle with pecans. Refrigerate for at least 2 hours. Serve with crackers. **Yield:** 2 servings.

HOT BROCCOLI DIP

(Pictured below)

I've increased this recipe to serve it at Super Bowl parties and wedding showers, and it's
always a favorite. To keep the dip warm, use a fondue pot or mini slow cooker.
—Carol Tobisch, Park Falls, Wisconsin

3/4 cup frozen chopped broccoli
1 package (3 ounces) cream cheese,
    cubed
3 tablespoons mayonnaise
1/8 teaspoon garlic salt
Dash lemon-pepper seasoning
1/3 cup chopped celery
2 tablespoons chopped onion
2 tablespoons chopped fresh
    mushrooms
1 tablespoon butter *or* margarine
Assorted crackers

In a microwave-safe bowl, microwave broccoli on high for 1-1/2 to 2 minutes or until tender, stirring once. Drain well. In another microwave-safe bowl, combine the cream cheese, mayonnaise, garlic salt and lemon-pepper until smooth. Add broccoli.

In a small saucepan, saute the celery, onion and mushrooms in butter until tender. Stir into cream cheese mixture. Before serving, microwave, uncovered, on high for 30-60 seconds or until warm, stirring once. Serve with crackers. **Yield:** 1 cup.

PRETZEL MUSTARD DIP

(Pictured below)

I make this tangy dip often because it's so easy and tastes so good. In addition to pretzels, it's good on ham. Dijon mustard gives it a more mellow flavor than yellow mustard.
—Bonnie Capper-Eckstein, Brooklyn Park, Minnesota

1/4 cup mayonnaise
1/4 cup prepared yellow *or* Dijon mustard
2 tablespoons finely chopped onion
1 tablespoon ranch salad dressing mix
2-1/4 teaspoons prepared horseradish
Pretzels

In a bowl, combine the mayonnaise, mustard, onion, salad dressing mix and horseradish. Cover and refrigerate for at least 30 minutes. Serve with pretzels. **Yield:** about 1/2 cup.

Nutritional Analysis: One 2-tablespoon serving of dip (prepared with fat-free mayonnaise and calculated without pretzels) equals 30 calories, 1 g fat (trace saturated fat), 2 mg cholesterol, 415 mg sodium, 5 g carbohydrate, 1 g fiber, 1 g protein. **Diabetic Exchange:** 1 vegetable.

SUPER NACHOS

This tried-and-true appetizer is my choice when we want a hearty snack. It's always a hit at family gatherings, including Christmas Eve.
—Shirley Murphy, Jacksonville, Illinois

1/4 pound lean ground beef
1 tablespoon chopped onion
1/8 teaspoon salt
Dash pepper
3/4 cup refried beans
2 tablespoons chopped green chilies
1/4 cup taco sauce
1 cup (4 ounces) shredded cheddar cheese
2 tablespoons sour cream
Tortilla chips, optional

In a small nonstick skillet, cook beef and onion over medium heat until meat is no longer pink; drain. Sprinkle with salt and pepper; set aside. Spread refried beans on bottom of a 9-in. pie plate coated with nonstick cooking spray. Top with meat mixture and chilies. Drizzle with taco sauce. Sprinkle with cheese. Bake, uncovered, at 400° for 10-15 minutes or until heated through and cheese is melted. Garnish with sour cream. Serve with tortilla chips if desired. **Yield:** 2-3 servings.

CITRUS COOLER

(Pictured at right)

We enjoy this refreshingly tart drink often, especially on hot summer days.
It pairs up nicely with a wide variety of appetizers.
—Carol Hemker, Phenix City, Alabama

1/2 cup grapefruit juice
1/2 cup orange juice
1 to 2 teaspoons lime juice
1 cup ginger ale, chilled
8 ice cubes
Lime and orange slices, optional

In a bowl, combine the grapefruit juice, orange juice, lime juice and ginger ale. Place ice cubes in two glasses. Pour citrus mixture into glasses. Garnish with lime and orange slices if desired. **Yield:** 2 servings.

Nutritional Analysis: One 1-cup serving (prepared with sugar-free ginger ale) equals 52 calories, trace fat (trace saturated fat), 0 cholesterol, 16 mg sodium, 12 g carbohydrate, trace fiber, 1 g protein. **Diabetic Exchange:** 1 fruit.

VEGETABLE BITES

(Pictured at right)

You save time by using a tube of refrigerated crescent rolls as the crust for these snacks.
I receive compliments every time I make them.
—Corey Henderson, Calgary, Alberta

1 tube (4 ounces) refrigerated crescent rolls
4 ounces cream cheese, softened
1 tablespoon mayonnaise
1-1/2 teaspoons ranch salad dressing mix
1/2 cup finely chopped fresh broccoli
1/2 cup finely chopped fresh cauliflower
3 tablespoons diced sweet red pepper
3 tablespoons diced green pepper

Unroll crescent dough onto a baking sheet, forming a 14-in. x 3-1/2-in. rectangle; seal perforations. Bake at 375° for 7-9 minutes or until golden brown. Cool completely on a wire rack.

In a bowl, combine the cream cheese, mayonnaise and salad dressing mix; spread evenly over crust. Sprinkle with vegetables; press down slightly. Cover with plastic wrap. Refrigerate until serving. Cut into squares. **Yield:** 4 servings.

Nutritional Analysis: One serving (prepared with reduced-fat cream cheese and fat-free mayonnaise) equals 191 calories, 11 g fat (5 g saturated fat), 16 mg cholesterol, 403 mg sodium, 16 g carbohydrate, 1 g fiber, 6 g protein. **Diabetic Exchanges:** 2 fat, 1 starch.

CITRUS COOLER
VEGETABLE BITES

EASY PEANUT BUTTER PRETZELS

My husband, who would gladly eat peanut butter every day of his life, says these pretzels are delicious. You can decorate them with colored sprinkles to match the occasion.
—Jeannie Berry, Perrysville, Ohio

1/2 cup peanut butter chips
3/4 to 1 teaspoon shortening
8 pretzel rods
Assorted sprinkles, optional

In a 1-cup microwave-safe bowl, combine peanut butter chips and shortening. Microwave, uncovered, at 50% power until melted, stirring every 30 seconds. Dip pretzels in peanut butter mixture. Place on waxed paper and dust with sprinkles if desired. Cool completely. **Yield:** 2 servings.

Editor's Note: This recipe was tested in an 850-watt microwave.

MARINATED MOZZARELLA

(Pictured at right)

This make-ahead appetizer picks up wonderful flavor from the vinegar and spices. I've made it with fat-free mozzarella, and it still tastes just as good.
—Rita Reinke, Wauwatosa, Wisconsin

1 piece (4 ounces) mozzarella cheese
1/3 cup olive *or* vegetable oil
2 tablespoons diced green pepper
2 tablespoons diced sweet red pepper
1 tablespoon white wine vinegar *or* cider vinegar
3/4 teaspoon dried oregano
3/4 teaspoon crushed red pepper flakes
3/4 teaspoon whole peppercorns
1/4 teaspoon dried thyme
1/8 teaspoon garlic powder

Cut mozzarella cheese into 1/2-in. cubes; prick with a fork. Place in a glass bowl. In a small saucepan, combine the remaining ingredients. Cook over medium heat for 5 minutes or until heated through, stirring occasionally. Remove from the heat; let cool to room temperature. Pour over cheese. Stir gently to coat. Cover and refrigerate for 24 hours. **Yield:** 1/4 pound.

APPLE SAUSAGE APPETIZERS

(Pictured at right)

Once you've tried these mini sausages, you won't go back to the traditional barbecued version. The apple and onion flavors blend as the sauce thickens to a glaze.
—Diane Hixon, Niceville, Florida

    1 **small onion, chopped**
1-1/2 **teaspoons butter** *or* **margarine**
    2 **tablespoons apple jelly**
    2 **tablespoons brown sugar**
    8 **ounces miniature smoked sausage links**
    1 **small apple, peeled and sliced**
  3/4 **teaspoon cornstarch**
1-1/2 **teaspoons water**

In a small saucepan, saute onion in butter until tender. Stir in apple jelly and brown sugar; add sausage links. Cook, uncovered, over medium-low heat for 15-20 minutes or until thickened, stirring occasionally. Add apple. Cover and cook over medium-low heat for 8-10 minutes or until apples are tender. Combine cornstarch and water until smooth; stir into saucepan. Bring to a boil; cook and stir for 1 minute or until thickened. Serve warm. **Yield:** 2-4 servings.

GUACAMOLE DIP

(Pictured on page 32)

Since guacamole is a favorite in this area with its emphasis on Mexican food, I decided to create my own recipe. I serve it as a dip for chips. My family also likes it on baked chicken and green salads.
—Virginia Burwell, Dayton, Texas

    1 **large ripe avocado, peeled**
1/4 **cup plain yogurt**
    2 **tablespoons picante sauce** *or* **salsa**
    1 **tablespoon finely chopped onion**
1/8 **teaspoon salt**
    2 **to 3 drops hot pepper sauce, optional**
Tortilla chips

In a small bowl, mash avocado until smooth. Stir in the yogurt, picante sauce, onion, salt and hot pepper sauce if desired. Cover and refrigerate until serving. Serve with tortilla chips. **Yield:** 2 servings (3/4 cup).

SOUPS, SALADS & SANDWICHES

If you're looking for a flavorful
salad to start a meal or you
want to create a hearty soup
and sandwich combination,
turn to this chapter for
48 tried-and-true options,
all of which are yummy.

VINEGAR NOODLES (P. 62)

GRILLED CHICKEN
CAESAR SALAD (P. 51)
BEAN CABBAGE SOUP (P. 50)
BROCCOLI HAM POCKETS (P. 50)

BROCCOLI HAM POCKETS

(Pictured on page 49)

*This hearty sandwich not only tastes great, it's attractive, too.
The creamy filling has wonderful flavor.*
—Nancy Robaidek, Krakow, Wisconsin

1/3 cup diced fully cooked ham
3 tablespoons finely chopped fresh broccoli
2 tablespoons shredded cheddar cheese
1 tablespoon diced sweet red pepper
2 tablespoons mayonnaise
1/4 teaspoon Dijon mustard, optional
1 tube (4 ounces) refrigerated crescent rolls
1 egg white, lightly beaten
1-1/2 teaspoons sliced almonds

In a bowl, combine the ham, broccoli, cheddar cheese, sweet pepper, mayonnaise and mustard if desired. Unroll crescent dough into two rectangles; seal seams and perforations. Spread filling down center of each rectangle. Fold dough over filling and pinch to seal; tuck ends under. Place seam side down on an ungreased baking sheet. Brush tops with egg white and sprinkle with almonds. Bake at 375° for 11-13 minutes or until golden brown. **Yield:** 2 servings.

BEAN CABBAGE SOUP

(Pictured on page 49)

*I used to love my Italian grandmother's homemade minestrone. She was very particular
about ingredients and where she bought them. Since I cook for only my husband and myself,
I have simplified her recipe and cut down on the amounts. If I do say so myself,
it's almost as good as Nonna Teresa's.*
—Joyce Anderson, Chico, California

2 tablespoons chopped celery
1 tablespoon chopped onion
1 teaspoon olive *or* canola oil
1 garlic clove, minced
1/3 cup cubed zucchini
1/3 cup cubed peeled potato
1/3 cup sliced carrot
1 can (14-1/2 ounces) beef broth
1/2 cup canned cannellini beans *or* white kidney beans, rinsed and drained
2 teaspoons minced fresh basil *or* 1/2 teaspoon dried basil
Dash pepper
1/2 cup coarsely chopped cabbage
1/4 cup cooked rice
1 tablespoon grated Parmesan cheese

In a saucepan, saute celery and onion in oil for 2-3 minutes. Add garlic and saute for 1 minute. Add the zucchini, potato and carrot; saute for 3 minutes. Stir in the beef broth, beans, basil and pepper. Bring to a boil. Stir in cabbage. Reduce heat; cover and simmer for 20 minutes or until potatoes are tender. Just before serving, stir in rice and cheese. **Yield:** 2 servings.

Nutritional Analysis: One 1-1/2-cup serving (prepared with reduced-sodium beef broth) equals 162 calories, 3 g fat (1 g saturated fat), 6 mg cholesterol, 566 mg sodium, 25 g carbohydrate, 5 g fiber, 7 g protein. **Diabetic Exchanges:** 2 vegetable, 1 starch.

GRILLED CHICKEN CAESAR SALAD

(Pictured on page 49)

This recipe is simple, but it always gets great reviews.
—Joan Boersema, Zeeland, Michigan

2 tablespoons butter *or* margarine, melted
1/4 teaspoon garlic powder
1/8 teaspoon seasoned salt
2 to 3 slices day-old bread, cut into 1/2-inch cubes
1/2 cup Italian salad dressing
2 boneless skinless chicken breast halves
6 cups torn romaine
1/2 cup shredded Parmesan cheese
1/3 cup Caesar salad dressing

In a bowl, combine the butter, garlic powder and seasoned salt; add bread cubes and toss to coat. Place on a baking sheet; bake at 350° for 8-10 minutes or until cubes are golden brown.

Pour the Italian salad dressing into a large resealable plastic bag; add the chicken. Seal the bag and turn to coat; refrigerate for at least 3 hours. Drain and discard the marinade. Grill the chicken, uncovered, over medium heat or broil 4-6 in. from the heat for 6-7 minutes on each side or until juices run clear. Cut into strips or cubes; refrigerate until chilled.

In a salad bowl, combine the romaine, cheese, croutons and chicken; toss gently to combine. Just before serving, drizzle with Caesar salad dressing; toss gently to coat. **Yield:** 2 servings.

CREAMY GREEN BEAN SALAD

(Pictured at right)

In our early years of marriage, my husband asked me to make bean salad like his mother's. Our whole family likes this one.
—Lorraine Mix, Remer, Minnesota

2 tablespoons sour cream
1 tablespoon prepared Italian salad dressing
1 can (8 ounces) cut green beans, drained
1 medium tomato, chopped and drained
2 tablespoons finely chopped onion
Lettuce leaves

In a bowl, combine sour cream and salad dressing; mix well. Stir in the beans, tomato and onion. Cover and refrigerate for 1 hour. Serve on lettuce. **Yield:** 2 servings.

STEWED VEGETABLES AND HAM SOUP

Here's a hearty soup that's not only good but good for you as well. Because of my schedule, I need to have simple yet satisfying dishes that take little time to prepare. This one fills the bill.
—Donna Carlson, Sartell, Minnesota

1 can (14-1/2 ounces) Italian stewed tomatoes, cut up
3/4 cup chicken broth
1 tablespoon minced fresh basil *or* 1 teaspoon dried basil
1/8 teaspoon pepper
1/2 cup frozen mixed vegetables
1/2 cup cubed fully cooked ham
1/2 cup frozen cut green beans
1/2 cup cooked spiral pasta

In a medium saucepan, combine the tomatoes, chicken broth, basil and pepper. Bring to a boil. Stir in the mixed vegetables, ham and beans. Return to a boil. Reduce heat; cover and simmer about 10 minutes or until vegetables are tender. Stir in pasta and heat through. **Yield:** 2 servings.

Nutritional Analysis: One 1-1/2-cup serving (prepared with reduced-sodium chicken broth) equals 187 calories, 2 g fat (1 g saturated fat), 11 mg cholesterol, 1,332 mg sodium, 32 g carbohydrate, 7 g fiber, 14 g protein. **Diabetic Exchanges:** 2 starch, 1 lean meat.

TORTELLINI SALAD

(Pictured at right)

I like this recipe because you can make it ahead of time. It's the perfect size for lunch. You can vary the dressing to suit your taste.
—Mary Jo Kempf, Lackawanna, New York

1-3/4 cups frozen cheese tortellini
1 small onion, chopped
1/2 cup chopped green *or* sweet red pepper
1 small tomato, seeded and diced
1/4 cup julienned pepper Jack cheese
1/4 cup Italian salad dressing

Cook tortellini according to package directions. Drain and rinse in cold water. In a bowl, combine tortellini with all of the remaining ingredients; toss gently to coat. Cover and refrigerate for at least 1 hour. **Yield:** 2 servings.

Nutritional Analysis: One 1-1/2-cup serving (prepared with fat-free salad dressing) equals 331 calories, 10 g fat (5 g saturated fat), 31 mg cholesterol, 861 mg sodium, 46 g carbohydrate, 1 g fiber, 16 g protein. **Diabetic Exchanges:** 3 starch, 1 lean meat, 1 fat.

CRAB SALAD POCKETS

(Pictured at right)

When I'm out of crab, I substitute albacore tuna with great results. This sandwich makes a nice, light lunch.
—Penny Bokovoy, Ulm, Montana

**2 ounces imitation crabmeat, flaked
or 2 ounces canned crabmeat,
drained, flaked and cartilage removed
1/4 cup finely chopped cucumber
2 tablespoons chopped sweet red
pepper
2 tablespoons chopped green pepper
1 tablespoon sliced green onion
1 tablespoon finely chopped celery
1/4 teaspoon seafood seasoning
2 tablespoons mayonnaise *or* salad
dressing
2 whole wheat pita pockets
(6 inches), halved and warmed**

In a bowl, combine the crab, cucumber, peppers, onion, celery and seafood seasoning. Stir in mayonnaise. Fill pita halves with crab mixture. **Yield:** 1 serving.

Nutritional Analysis: One sandwich (prepared with fat-free mayonnaise) equals 219 calories, 3 g fat (trace saturated fat), 7 mg cholesterol, 786 mg sodium, 42 g carbohydrate, 6 g fiber, 10 g protein. **Diabetic Exchanges:** 2-1/2 starch, 1 very lean meat.

TACO CHILI

Our family loves tacos and taco salad, so I thought it would be fun to make soup that tastes like a taco. Whenever someone new tries it, they ask for the recipe.
—Janalee Watkins, Vernal, Utah

**1/4 pound ground beef
1 can (14-1/2 ounces) stewed
tomatoes, cut up
3/4 cup canned kidney beans, rinsed
and drained
3/4 cup frozen corn, thawed
2 tablespoons taco sauce *or* salsa
1 tablespoon canned chopped green
chilies *or* jalapenos
1 to 1-1/2 teaspoons chili powder
Dash garlic salt
Dash onion salt
Crushed tortilla chips, shredded cheddar
cheese and sour cream**

In a large saucepan, cook beef over medium heat until no longer pink; drain. Add the tomatoes, kidney beans, corn, taco sauce, chilies, chili powder, garlic salt and onion salt. Bring to a boil. Reduce heat; cover and simmer for 10 minutes. Serve over crushed tortilla chips. Garnish with cheese and sour cream. **Yield:** 2 servings.

CUCUMBER MELON SALAD

(Pictured at right)

This colorful salad is tangy and delicious. The unexpected combination is such a pleasant surprise. You can use whatever type of melon you have on hand.
—Edie Farm, Farmington, New Mexico

2 tablespoons canola *or* vegetable oil
1 tablespoon lemon juice
1/2 teaspoon sugar
Dash pepper
1 unpeeled small cucumber
1 cup cubed melon of your choice

In a small bowl, combine the oil, lemon juice, sugar and pepper. Cut a few slices from cucumber and set aside for garnish. Cut remaining cucumber into quarters, then cut into pieces. In a serving bowl, combine cucumber and melon. Pour dressing over all; toss gently to coat. Garnish with reserved cucumber slices. **Yield:** 2 servings.

Nutritional Analysis: One 1-1/2-cup serving equals 92 calories, 7 g fat (1 g saturated fat), 0 cholesterol, 4 mg sodium, 7 g carbohydrate, 1 g fiber, 1 g protein. **Diabetic Exchanges:** 1-1/2 fat, 1 vegetable.

GRAPEFRUIT GELATIN MOLDS

(Pictured at right)

I found this recipe in a magazine back in the '50s. It's a nice salad, particularly with a heavy meal. It's a refreshing snack as well.
—Dorothy Eissinger, Hazen, North Dakota

1 envelope unflavored gelatin
2 tablespoons cold water
1/3 cup sugar
1/3 cup water
1/2 cup grapefruit juice
3 tablespoons orange juice
4 teaspoons lemon juice

In a small bowl, sprinkle gelatin over cold water; let stand for 1 minute. In a saucepan, combine sugar and water; bring to a boil. Reduce heat; stir in gelatin until dissolved. Stir in juices; pour into three 1/2-cup or one 2-cup mold coated with nonstick cooking spray. Refrigerate for 4-5 hours or until set. **Yield:** 2-3 servings.

SERVING SUGGESTION
Freeze extra fruit juice in ice cube trays. Then add these flavorful ice cubes to lemon-lime sodas or fruit punch.

CUCUMBER MELON SALAD
GRAPEFRUIT GELATIN MOLDS

CRANBERRY PEAR SALAD

My husband and I recently celebrated our 48th wedding anniversary—which is also how long I've had this recipe. I like to serve the salad on a bed of green or red leaf lettuce and sometimes garnish it with dates. This delicious salad is easy to prepare when time is short.
—Edna Hoffman, Hebron, Indiana

1 can (8 ounces) pear halves
Lettuce leaves
1/2 cup whole-berry cranberry sauce
Toasted sliced almonds, optional

Drain pears, reserving 1 tablespoon juice (discard remaining juice or refrigerate for another use). Place pears cut side up on a lettuce-lined plate. Combine the cranberry sauce and reserved pear juice; spoon over pears. Sprinkle with almonds if desired. **Yield:** 2 servings.

SALAMI CALZONES

Melted cheddar cheese and zesty salami combine for a mouth-watering hot sandwich from our Test Kitchen home economists.

1/3 cup chopped salami
1/3 cup shredded cheddar cheese
1/4 teaspoon garlic powder
1/4 teaspoon dried oregano
2 frozen bread dough rolls, thawed
Milk, optional

In a bowl, combine the salami, cheese and seasonings; set aside. On a lightly floured surface, roll each bread dough roll into a 5-in. circle. Spoon half of salami mixture onto the center of each circle to within 1 in. of edge. Fold dough over filling; pinch edges to seal. Place on a greased baking sheet and brush with milk if desired. Bake at 375° for 18-20 minutes or until golden brown. **Yield:** 1-2 servings.

TANGY FLORET SALAD

One of my favorite and most-used recipes, this salad is easy to prepare for two or 20! I often improvise with other fresh ingredients such as carrots, onions, celery, parsley and even crunchy water chestnuts.
—Sally Frizzell, New London, Ohio

1 cup broccoli florets
1 cup cauliflowerets
1 cup frozen peas
1/2 cup mayonnaise
1 tablespoon sugar
1 tablespoon vinegar
1/2 teaspoon salt
1/8 teaspoon pepper

In a bowl, combine the first three ingredients. In a small bowl, combine the mayonnaise, sugar, vinegar, salt and pepper; mix well. Spoon over vegetables and toss to coat. **Yield:** 2-3 servings.

HEARTY WALLEYE SANDWICHES

(Pictured at right)

Our family likes to fish, so I'm always looking for different ways to prepare our catch. This one has turned out to be a family favorite.
—Carmen Henderson, Hereford, Texas

- **1 walleye fillet (about 12 ounces), cut in half**
- **1 tablespoon lemon juice**
- **1/4 teaspoon salt**
- **1/8 to 1/4 teaspoon pepper**
- **1/4 cup cornmeal**
- **4 bacon strips**
- **1 tablespoon butter *or* margarine, softened**
- **2 submarine buns, split**
- **1/4 cup mayonnaise**
- **1 garlic clove, minced**
- **Lettuce leaves**
- **Tomato slices**

Sprinkle fillet with lemon juice, salt and pepper. Coat with cornmeal and set aside. In a skillet, cook bacon over medium heat until crisp. Remove to paper towels; drain, reserving 2 tablespoons drippings.

In the same skillet, cook fillet in reserved drippings for about 4 minutes on each side or until fish flakes easily with a fork. Meanwhile, butter cut sides of buns. Place buttered side up on a baking sheet. Toast under broiler for about 1 minute or until golden brown. In a small bowl, combine mayonnaise and garlic; spread on buns. Top with lettuce, tomato slices and fish. **Yield: 2 servings.**

GRILLED 'PBJ' SANDWICHES

I was going to make grilled cheese sandwiches one day and had already buttered several slices of bread when I found I was out of cheese. So I pulled out some peanut butter and jelly, and the result was this tasty variation of a popular classic.
—Barb Trautmann, Ham Lake, Minnesota

- **4 tablespoons peanut butter**
- **2 tablespoons strawberry jam**
- **4 slices English muffin *or* white toasting bread**
- **2 tablespoons butter *or* margarine, softened**
- **Confectioners' sugar, optional**

Spread peanut butter and jam on two slices of bread; top with remaining bread. Butter the outsides of sandwiches; cook in a large skillet over medium heat until golden brown on each side. Dust with confectioners' sugar if desired. **Yield: 2 servings.**

BAKED HAM AND CHEESE SANDWICHES

(Pictured below)

I collect cookbooks and enjoy reading them much like a novel. But when I start cooking, I create my own recipes to suit my taste. This sandwich is one of my creations.
—Norma Curtis, Ithaca, Michigan

4 slices bread
2 slices fully cooked ham
2 slices cheddar cheese
2 eggs
1-1/4 cups milk
1 tablespoon prepared mustard
1 tablespoon minced fresh parsley
    or 1 teaspoon dried parsley flakes
Fresh asparagus tips, cooked
Shredded cheddar cheese, optional

Place two slices of bread in a greased 11-in. x 7-in. x 2-in. baking dish or two individual baking dishes. Top each with a slice of ham and cheese; top with remaining bread. In a small bowl, beat the eggs, milk, mustard and parsley. Pour over sandwiches. Let stand for 5 minutes; carefully turn sandwiches over and let stand 5 minutes longer.

Bake, uncovered, at 350° for 30-35 minutes. Top with asparagus and shredded cheese if desired. Bake 5 minutes longer or until cheese is melted and a knife inserted into the egg mixture comes out clean. Serve immediately. **Yield:** 2 servings.

PERFECT CHICKEN SALAD

My godchild doesn't care for vegetables, but he loves this salad...even the peas and carrots!
—Lora Schnurr, Fort Wayne, Indiana

2 cups cubed cooked chicken
1/2 cup frozen peas, thawed
1/4 cup chopped ripe olives
2 tablespoons shredded carrot
2 tablespoons minced onion
DRESSING:
1/2 cup mayonnaise
1 tablespoon yellow *or* spicy brown
    mustard
1/4 teaspoon Worcestershire sauce
1/4 teaspoon seasoned salt
1/8 teaspoon pepper

In a medium bowl, combine the chicken, peas, olives, carrot and onion. Mix dressing ingredients in a small bowl; pour over salad and toss to coat. Refrigerate until serving. **Yield:** 2-3 servings.

ITALIAN PORK HOAGIES

I received this recipe from the parents of one of the preschoolers where I teach.
They're pork producers. This works well as a quick lunch or pre-game meal.
—Nancy Heesch, Sioux Falls, South Dakota

2 boneless pork loin chops (4 ounces
  each), cut into strips
3 tablespoons prepared Italian salad
  dressing
2 hard rolls *or* other small sandwich
  rolls
4 teaspoons pizza sauce
1/4 cup shredded mozzarella cheese
3 tablespoons chopped green onions

Place pork in a resealable plastic bag; add salad dressing. Seal bag and turn to coat; refrigerate for at least 2 hours.

Drain and discard marinade. In a skillet, cook the strips over medium heat until no longer pink; set aside. Meanwhile, place open sandwich buns on a baking sheet. Spread pizza sauce on the bottom half of each bun. Top with pork strips, cheese and onions. Bake at 350° for 5 minutes or until cheese is melted and bun is lightly toasted. **Yield:** 2 servings.

Nutritional Analysis: One sandwich (prepared with part-skim mozzarella cheese) equals 458 calories, 20 g fat (5 g saturated fat), 80 mg cholesterol, 637 mg sodium, 34 g carbohydrate, 2 g fiber, 33 g protein. **Diabetic Exchanges:** 3 lean meat, 3 fat, 2 starch.

ANNIVERSARY CHOWDER

(Pictured at right)

We celebrated our 35th wedding anniversary with dinner at a lovely pre-Revolutionary War restaurant in Pennsylvania, where I enjoyed a wonderful salmon chowder. I wanted to duplicate it, so I put this recipe together, using salmon we had purchased in Alaska.
—Barbara Harrison, Ringoes, New Jersey

2 small red potatoes, cubed
1/2 medium carrot, finely chopped
1/4 cup finely chopped onion
2 tablespoons butter *or* margarine
2 cups half-and-half cream
1 can (6 ounces) boneless skinless
  salmon, drained and flaked
1/2 cup fresh *or* frozen corn
1/4 teaspoon dried rosemary, crushed
1/4 teaspoon dried parsley flakes
1/4 teaspoon salt
1/8 teaspoon pepper
1/8 teaspoon rubbed sage
1/8 teaspoon dried thyme

In a large saucepan, saute the potatoes, carrot and onion in butter until tender. Reduce heat; stir in remaining ingredients. Cook and stir for 10 minutes or until soup is heated through. **Yield:** 2 servings.

PEPPER STEAK SANDWICHES

(Pictured at right)

These wonderful sandwiches are very satisfying. I like to serve them with raw veggies and fresh fruit. Onion plus the green and red pepper give the sandwiches zip.
—Patricia Schnaidt, Olympia, Washington

2 tablespoons butter *or* margarine, softened
2 French *or* submarine rolls, split
1/2 medium green pepper, julienned
1/2 medium sweet red pepper, julienned
1 small onion, sliced and separated into rings
Salt and pepper to taste
1-1/2 teaspoons vegetable oil
1/2 pound beef flank steak, cut into strips
1/2 cup shredded Swiss cheese

Butter rolls and place buttered side up on a baking sheet. Bake at 375° for 3-4 minutes or until lightly toasted.

Meanwhile, in a skillet, combine the green pepper, red pepper and onion. Sprinkle with salt and pepper. Saute in oil until vegetables are crisp-tender. Remove and keep warm.

To the skillet, add the steak. Cook and stir until steak reaches desired doneness. Return peppers to pan; heat through. Spoon beef mixture onto rolls. Sprinkle with cheese. Replace roll tops. **Yield:** 2 servings.

KENTUCKY HOT BROWN SANDWICHES

(Pictured at right)

Hot Brown Sandwiches are as popular in Kentucky as The Derby. Some recipes stack both turkey and ham, although we prefer it without ham. Paired with a side salad, this sandwich makes a hearty meal.
—Margaret Evans, Frankfort, Kentucky

4-1/2 teaspoons butter *or* margarine
4-1/2 teaspoons all-purpose flour
2/3 cup milk
3/4 teaspoon chicken bouillon granules
2 slices bread, toasted
4 thin slices deli turkey
2 slices cheddar cheese
4 to 6 slices tomato
2 bacon strips, cooked and crumbled

In a small saucepan, melt butter. Stir in flour until smooth; gradually stir in milk and bouillon. Bring to a boil; cook and stir for 1 minute or until thickened. Remove from the heat; set aside.

Place toast in a baking pan. Top each with 2 slices of turkey; spoon reserved white sauce over turkey. Top each with one cheese slice and 2-3 tomato slices. Bake, uncovered, at 350° for 25-30 minutes or until lightly browned. Sprinkle with bacon. **Yield:** 2 servings.

PEPPER STEAK SANDWICHES
KENTUCKY HOT BROWN SANDWICHES

VINEGAR NOODLES

(Pictured on page 48)

*I work in a beauty salon, and one of my clients shared this recipe with me many years ago.
The name of this dish intrigued me, so I gave it a try. It's a refreshing summer favorite.*
—Jeanette Fuehring, Concordia, Missouri

1 cup uncooked spiral noodles
1/2 cup thinly sliced cucumber
1/4 cup thinly sliced onion
6 tablespoons sugar
1/4 cup water
3 tablespoons vinegar
3/4 teaspoon prepared mustard
3/4 teaspoon dried parsley flakes
1/4 to 1/2 teaspoon pepper
1/4 teaspoon salt
1/8 teaspoon garlic salt

Cook noodles according to package directions. Drain and rinse in cold water. Place in a bowl; add cucumber and onion. In a jar with tight-fitting lid, combine remaining ingredients; shake well. Pour over noodle mixture and toss to coat. Cover and refrigerate for at least 1 hour. **Yield:** 2 servings.

TURKEY BLT

*As much as my family loves them, leftover turkey sandwiches can get pretty boring.
This recipe dresses them up and adds a nice twist to a traditional treat.*
—Deborah Westbrook, York Springs, Pennsylvania

2 tablespoons mayonaise
1 tablepoon spicy brown mustard
1 tablespoon honey
2 large pumpernickel rolls, split
4 slices cooked turkey
4 bacon strips, cooked
2 slices Swiss cheese
4 slices tomato
Letuce leaves

In a small bowl, combine mayonaise, mustard and honey; spread on cut sides of rolls. On bottom of rolls, layer turkey, bacon and cheese. Broil 4 in. from the heat for 2-3 minutes or until cheese begins to melt. Top with tomato and lettuce; replace roll tops. **Yield:** 2 servings.

TOMATO AVOCADO SALAD

*I came up with this recipe one day when avocados were on sale at the market.
It's a nice change from a lettuce salad, plus it's quick to make.*
—Pamela Bures Raybon, Edna, Texas

1-1/2 teaspoons lemon juice
3/4 teaspoon lime juice
1/8 to 1/4 teaspoon garlic powder
1/8 teaspoon salt
1/8 teaspoon pepper
1/2 cup cubed tomato
1/4 cup chopped red onion
1 medium ripe avocado, peeled and cubed

In a bowl, combine the lemon juice, lime juice, garlic powder, salt and pepper. Stir in tomato and onion. Add avocado and toss gently to coat. Refrigerate for 30 minutes before serving. **Yield:** 2 servings.

SOURDOUGH CHICKEN SANDWICHES

(Pictured below)

My family loves chicken, so I created this easy sandwich recipe. The chicken stays moist and tasty prepared this way. With potatoes or fries and a salad, it's a complete meal.
—Joe Urban, West Chicago, Illinois

2 **boneless skinless chicken breast halves (about 6 ounces** *each***)**
1 **egg, beaten**
1/2 **cup seasoned bread crumbs**
2 **tablespoons butter** *or* **margarine**
4 **slices sourdough bread**
2 **to 3 teaspoons mayonnaise, optional**
2 **lettuce leaves**
2 **slices Swiss cheese**
2 **slices tomato**
2 **bacon strips, cooked**

Pound chicken to 1/4-in. thickness. Dip chicken in egg, then coat with crumbs. Let stand for 5 minutes. In a skillet, cook chicken in butter over medium-high heat for 4 minutes on each side until juices run clear. Spread bread with mayonnaise if desired. Top two slices with the lettuce, cheese, tomato, bacon and chicken. Top with the remaining bread. **Yield:** 2 servings.

ORANGE BANANA SALAD

I love fresh fruit salads. With this simple recipe, I can enjoy one even in January! This colorful salad complements most any entree.
—Mary Danks, Grand Rapids, Michigan

1 **medium navel orange, sectioned**
2 **tablespoons flaked coconut, toasted**
2 **tablespoons orange juice**
1/8 **teaspoon ground cinnamon, optional**
1 **medium ripe banana, sliced**

Cut orange sections into bite-size pieces. In a bowl, combine the orange, coconut, orange juice and cinnamon if desired; toss gently. Refrigerate until chilled. Just before serving, add banana and toss gently. **Yield:** 2 servings.

Nutritional Analysis: One 1/2-cup serving equals 116 calories, 2 g fat (1 g saturated fat), 0 cholesterol, 13 mg sodium, 27 g carbohydrate, 4 g fiber, 1 g protein. **Diabetic Exchange:** 2 fruit.

CURRIED PEA SOUP

Wonderful for a winter day, this soup gets subtle flavor from curry.
I serve it with salad and a toasted baguette.
—Marion Lowery, Medford, Oregon

1/2 cup water
  1 teaspoon chicken bouillon granules
  1 garlic clove, minced
1/2 teaspoon curry powder
1/4 to 1/2 teaspoon salt
1/8 teaspoon white pepper
Dash to 1/8 teaspoon dried mint flakes
  1 package (10 ounces) frozen peas
  1 celery rib, finely chopped
1/2 cup milk
1/2 cup whipping cream
  2 tablespoons lemon juice
Fresh mint, optional

In a saucepan, bring water, bouillon, garlic, curry powder, salt, pepper and mint to a boil. Stir in peas and celery. Return to a boil. Reduce heat; cover and simmer for 6-8 minutes or until peas and celery are tender. Cool slightly.

Place pea mixture and milk in a blender or food processor; cover and process until smooth. Return to saucepan. Stir in cream; heat through (do not boil). Stir in lemon juice. Garnish with fresh mint if desired. **Yield:** 2 servings.

CARROT RAISIN SALAD

(Pictured below)

My mother made this healthy salad every holiday, using either regular or golden raisins.
This was one of the first recipes I tried on my husband when we were newlyweds. He was
skeptical because he didn't like raisins, but now this is one of his favorite salads.
—Marlene Reilly, Nescopeck, Pennsylvania

1/2 pound carrots, shredded
1/3 cup golden raisins
1/3 cup plain yogurt
  2 tablespoons mayonnaise
  1 teaspoon honey
Dash cinnamon, optional
Lettuce leaves

In a small bowl, combine the carrots, raisins, yogurt, mayonnaise, honey and cinnamon if desired. Refrigerate for several hours or overnight. Serve in a lettuce-lined bowl. **Yield:** 2 servings.

Nutritional Analysis: One serving (prepared with fat-free yogurt and fat-free mayonnaise) equals 159 calories, 1 g fat (trace saturated fat), 2 mg cholesterol, 185 mg sodium, 39 g carbohydrate, 5 g fiber, 4 g protein. **Diabetic Exchanges:** 2 fruit, 1/2 fat-free milk.

WINTER VEGETABLE SOUP

(Pictured at right)

I've enjoyed this soup for years because it tastes good, is simple to make and doesn't leave a lot of leftovers. Whenever there's a chill in the air, a steaming bowl of this savory soup is welcome.
—Mavis Diment, Marcus, Iowa

1/2 cup sliced green onions
1 tablespoon canola *or* vegetable oil
1 can (14-1/2 ounces) chicken broth
1 small potato, peeled and cubed
1 large carrot, sliced
1/4 teaspoon dried thyme
1 cup broccoli florets
1/4 teaspoon salt, optional
1/8 teaspoon pepper

In a medium saucepan, saute onions in oil until tender. Add the broth, potato, carrot and thyme; bring to a boil. Reduce heat; simmer, uncovered, for 5 minutes. Add the broccoli, salt if desired and pepper; simmer, uncovered, for 7 minutes or until vegetables are tender. **Yield:** 2 servings.

Nutritional Analysis: One serving (prepared with reduced-sodium broth and without salt) equals 164 calories, 7 g fat (1 g saturated fat), 0 cholesterol, 581 mg sodium, 21 g carbohydrate, 4 g fiber, 5 g protein. **Diabetic Exchanges:** 1 starch, 1 vegetable, 1 fat.

OPEN-FACED MOZZARELLA SANDWICHES

These zesty sandwiches are a family favorite at our house. They have a distinctly Italian flavor, plus a fresh-from-the-garden taste that can't be beat.
—Valerie Hart, Mt. Dora, Florida

1 cup seeded chopped plum tomatoes
3 tablespoons olive *or* vegetable oil
1 garlic clove, minced
1 teaspoon thinly sliced green onion
1 teaspoon chopped fresh basil *or* 1/4
   teaspoon dried basil
1/4 teaspoon salt
1/8 teaspoon pepper
Dash cayenne pepper
4 slices Italian bread (3/4 inch thick)
1/2 cup shredded mozzarella cheese

In a small bowl, combine the first eight ingredients. Cover and refrigerate for at least 1 hour. Drain 2 teaspoons liquid from the tomato mixture; brush onto one side of each slice of bread. Broil 5 in. from the heat for 2 minutes or until crisp. Spoon 1/4 cup tomato mixture on each piece of bread; sprinkle with cheese. Broil 1-2 minutes longer or until bubbly. **Yield:** 2 servings.

BACON TOMATO CHOWDER

(Pictured at right)

This soup recipe is so warm and inviting for any occasion, but most of all, I like to cook it for just my husband and me.
—Heidi Sollinger, Bechtelsville, Pennsylvania

   3 bacon strips, diced
1/4 cup butter *or* margarine
1/4 cup all-purpose flour
Dash ground nutmeg
   1 can (14-1/2 ounces) chicken broth
3/4 cup canned diced tomatoes with juice
2/3 cup half-and-half cream

In a saucepan, cook bacon over medium heat until crisp. Using a slotted spoon, remove to paper towels to drain. Discard drippings. In same pan, melt butter. Stir in flour and nutmeg until smooth. Gradually whisk in broth. Bring to a boil; cook and stir for 2 minutes or until thickened. Stir in tomatoes; heat through. Reduce heat; stir in cream. Heat through (do not boil). Add bacon. **Yield:** 2 servings.

CHUNKY TURKEY VEGETABLE SOUP

(Pictured at right)

It's been 25 years since I cut this recipe out of a newspaper, and I've made it countless times since then. We like it so well that I always boil the leftover turkey bones and freeze the broth with turkey meat in quart containers, so it's available whenever I want to make soup.
—Suzanne Fawkes, Cameron, Missouri

   3 cups chicken broth
1/2 cup frozen baby lima beans, thawed
1/3 cup cubed peeled potato
1/3 cup sliced carrot
1/3 cup sliced celery
   2 tablespoons chopped onion
3/4 cup cubed cooked turkey *or* chicken
1/2 cup cooked spiral pasta
   1 tablespoon minced fresh parsley

In a saucepan, combine the broth, lima beans, potato, carrot, celery and onion. Bring to a boil. Reduce heat; cover and cook for 15 minutes or until vegetables are tender. Add turkey and pasta; cook until heated through. Stir in parsley. **Yield:** 2 servings.

Nutritional Analysis: One 1-1/2-cup serving (prepared with reduced-sodium chicken broth) equals 242 calories, 3 g fat (1 g saturated fat), 51 mg cholesterol, 284 mg sodium, 27 g carbohydrate, 4 g fiber, 25 g protein. **Diabetic Exchanges:** 2 vegetable, 2 lean meat, 1 starch.

TIMELY TIP
To store unbroken egg yolks, place in a container and cover with water. Tightly cover the container and refrigerate for 2-4 days.

BACON TOMATO CHOWDER
CHUNKY TURKEY VEGETABLE SOUP

CARROT CHEESE SOUP

(Pictured below)

I thought this sounded like a compatible mix of ingredients when I read the recipe for the first time—and it is delicious. It's a pretty color and makes a hearty soup to serve during the winter months.
—Terese Snyder, Marquette, Michigan

2 to 3 tablespoons butter *or* margarine
2 tablespoons all-purpose flour
1 medium carrot, diced
2 green onions, sliced
2 tablespoons diced fully cooked ham
2 cups hot chicken broth
1/3 cup shredded cheddar cheese
1 tablespoon minced fresh parsley
1/8 teaspoon pepper
Dash hot pepper sauce

In a saucepan, melt the butter; stir in flour until smooth. Cook and stir over medium heat for 2 minutes. Add carrot, onions and ham; cook and stir for 1 minute. Gradually add broth. Bring to a boil; cook and stir for 2 minutes or until thickened. Reduce heat. Add the cheese, parsley, pepper and hot pepper sauce; heat until the cheese is melted and the vegetables are tender. **Yield:** 2 servings.

CHUNKY VEGGIE PASTA SALAD

You can vary this salad based on the season or your own preferences. Mushrooms, sliced cucumber and diced or shredded carrots taste good in it. To make a main-dish salad, simply add shredded cheddar cheese and cubed cooked ham.
—Sheri Kratcha, Avoca, Wisconsin

1/3 cup uncooked small pasta
1/4 cup small cauliflowerets
1/4 cup small broccoli florets
1/4 cup diced seeded tomato
1/4 cup chopped green pepper
1/4 cup diced onion
2 tablespoons sliced ripe olives
1/4 cup Italian salad dressing

Cook pasta according to package directions; drain and rinse in cold water. In a bowl, combine pasta with the remaining ingredients; toss gently to coat. Cover and refrigerate for 3 hours or overnight. **Yield:** 2 servings.

Nutritional Analysis: One 1-cup serving (prepared with fat-free salad dressing) equals 112 calories, 2 g fat (trace saturated fat), 1 mg cholesterol, 510 mg sodium, 21 g carbohydrate, 2 g fiber, 4 g protein. **Diabetic Exchanges:** 1 starch, 1 vegetable.

VEGGIE CALZONES

Our Test Kitchen home economists created this recipe for a flavorful sandwich that blends fresh herbs and three kinds of cheese.

1 cup chopped sweet onion
1/2 cup chopped sweet red pepper
1/4 cup chopped fresh mushrooms
2 tablespoons olive *or* vegetable oil
1/2 cup chopped fresh spinach
2 teaspoons *each* shredded Swiss,
  mozzarella and Parmesan cheese
1 teaspoon minced chives
1 teaspoon minced fresh basil *or* 1/4
  teaspoon dried basil
1/2 teaspoon minced fresh dill *or* 1/8
  teaspoon dill weed
Salt and pepper to taste
1 egg, *separated*
4 frozen bread dough rolls, thawed
Fresh dill sprigs, optional

In a skillet, saute the onion, red pepper and mushrooms in oil until tender. Remove from the heat and stir in the spinach, cheeses, seasonings and egg white; set aside. On a lightly floured surface, roll each ball of dough into a 5-in. circle. Spoon a fourth of vegetable mixture onto the center of each circle to within 1 in. of edge. Fold dough over filling; pinch edges to seal.

Place on a greased baking sheet. Place a fresh dill sprig on each if desired. Beat egg yolk and brush over tops. Bake at 375° for 18-20 minutes or until golden brown. **Yield:** 2 servings.

SLOPPY TOMS

These hearty sandwiches are called "Toms" rather than "Joes" because they're made with leftover turkey. I've always loved to cook. I can remember checking out cookbooks from the grade school library, and I worked in the cafeteria from third through sixth grade.
—Barbara Blackmore, Lewisburg, Tennessee

2 bacon strips, cut into 1-inch pieces
1 celery rib, chopped
1 cup diced cooked turkey
1 can (8 ounces) tomato sauce
1/4 cup water
2 to 3 teaspoons onion soup mix
1-1/2 teaspoons brown sugar
1/2 teaspoon prepared mustard
Dash pepper
2 sesame seed hamburger buns,
  toasted

In a small skillet, cook bacon over medium heat until crisp. Using a slotted spoon, remove bacon to drain on paper towels and set aside. Saute celery in bacon drippings; drain. Add the turkey, tomato sauce, water, soup mix, brown sugar, mustard and pepper. Bring to a boil. Reduce heat; simmer, uncovered, for 15 minutes or until thickened. Serve on hamburger buns. Sprinkle with bacon. **Yield:** 2 servings.

TIMELY TIP
Leftover water chestnuts add a nutty crunch to salads, stir-fries or casseroles. Refrigerate, covered, in their liquid for up to 1 week.

ORIENTAL CHICKEN GRILL

(Pictured at right)

Since my husband and I are empty nesters, this recipe is great for just the two of us, although it could be increased. We both love these tasty sandwiches— especially my husband, who "lives to eat" rather than "eats to live"!
—Rosemary Splittgerber, Mesa, Arizona

  2 boneless skinless chicken breast halves
1/2 cup orange juice
  2 tablespoons honey
  2 tablespoons soy sauce
  1 teaspoon lemon-pepper seasoning
  1 teaspoon ground ginger
1/2 teaspoon garlic powder
  2 hamburger buns, split
Lettuce leaves and tomato slices, optional

Pound chicken breasts to 3/8-in. thickness. In a small bowl, combine the juice, honey, soy sauce and seasonings; mix well. Pour 1/2 cup into a resealable plastic bag; add chick-en. Seal bag and turn to coat; refrigerate overnight. Cover and refrigerate remaining marinade.

Drain and discard marinade. Grill chicken, uncovered, over medium heat for 6-8 minutes on each side or until juices run clear. Baste several times with reserved marinade. Serve on buns with lettuce and tomato if desired. **Yield:** 2 servings.

CRAB PASTA SALAD

My mother shared this recipe with me. It's one of my standby meals for a light summer lunch.
—Diane Brondyke, Dubuque, Iowa

2/3 cup uncooked spiral pasta
1/2 cup canned crabmeat, drained, flaked and cartilage removed *or* 1 cup imitation crabmeat
1/3 cup broccoli florets
  3 tablespoons chopped seeded tomato
  2 tablespoons chopped green pepper
  1 tablespoon sliced green onion
  3 tablespoons mayonnaise
  1 tablespoon prepared Italian salad dressing
1/4 teaspoon grated Parmesan cheese

Cook pasta according to package directions; drain and rinse in cold water. In a bowl, combine the pasta, crab, broccoli, tomato, green pepper and green onion. In a small bowl, combine the mayonnaise, salad dressing and Parmesan cheese. Pour over salad mixture; toss gently to coat. **Yield:** 2 servings.

Nutritional Analysis: One 1-cup serving (prepared with fat-free mayonnaise and fat-free salad dressing) equals 148 calories, 2 g fat (trace saturated fat), 33 mg cholesterol, 410 mg sodium, 22 g carbohydrate, 2 g fiber, 10 g protein. **Diabetic Exchanges:** 1 starch, 1 vegetable, 1 lean meat.

PIZZA BURGERS

*My husband loved the pizza burgers at a restaurant back home in New York.
We can't get them as often anymore since we moved to Delaware, so I decided to
try to duplicate the recipe. It must have worked; my husband says they're great.*
—Cheryl Parker, Seaford, Delaware

1 egg
1 tablespoon dry bread crumbs
1/2 teaspoon dried oregano
1/4 teaspoon salt
1/4 teaspoon lemon-pepper seasoning
1/8 teaspoon garlic powder
1/8 teaspoon dried marjoram
1/8 teaspoon dried basil
1/2 pound ground beef
2 slices provolone cheese
2 hamburger buns, split and toasted
  if desired
2 tablespoons pizza sauce

In a bowl, combine the first eight ingredients. Crumble beef over mixture and mix well. Shape into two 4-in. patties. In a skillet, fry patties for 4-5 minutes on each side or until no longer pink. Top each patty with cheese. Serve on buns with pizza sauce. **Yield:** 2 servings.

TOMATOES WITH BASIL-GARLIC DRESSING

(Pictured below)

*In summer when it's peak time for fresh, ripe tomatoes, this is the salad to serve! Meaty
tomatoes topped with a touch of this dressing will bring on rave reviews.*
—Ruby Williams, Bogalusa, Louisiana

2 medium tomatoes, sliced
Pepper to taste
2 tablespoons chopped green onions
2 tablespoons plain yogurt
1 tablespoon cider vinegar
1 teaspoon minced fresh basil *or* 1/2
  teaspoon dried basil
1 garlic clove, minced

Arrange tomatoes on salad plates; sprinkle with pepper. In a small bowl, combine the remaining ingredients; mix well. Spoon over tomatoes. **Yield:** 2 servings.

Nutritional Analysis: One serving (prepared with fat-free yogurt) equals 38 calories, trace fat (trace saturated fat), trace cholesterol, 21 mg sodium, 8 g carbohydrate, 2 g fiber, 2 g protein. **Diabetic Exchange:** 1 vegetable.

ITALIAN-SAUSAGE PEPPER SANDWICHES

I don't remember where I got this recipe. It's been around for years. These sandwiches are great on a busy weeknight because they're easy to prepare yet very tasty.
—Jan Dee Vardaman, Van Nuys, California

2 uncooked Italian sausage links
1 small red onion, thinly sliced
1/2 medium green pepper, julienned
1/2 medium sweet red pepper, julienned
1 garlic clove, chopped
1 tablespoon canola *or* vegetable oil
1 large tomato, seeded and chopped
1/2 teaspoon dried oregano
Salt and pepper to taste, optional
2 French *or* submarine rolls, split and toasted

In a skillet, cook sausage over medium heat until browned. Let stand until cool enough to handle. Cut into 1/2-in. slices. Return to pan and cook until no longer pink; drain and set aside.

In same skillet, saute the onion, green pepper, red pepper and garlic in oil until crisp-tender. Add the sausage, tomato, oregano and salt and pepper if desired. Cook until tomatoes are heated through. Spoon sausage mixture into rolls. **Yield:** 2 servings.

Nutritional Analysis: One sandwich (prepared with turkey Italian sausage and calculated without salt) equals 291 calories, 12 g fat (2 g saturated fat), 15 mg cholesterol, 466 mg sodium, 38 g carbohydrate, 4 g fiber, 11 g protein. **Diabetic Exchanges:** 2 starch, 2 lean meat, 1 vegetable.

ASPARAGUS CHEESE SOUP

Although I came from a large family, I had to adjust to cooking for two during the years I had a roommate. This soup is a springtime favorite.
—Don Laugherty, Connellsville, Pennsylvania

2 cups water, *divided*
1 teaspoon chicken bouillon granules
1/4 teaspoon seasoned salt
1/4 teaspoon lemon-pepper seasoning
1/4 teaspoon white pepper
3/4 pound fresh asparagus spears, trimmed
4 slices process American cheese, cut up
1 bacon strip, cooked and crumbled

In a small skillet, combine 1 cup water, bouillon, seasoned salt, lemon-pepper and white pepper. Add asparagus. Bring to a boil. Reduce heat; cover and simmer for 8-10 minutes or until asparagus is tender. Remove asparagus; cool slightly.

Cut off several asparagus tips and set aside. Cut remaining asparagus into large pieces. Place asparagus pieces and cooking liquid in a blender or food processor; cover and process until smooth. In a saucepan, combine asparagus mixture and remaining water; heat through. Reduce heat; stir in cheese just until melted. Garnish with bacon bits and reserved asparagus tips. **Yield:** 2 servings.

TUNA FISH SPECIAL

(Pictured below)

This was my children's favorite salad when they were growing up. Whenever we would go on a picnic, they requested the "tuna fish special". The variety of flavors gives it a taste everyone loves.
—Gerry Tressler, St. Petersburg, Florida

1 can (6 ounces) tuna, drained and flaked
1 cup frozen peas, thawed
1/2 cup chopped celery
1/4 cup sliced green onions
1/3 cup mayonnaise
1 teaspoon lemon juice
1/2 teaspoon soy sauce
1/8 teaspoon curry powder
Dash garlic powder
2 tablespoons slivered almonds, toasted
1 cup chow mein noodles
Lettuce leaves, optional

In a bowl, combine the tuna, peas, celery and onions. In another bowl, combine the mayonnaise, lemon juice, soy sauce, curry powder and garlic powder; stir into tuna mixture. Stir in almonds; top with noodles. Serve on lettuce if desired. **Yield:** 2 servings.

CHICKEN VEGGIE POCKETS

I came up with this recipe when I wanted to make something a little more special than ordinary sandwiches. It's good with leftover turkey, too.
—Linda Kelly, Columbia, Tennessee

1 package (3 ounces) cream cheese, softened
1 tablespoon milk
1/4 to 1/2 teaspoon Italian seasoning
1/4 teaspoon salt
1/8 teaspoon pepper
1 cup cubed cooked chicken
2 small fresh mushrooms, sliced
1/4 cup frozen corn, thawed and patted dry
3 tablespoons frozen cut green beans, thawed and patted dry
1 can (4 ounces) refrigerated crescent rolls

In a small mixing bowl, beat cream cheese and milk until blended. Stir in Italian seasoning, salt and pepper; mix well. Stir in the chicken, mushrooms, corn and green beans. Unroll crescent roll dough and separate into two rectangles; seal perforations. Place half of filling on one side of each rectangle. Fold in half; seal edges (pockets will be full). Place on an ungreased baking sheet. Bake at 375° for 15-20 minutes or until golden brown. **Yield:** 2 servings.

ZIPPY EGG SALAD

(Pictured below)

Egg salad is a refreshing, tasty change from lunch meat or peanut butter sandwiches. The extra preparation time is worth the effort. A touch of mustard and lemon juice give it zip.
—Annemarie Pietila, Farmington Hills, Michigan

3 tablespoons mayonnaise
1-1/2 teaspoons prepared mustard
1/8 teaspoon salt
1/8 teaspoon pepper
1/8 teaspoon lemon juice
3 hard-cooked eggs, coarsely chopped
1 tablespoon minced green onion
Bread *or* crackers
Sliced tomato, optional

In a small bowl, combine the mayonnaise, mustard, salt, pepper and lemon juice. Stir in the eggs and onion. Serve on bread or crackers; top with tomato if desired. **Yield:** 2 servings.

SESAME STEAK SANDWICH

I found this recipe in a book that I bought in a hospital gift shop more than 25 years ago. It's a hit with family and friends every time I make it.
—Susan Mielke, Hartland, Wisconsin

1/4 teaspoon salt
1/8 teaspoon pepper
1 beef cube steak
1-1/2 teaspoons vegetable oil
1 sesame seed hamburger bun, split
1 slice mozzarella cheese
1 tablespoon mayonnaise
1 lettuce leaf
1 tomato slice

Sprinkle salt and pepper over meat. In a skillet, cook meat in oil for 3-5 minutes on each side or until browned. Place meat and a slice of cheese on the bottom of the bun. Broil open-faced sandwich 4-6 in. from the heat for 2 minutes or until cheese is melted and bun is toasted. Spread mayonnaise over bun top. Place lettuce and tomato slices on cheese. Cover with bun top. **Yield:** 1 serving.

HERBED CREAM OF POTATO SOUP

I think white sauce is the best base for cream soup. One day I added complementary herbs to plain potato soup. Yum! Now we always have our potato soup "herbed".
—Juanita McDade, Paris, Tennessee

3/4 cup cubed peeled potatoes
 1 tablespoon cold water
 2 teaspoons beef bouillon granules
1/4 cup boiling water
 1 tablespoon chopped onion
 3 tablespoons butter *or* margarine
 3 tablespoons all-purpose flour
 2 cups milk
1-1/2 teaspoons dried parsley flakes
1/8 to 1/4 teaspoon dried thyme
1/8 teaspoon dried rosemary, crushed
1/8 teaspoon garlic salt

Place potatoes and cold water in a microwave-safe bowl. Cover and microwave on high for about 1-1/2 minutes or until potatoes are tender; drain and set aside. In a small bowl, dissolve bouillon in boiling water; set aside.

In a saucepan, saute onion in butter until tender. Stir in flour until blended. Gradually stir in milk. Bring to a boil; cook and stir for 1-2 minutes or until thickened. Stir in the parsley, thyme, rosemary and garlic salt. Stir in potatoes and bouillon mixture; heat through. **Yield:** 2 servings.

Editor's Note: This recipe was tested in an 850-watt microwave.

HOMEMADE CREAM-STYLE SOUP MIX

This easy-to-make soup mix is great to have on hand for those nights when you need to whip up supper in a hurry. It's also a great substitute for canned cream soup in a recipe.
—DeAnn Alleva, Worthington, Ohio

2 cups instant nonfat dry milk
  powder
1/2 cup plus 2 tablespoons cornstarch
1/2 cup mashed potato flakes
1/4 cup chicken bouillon granules
 2 tablespoons dried vegetable flakes
 1 teaspoon onion powder
1/2 teaspoon dried marjoram
1/4 teaspoon garlic powder
1/8 teaspoon white pepper

In a food processor or blender, combine all the ingredients; cover and process until vegetable flakes are finely chopped. Store in an airtight container in a cool dry place for up to 1 year. **Yield:** 3 cups total.

Editor's Note: Use as a substitute for half a 10-3/4-ounce can of condensed cream of chicken, mushroom or celery soup.

For half of a can of soup, in a microwave-safe dish, whisk together 2/3 cup water and 3 tablespoons soup mix. Microwave, uncovered, on high for 2 to 2-1/2 minutes, whisking occasionally.

For mushroom soup, add 1/4 to 1/2 cup sauteed sliced mushrooms. For celery soup, add 1/8 teaspoon celery salt or one sauteed, sliced or chopped celery rib.

MEALS FOR ONE OR TWO

If you're too busy to
plan meals, don't worry.
This handy chapter features
20 complete menus.
You can mix and match
for even more
delicious combinations.

DEVILED CRAB CASSEROLE MEAL (P. 86)

MUSHROOM SPINACH SALAD

This salad is especially delicious made with spinach fresh from the garden.
—Patty Kile, Greentown, Pennsylvania

3 cups torn fresh spinach
1/2 cup sliced fresh mushrooms
1/2 cup seasoned croutons
2 tablespoons vegetable oil
1 tablespoon cider vinegar *or* white
    wine vinegar
1-1/2 teaspoons sugar
1 teaspoon lemon juice
1/8 teaspoon salt

1/8 teaspoon pepper
1 tablespoon crumbled cooked bacon

In a bowl, combine the spinach, mushrooms and croutons. In a jar with a tight-fitting lid, combine oil, vinegar, sugar, lemon juice, salt and pepper; shake well. Drizzle over salad and toss to coat. Sprinkle with crumbled bacon. **Yield:** 2 servings.

STEAKS WITH SQUASH MEDLEY

This recipe dates back to the 1960s, yet it's still a favorite today.
—Jim Tusing, Oklahoma City, Oklahoma

2 rib eye steaks (10 ounces *each*)
3 tablespoons olive *or* vegetable oil, *divided*
1/2 cup chopped onion
1/2 cup chopped yellow summer squash
1/2 cup chopped zucchini
1/2 cup sliced okra, optional
1 garlic clove, minced
1/4 cup tomato sauce
3 tablespoons vinegar
1/2 teaspoon dried rosemary, crushed
1/2 teaspoon dried thyme
1/8 teaspoon pepper

In a skillet over medium heat, brown steaks on both sides in 2 tablespoons oil. Cook 8 minutes longer or until the meat reaches desired doneness (for rare, a meat thermometer should read 140°; medium, 160°; well-done, 170°). Remove and keep warm.

Drain skillet. Saute onion, squash, zucchini, okra if desired and garlic in remaining oil for 6 minutes or until tender. Stir in the tomato sauce, vinegar, rosemary, thyme and pepper. Cook 3-4 minutes longer or until heated through. Serve over steaks. **Yield:** 2 servings.

CASHEW RICE

The vegetables add color while the cashews give this economical dish a classy touch.
—Pat Habiger, Spearville, Kansas

1/2 cup beef *or* chicken broth
2 tablespoons shredded carrot
2 tablespoons finely chopped celery
1 tablespoon sliced green onion
1 teaspoon butter *or* margarine
Dash pepper
1/2 cup uncooked instant rice
Chopped cashews

In a small saucepan, combine broth, carrot, celery, onion, butter and pepper. Bring to a boil; remove from the heat. Stir in rice; cover and let stand for 5 minutes or until the liquid is absorbed. Sprinkle with cashews. **Yield:** 2 servings.

PEACH COBBLER FOR TWO

Orange peel enhances the color and gives this traditional dessert a delicious distinction.
——Betty Clark, Mt. Vernon, Missouri

3 tablespoons brown sugar
2 teaspoons cornstarch
1/4 cup water
1-1/2 cups sliced fresh *or* frozen peaches
1 tablespoon butter *or* margarine
1 teaspoon lemon juice
TOPPING:
1/3 cup all-purpose flour
2 tablespoons sugar
1/2 teaspoon baking powder
Pinch salt
2 tablespoons milk
4-1/2 teaspoons butter *or* margarine, melted

1/4 teaspoon grated orange peel

In a small saucepan, combine brown sugar, cornstarch and water until smooth. Add peaches; bring to a boil. Cook and stir for 2 minutes. Reduce heat to low; stir in butter and lemon juice.

For topping, combine flour, sugar, baking powder and salt in a bowl. Stir in milk, butter and orange peel. Transfer hot peach mixture to an ungreased 1-qt. baking dish. Spoon topping over peaches. Bake, uncovered, at 400° for 25 minutes or until golden brown. **Yield:** 2 servings.

DILLED NOODLES

*This recipe is as simple as it is delicious. I tried it the first year I had
an herb garden, and I've been making it ever since.*
—Anna Prenni, Saltsburg, Pennsylvania

1-1/2 cups medium egg noodles
  1/2 cup small-curd cottage cheese
    1 to 2 tablespoons snipped fresh dill
      or 1 to 2 teaspoons dill weed
  1/4 teaspoon salt
Dash pepper

In a saucepan, cook noodles according to package directions. Meanwhile, combine the remaining ingredients. Drain noodles; add to cottage cheese mixture and toss gently. Serve immediately. **Yield:** 2 servings.

MINI TUNA CASSEROLES

I can whip up this dish in a hurry, and it's perfect for a light supper or lunch.
I always have a can of tuna on my pantry shelf, so it's convenient, too.
—Rebecca Reese, Jacksboro, Texas

1/2 cup chopped green onions
　2 tablespoons butter *or* margarine
　2 tablespoons all-purpose flour
3/4 cup milk
　1 can (6 ounces) tuna, drained
　1 cup crushed potato chips, *divided*
1/4 teaspoon pepper

In a saucepan, saute onions in butter. Stir in flour until blended. Gradually stir in milk. Bring to a boil over medium heat; cook and stir for 2 minutes or until thickened. Remove from the heat. Stir in the tuna, 1/2 cup of potato chips and pepper. Pour into two greased 8-oz. baking dishes. Sprinkle with remaining potato chips. Bake, uncovered, at 350° for 20-25 minutes or until hot and bubbly. **Yield:** 2 servings.

COLORFUL CABBAGE SKILLET

Crunchy and colorful, this side dish has the flavor and texture of creamy coleslaw,
but it's served warm. It's a nice change from typical vegetable dishes.
—Bernice Knutson, Soldier, Iowa

　1 cup coarsely shredded cabbage
1/3 cup sliced celery
1/3 cup julienned carrot
　2 tablespoons chopped onion
　2 tablespoons butter *or* margarine
1/2 teaspoon salt
Dash pepper
　3 tablespoons half-and-half cream
Minced fresh parsley

In a skillet, saute the cabbage, celery, carrot and onion in butter for 12 minutes or until crisp-tender. Sprinkle with salt and pepper. Reduce heat; stir in cream. Cook and stir for 3 minutes or until heated through. Sprinkle with parsley. **Yield:** 2 servings.

RASPBERRY CREAM

I discovered this recipe over 40 years ago. It's a refreshing summer dessert.
If you need a great-looking, tasty treat to end a meal, this is it!
—Christl Bennett, Burlington, Kentucky

　1 package (3 ounces) raspberry
　　gelatin
1/2 cup boiling water
　1 package (10 ounces) frozen
　　sweetened raspberries
　1 cup vanilla ice cream, softened
Whipped cream

In a bowl, dissolve gelatin in boiling water. Stir in raspberries and ice cream until blended. Spoon into two dessert dishes. Cover and refrigerate for at least 1 hour. Top with a dollop of whipped cream. **Yield:** 2 servings.

COPPER CARROTS

(Not pictured)

This has been one of my favorites since I first had it back in 1942.
—Billie Scoggins, Long Beach, Mississippi

3 medium carrots, julienned
2 teaspoons sugar
1/2 teaspoon cornstarch
1/4 teaspoon salt
1/8 teaspoon ground ginger
2 tablespoons orange juice
1 tablespoon butter *or* margarine

Place 1 in. water in a small saucepan; add carrots. Bring to a boil. Cover and cook until tender; drain. Remove carrots; set aside and keep warm. In the same saucepan, combine the sugar, cornstarch, salt and ginger. Gradually stir in orange juice until smooth. Bring to a boil; cook and stir for 2 minutes or until thickened. Add butter. Return carrots to pan; heat through. **Yield:** 2 servings.

LAZY LASAGNA

*This recipe makes two hearty servings and calls for prepared spaghetti sauce.
It's a great one-pot meal on hectic days.*
—Carol Mead, Los Alamos, New Mexico

1 cup spaghetti sauce
1/2 cup cottage cheese
3/4 cup shredded mozzarella cheese
1-1/2 cups cooked wide noodles
2 tablespoons grated Parmesan
cheese

Warm the spaghetti sauce; stir in cottage cheese and mozzarella. Fold in the noodles. Pour into two greased 2-cup casseroles. Sprinkle with Parmesan cheese. Bake, uncovered, at 375° for 20 minutes or until bubbly. **Yield:** 2 servings.

CHEESE BREAD

I like to dress up plain bread for a flavorful oven-fresh sensation.
—Cookie Curci-Wright, San Jose, California

1 Italian-style roll (6 inches)
1 tablespoon butter *or* margarine,
melted
1 garlic clove, minced
1 tablespoon grated Parmesan cheese

Cut roll in half lengthwise. Combine butter, garlic and cheese; spread on cut sides of roll. Broil 4 in. from heat for 2-3 minutes. **Yield:** 2 servings.

LITTLE CHOCOLATE CAKE

This cute cake is sized perfectly for two, and it's topped with an irresistible fudgy frosting.
—Paula Anderson, Springfield, Illinois

2 squares (1 ounce *each*)
unsweetened chocolate
1/2 cup boiling water
1 cup sugar
1/4 cup shortening
1 egg
1/2 teaspoon vanilla extract
1 cup all-purpose flour
1/2 teaspoon baking soda
1/2 teaspoon salt
1/4 cup sour milk*
FROSTING:
1-1/2 cups sugar
1/3 cup milk
2 squares (1 ounce *each*)
unsweetened chocolate, melted
2 tablespoons shortening
1 tablespoon corn syrup
1/4 teaspoon salt
2 tablespoons butter *or* margarine

1 teaspoon vanilla extract

In a mixing bowl, stir chocolate and water until blended. Cool. Add the sugar, shortening, egg and vanilla; mix well. Combine flour, baking soda and salt; gradually add to the chocolate mixture alternately with sour milk. Pour into a greased 8-in. square baking pan. Bake at 350° for 30-35 minutes or until a toothpick inserted in the center comes out clean. Cool completely.

For the frosting, combine the first six ingredients in a saucepan; bring to a boil. Boil for 1-1/2 minutes; remove from the heat. Set pan in a larger pan of ice water. Beat for 1 minute. Add butter and vanilla. Beat 10 minutes longer or until frosting is desired spreading consistency. Frost cake. **Yield:** 4 servings. ***Editor's Note:** To sour milk, place 1 teaspoon white vinegar in a measuring cup; add milk to equal 1/4 cup.

ORANGE-GLAZED CHICKEN

*A friend gave me this chicken recipe right after I finished college.
It's a sweet and tangy way to dress up a chicken breast.*
—Diane Madonna, Brunswick, Ohio

  1 tablespoon all-purpose flour
1/2 teaspoon salt
1/4 teaspoon pepper
  1 boneless skinless chicken breast
    half
  2 teaspoons vegetable oil
1/2 teaspoon orange marmalade
Dash ground nutmeg
1/2 cup orange juice

Combine flour, salt and pepper; coat chicken breast. In a skillet, heat oil on medium; brown chicken. Spread marmalade on top of chicken; sprinkle with nutmeg. Add orange juice and simmer for 10-15 minutes or until the chicken juices run clear. **Yield:** 1 serving.

HERBED RICE

I shared this recipe in a cookbook for others who cook for one.
—John Davis, Mobile, Alabama

1/4 cup uncooked long grain rice
1 green onion with top, cut into 1-inch pieces
1 tablespoon butter *or* margarine
1/8 teaspoon *each* dried tarragon, thyme, basil, parsley flakes and pepper
1/2 cup chicken broth

In a small saucepan, cook rice and onion in butter until onion is tender. Add the seasonings; cook for 1 minute. Add broth and salt if desired; bring to a boil. Cover and simmer for 15 minutes or until liquid is absorbed and rice is tender. **Yield:** 1 serving.

FRENCH PEAS

This medley of peas, onions and mushrooms goes with nearly any main meal.
—John Davis, Mobile, Alabama

1 teaspoon butter *or* margarine
2 teaspoons water
2 medium fresh mushrooms, thinly sliced
1/2 cup frozen peas

2 thin onion slices
Pinch salt

Melt butter in a small saucepan; add all remaining ingredients. Cover and cook until the peas are tender, stirring occasionally. **Yield:** 1 serving.

COCONUT MACADAMIA SQUARES

(Not pictured)

I came across this keeper when I visited my hometown in Florida. They never last long.
—Michelle Krzmarzick, Redondo Beach, California

1/4 cup butter *or* margarine, softened
1/2 cup sugar
1/4 cup packed brown sugar
1 egg
1/2 teaspoon vanilla extract
3/4 cup plus 2 tablespoons all-purpose flour
1/2 teaspoon baking powder
1/4 teaspoon salt
1/4 cup chopped macadamia nuts
TOPPING:
1/4 cup packed brown sugar
1 tablespoon butter *or* margarine, melted
1 tablespoon milk
1 tablespoon light corn syrup
1/2 cup flaked coconut
1/4 cup chopped macadamia nuts

2 tablespoons semisweet chocolate chips

In a small mixing bowl, cream butter and sugars. Beat in egg and vanilla; mix well. Combine the flour, baking soda and salt; gradually add to creamed mixture and mix well. Stir in macadamia nuts. Spread into a greased 8-in. square baking dish. Bake at 350° for 15-20 minutes or until golden brown.

For topping, in another small mixing bowl, combine the sugar and butter. Stir in milk and corn syrup; mix well. Stir in coconut and macadamia nuts. Drop mixture evenly over top of warm bars. Return to the oven and broil 4 in. from the heat for 1-2 minutes or until mixture is bubbly. Immediately sprinkle with chocolate chips. Allow chips to soften for a few minutes, then spread over bars. Cool on a wire rack. **Yield:** 16 bars.

CRANBERRY PEARS

I devised this yummy recipe one summer when I had an abundant crop of pears. I started with a recipe for chunky applesauce, substituting pears for apples, with great results.
—Leila Ryan, McDonough, Georgia

3/4 cup water
1/2 cup sugar
1/2 teaspoon ground cinnamon
  2 large ripe pears, peeled and quartered
1/2 cup fresh *or* frozen cranberries

In a saucepan, combine water, sugar and cinnamon. Add pears; bring to a boil over medium heat. Stir in cranberries. Reduce heat; cover and simmer for 10 minutes or until tender, stirring occasionally. Serve warm or chilled. **Yield:** 2 servings.

DEVILED CRAB CASSEROLE

I serve this entree often, since it's so easy to assemble. The crab makes it taste special.
—Helen Bachman, Champaign, Illinois

1 can (6 ounces) crabmeat, drained,
   flaked and cartilage removed
1 cup dry bread crumbs, *divided*
3/4 cup milk
1/4 cup chopped green onions
2 hard-cooked eggs, chopped
1/2 teaspoon salt
1/4 teaspoon Worcestershire sauce
1/8 teaspoon ground mustard
1/8 teaspoon pepper
6 tablespoons butter *or* margarine,
   melted, *divided*
Paprika

In a bowl, combine crab, 3/4 cup of bread crumbs, milk, onions, eggs, salt, Worcestershire sauce, mustard and pepper. Add 4 tablespoons of butter; mix well. Spoon into a greased 1-qt. baking dish.

Combine remaining bread crumbs and butter; sprinkle over casserole. Sprinkle with paprika. Bake, uncovered, at 425° for 16-18 minutes or until golden brown and edges are bubbly. **Yield:** 2 servings.

WHITE BEANS AND SPINACH

This is a variation of a recipe I received from my Italian mother.
It complements a variety of main courses.
—Lucia Johnson, Massena, New York

8 cups torn fresh spinach
2 tablespoons water
2 garlic cloves, minced
1/4 teaspoon salt
Dash cayenne pepper
Dash ground nutmeg
3/4 cup canned white kidney *or* great
   northern beans

Combine spinach, water and garlic in a skillet; cover and cook over medium heat for 3 minutes or until tender, stirring occasionally. Sprinkle with salt, cayenne and nutmeg. Gently stir in beans; heat through. **Yield:** 2 servings.

CHOCOLATE PUDDING CAKE

This is a satisfying dessert topped with ice cream or whipped cream.
—Helene Belanger, Denver, Colorado

1/2 cup biscuit/baking mix
2 tablespoons sugar
2 teaspoons baking cocoa
3 tablespoons milk
1/2 teaspoon vanilla extract
TOPPING:
3 tablespoons brown sugar
1 tablespoon baking cocoa
1/2 cup boiling water
Ice cream *or* whipped cream, optional

In a small bowl, combine baking mix, sugar and cocoa. Stir in milk and vanilla. Spoon into two greased 8- or 10-oz. custard cups.

For topping, combine the brown sugar and cocoa in a bowl. Stir in boiling water. Pour over batter. Bake at 350° for 25 minutes or until a toothpick inserted in the cake layer comes out clean. Top with ice cream or whipped cream if desired. **Yield:** 2 servings.

SKILLET SQUASH AND POTATOES

My niece suggested I try cooking squash and potatoes together, so I made up this recipe.
It turned out to be a winner—a great side dish for just about any entree.
—Bonnie Milner, DeRidder, Louisiana

1 **small potato, peeled and thinly**
   sliced
1/4 **cup chopped onion**
1 **tablespoon vegetable oil**
1 **small yellow summer squash, sliced**
1/4 **teaspoon salt**
1/8 **teaspoon pepper**
Dash paprika

In a covered skillet over medium-low heat, cook the potato and onion in oil for 12 minutes. Add squash; cook, uncovered, for 8-10 minutes or until the vegetables are tender, stirring occasionally. Season with salt, pepper and paprika. **Yield:** 2 servings.

STUFFED PEPPERS FOR TWO

My husband likes stuffed peppers, but my old recipe made too much.
I devised this recipe to accommodate just the two of us.
—Elaine Carpenter, Horseshoe Bay, Texas

2 medium green peppers
1/2 pound ground beef
1 can (8 ounces) tomato sauce,
   divided
1/4 cup uncooked instant rice
3 tablespoons shredded cheddar
   cheese, *divided*
1 tablespoon chopped onion
1/2 teaspoon Worcestershire sauce
1/2 teaspoon salt
1/4 teaspoon pepper
1 egg, beaten

Cut tops off peppers and discard; remove seeds. Blanch peppers in boiling water for 5 minutes. Drain and rinse in cold water; set aside. In a bowl, combine beef, 1/4 cup of tomato sauce, rice, 2 tablespoons of cheese, onion, Worcestershire sauce, salt, pepper and egg; mix well. Stuff peppers; place in an ungreased 1-1/2-qt. baking dish. Pour remaining tomato sauce over peppers.

Cover and bake at 350° for 45-60 minutes or until meat is no longer pink and peppers are tender. Sprinkle with remaining cheese; return to the oven for 5 minutes or until cheese is melted. **Yield:** 2 servings.

FRUITY COLESLAW

The tartness of the slaw and the sweetness of the fruit give this dish a unique flavor.
—Margaret Wamper, Butler, Pennsylvania

1 can (8 ounces) pineapple chunks
2 cups shredded cabbage
3/4 cup mandarin oranges
1 carrot, thinly sliced
1 tablespoon finely chopped onion
1 tablespoon vegetable oil
1-1/2 teaspoons cider vinegar
1 teaspoon sugar
1/8 teaspoon salt
1/8 teaspoon pepper

Drain pineapple, reserving 1 tablespoon of the juice. In a large bowl, combine the pineapple, shredded cabbage, mandarin oranges and carrot; mix well. Combine the onion, oil, vinegar, sugar, salt, pepper and reserved pineapple juice; stir into the cabbage mixture. Cover and refrigerate until serving. **Yield:** 2 servings.

COCONUT MACAROONS

I won a first-place ribbon at the county fair with this recipe, which is my husband's favorite.
—Penny Ann Habeck, Shawano, Wisconsin

1-1/3 cups flaked coconut
1/3 cup sugar
2 tablespoons all-purpose flour
1/8 teaspoon salt
2 egg whites
1/2 teaspoon vanilla extract

In a bowl, combine coconut, sugar, flour and salt. Stir in egg whites and vanilla; mix well. Drop by rounded teaspoonfuls onto greased baking sheets. Bake at 325° for 18-20 minutes or until golden. Cool on a wire rack. **Yield:** about 1-1/2 dozen.

BANANA ORANGE SALAD

I came up with this salad when an unexpected guest showed up for lunch and I had to make do with what was on hand. I thought it would complement homemade soup, and it did. It's a refreshing salad that's also very attractive.
—Mary Paulson, Hopkins, Minnesota

1 medium navel orange, peeled and sliced
1 to 2 tablespoons honey
1 teaspoon whole cloves
2 cups torn salad greens
1 medium firm banana, sliced
1 to 2 teaspoons flaked coconut, toasted

Place orange slices in a bowl. Combine the honey and cloves; pour over oranges. Cover and refrigerate for at least 1 hour. Discard cloves. Arrange greens on salad plates. Top with orange and banana slices. Drizzle with honey mixture. Sprinkle with coconut. **Yield:** 2 servings.

CUBE STEAK SKILLET SUPPER

I first made this delicious dish in the '70s for a progressive dinner party. It's easy to prepare.
—Karen Rodgers, Verona, Virginia

1/4 cup all-purpose flour
1/4 teaspoon salt
Dash pepper
2 cube steaks
1 to 2 tablespoons vegetable oil
1 small onion, sliced
1 can (15 ounces) sliced potatoes, drained
1 can (14-1/2 ounces) French-style green beans, drained
1 can (10-3/4 ounces) condensed golden mushroom soup, undiluted
Paprika

In a large resealable plastic bag, combine flour, salt and pepper. Add steaks and shake to coat. In a skillet, brown steaks on both sides in oil. Set aside and keep warm. Add onion, potatoes and beans to skillet; stir in soup. Return steaks to skillet. Cover and simmer for 15 minutes or until meat is tender. Sprinkle with paprika. **Yield:** 2 servings.

FRENCH ONION SOUP

I adapted a basic recipe to copy the onion soup served at my favorite restaurant.
—Barbara Brunner, Steelton, Pennsylvania

2 medium onions, chopped
1 teaspoon sugar
6 tablespoons butter *or* margarine, *divided*
1 tablespoon all-purpose flour
1/8 teaspoon pepper
Dash ground nutmeg
2-1/2 cups beef broth
2 tablespoons grated Parmesan cheese
2 slices French bread (1 inch thick)
4 slices provolone cheese

In a saucepan, saute onions and sugar in 3 tablespoons of butter until golden brown. Stir in the flour, pepper and nutmeg until blended. Gradually stir in broth. Bring to a boil; cook and stir for 2 minutes. Reduce heat; cover and simmer for 30 minutes. Stir in the Parmesan cheese.

Meanwhile, in a skillet, melt remaining butter; add bread. Cook until golden brown on both sides. Ladle soup into two ovenproof bowls. Place a slice of cheese in each bowl; top with bread and remaining cheese. Bake at 375° for 10 minutes or until the cheese is bubbly. **Yield:** 2 servings.

APPLE GRAHAM DESSERT

Years ago, my favorite after-school snack was applesauce with graham crackers.
This version is my creation.
—Rita Ferro, Alameda, California

6 cinnamon graham crackers (4-3/4 inches x 2-1/2 inches)
1 cup applesauce
1 cup whipped topping
Chopped walnuts, optional

Place one graham cracker on a serving plate. Spread with 2 heaping tablespoons of applesauce. Repeat layers, ending with applesauce. Spread the whipped topping over top and sides. Sprinkle with nuts if desired. Refrigerate for 2 hours before slicing. **Yield:** 2 servings.

SWEETHEART SORBET

*This not-too-sour, not-too-sweet lemony confection from our
Test Kitchen home economists is a refreshingly frosty finish.*

1 cup sugar
1 cup water
1/2 cup lemon juice
1 tablespoon grated lemon peel

In a bowl, combine all ingredients; whisk until sugar is dissolved. Pour into the cylinder of an ice cream freezer. Freeze according to manufacturer's directions. **Yield:** 2 cups.

COUPLE'S CATCH OF THE DAY

Here's a match made in heaven—two tasty fish fillets in a Valentine's Day shape!
Moist and tender, this succulent orange roughy from our Test Kitchen staff
will win hearts with its memorable blend of garlic, dill and lemon.

2 **parchment paper squares
(12 inches** *each***)**
2 **tablespoons butter** *or* **margarine,
melted,** *divided*
2 **orange roughy fillets (about 3/4
pound)**
1 **teaspoon snipped fresh dill**
1/4 **teaspoon lemon-pepper seasoning**
1/8 **teaspoon garlic powder**
1/2 **medium lemon, cut into 1/4-inch
slices**
2 **fresh dill sprigs**

Cut each piece of parchment paper into a 12-in. heart. Brush paper with 1 tablespoon butter. Place a fillet on one side of each heart. Sprinkle with dill, lemon-pepper and garlic powder. Drizzle with remaining butter. Arrange lemon slices over fish.

Fold parchment hearts in half. Beginning at the tip of the heart, fold edges together, 2 in. at a time. Place on a large baking sheet. Bake at 375° for 20-25 minutes. With a scissors, cut an X through top of parchment; fish should flake easily with a fork. Transfer each parchment heart to a plate. Garnish with dill sprigs. **Yield:** 2 servings.

LOVE KNOT VEGETABLES

Tie these veggies from our home economists into a romantic meal plan—your sweetheart will get
attached fast! Simply soften carrots and zucchini so they're flexible enough to intertwine.

2 **medium carrots**
6 **cups water,** *divided*
1 **medium zucchini**
1 **teaspoon cornstarch**
1/2 **cup chicken broth**
1/2 **teaspoon dried oregano**

Peel carrots; cut each end at a diagonal. In a large saucepan, bring 4 cups water to a boil; add carrots. Cover and cook for 10-12 minutes or until crisp-tender. Cool slightly.

Using a vegetable peeler, peel carrots into lengthwise strips; cut each 1/2 in. wide. Stack two strips together; loosely tie into a knot. Repeat to make five more carrot knots. Set knots and remaining strips aside. Cut zucchini ends at an angle. Using the peeler, peel zucchini into thin strips; cut each 1/2 in. wide. Bring remaining water to a boil; add zucchini strips. Cook for 2 minutes or just until tender. Make six zucchini knots, following directions for carrot knots.

In a saucepan, combine the cornstarch, broth and oregano until smooth. Bring to a boil; cook and stir for 1 minute or until thickened. Add vegetable knots and strips; heat through. Place strips in a serving bowl; top with knots. **Yield:** 2 servings.

TIMELY TIP

*Freeze leftover vegetables, such as corn, cabbage, tomatoes,
carrots and broccoli, in a container just for soup.
When you have enough, add canned broth for a one-of-a-kind soup.*

Oatmeal Apricot Squares

*Easy to prepare, these squares contain a marvelous blend of flavors.
This dessert can be stirred up in no time to satisfy a sweet tooth
warm from the oven or as a treat later.*
—Veronica Roza, Bayport, New York

1 cup all-purpose flour
1 cup quick-cooking oats
1/2 cup packed brown sugar
1/4 teaspoon salt
1/4 teaspoon baking soda
1/2 cup cold butter *or* margarine
3/4 cup apricot preserves

In a bowl, combine the first five ingredients. Cut in butter until the mixture resembles coarse crumbs. Press half of the mixture into a greased 8-in. square baking pan. Spread with preserves. Sprinkle with remaining oat mixture; gently press down. Bake at 350° for 38-42 minutes or until golden brown. Cool on a wire rack. Cut into squares. **Yield:** 16 servings.

RED PEPPER 'N' CORN SKILLET

This is an old recipe we used when I was growing up in Kentucky.
We called it "fried corn" and made it as long as we could get fresh corn on the cob.
—Barbara Marshall, Concord, California

1 bacon strip, diced
3/4 cup fresh *or* frozen corn
1/3 cup chopped onion
1/2 cup chopped sweet red *or*
    green pepper
1/4 cup chicken broth
1/2 teaspoon salt
1/4 teaspoon pepper
  1 tablespoon cider vinegar

2 teaspoons minced fresh sage *or* 1/4
    teaspoon rubbed sage

In a skillet, cook bacon over medium heat until nearly crisp. Add the corn, onion and red pepper. Cook and stir over medium heat about 5 minutes, until tender. Stir in the broth, salt and pepper. Cook for 5 minutes or until liquid is almost absorbed. Stir in vinegar and sage. **Yield:** 2 servings.

CARAMELIZED APPLE RINGS

When my children were little, this was one of their favorites. One taste and you'll see why.
—Helen Steele, Polk City, Florida

1 large tart apple, cored and sliced
    1/2 inch thick
2 tablespoons butter *or* margarine
1/4 cup packed brown sugar

In a skillet, cook apples in butter until tender. Sprinkle with brown sugar. Cook until apples are golden brown and caramelized, about 5 minutes. **Yield:** 2 servings.

TURKEY TURNOVERS

I make this dish after the holidays, when there's leftover turkey in the refrigerator or freezer.
—Julie Wagner, Northville, Michigan

1 package (3 ounces) cream cheese,
    softened
1 tablespoon milk
1/2 cup cubed cooked turkey
1/2 cup cooked peas
  4 teaspoons sliced almonds
1 tablespoon minced fresh parsley
1 tablespoon finely chopped onion
1-1/2 teaspoons diced pimientos
Dash *each* salt, pepper and garlic powder
1 cup biscuit/baking mix
1/4 cup cold water
1 tablespoon butter *or* margarine,
    melted
1/2 to 3/4 cup condensed cream
    of chicken soup, undiluted
    or chicken gravy

In a mixing bowl, beat cream cheese and milk until smooth. Stir in the turkey, peas, almonds, parsley, onion, pimientos, salt, pepper and garlic powder; set aside.

In a bowl, combine biscuit mix and water until a soft dough forms. On a floured surface, knead gently 5-6 times or until dough is no longer sticky. Gently roll into an 11-in. x 7-in. rectangle; cut in half. Spoon half of the turkey mixture onto each. Carefully fold pastry over filling; seal edges tightly with a fork. Brush tops with butter.

Place on a greased baking sheet. Bake at 350° for 30-35 minutes or until golden brown. Meanwhile, heat soup; serve with turnovers. **Yield:** 2 servings.

BEEF TENDERLOIN IN MUSHROOM SAUCE

It doesn't take much fuss to fix a special meal for two. Here's the delicious proof.
—Denise McNab, Warrington, Pennsylvania

1 teaspoon vegetable oil
4 tablespoons butter *or* margarine, *divided*
2 beef tenderloin steaks *or* fillets (1 inch thick)
1/2 cup chopped fresh mushrooms
1 tablespoon chopped green onions
1 tablespoon all-purpose flour
1/8 teaspoon salt
Dash pepper
2/3 cup chicken *or* beef broth
1/8 teaspoon browning sauce, optional

In a skillet, heat oil and 2 tablespoons of butter over medium-high heat. Cook steaks for 6-7 minutes on each side or until meat is done (for rare, a meat thermometer should read 140°; medium, 160°; well-done, 170°). Remove to a plate; keep warm.

To pan juices, add mushrooms, onions and remaining butter; saute until vegetables are tender. Add flour, salt and pepper; gradually stir in broth until smooth. Add browning sauce if desired. Bring to a boil; boil and stir for 2 minutes. Spoon over the steaks. Serve immediately. **Yield:** 2 servings.

VEGETABLE RAMEKINS

We eat this dish often since we can pull fresh vegetables from our garden all year.
—Dona Alsover, Upland, California

1 small zucchini *or* yellow summer squash, halved and cut into 1/2-inch slices
1/4 cup chopped green pepper
1/3 cup broccoli florets
1 medium carrot, julienned
1 medium potato, peeled, cooked and cubed
2 tablespoons butter *or* margarine
2 tablespoons all-purpose flour
3/4 cup milk
1/4 teaspoon garlic salt
1/8 teaspoon coarse black pepper
1/4 cup shredded cheddar cheese
1 tablespoon minced fresh parsley
1 tablespoon chopped walnuts

In a saucepan over medium heat, cook squash, green pepper, broccoli and carrot in boiling water until crisp-tender; drain. Stir in the potato. Spoon into two greased ovenproof 10-oz. custard cups or casseroles.

In a saucepan, melt the butter; stir in flour, milk, garlic salt and pepper until smooth. Cook for 2-3 minutes, gradually adding cheese in small amounts; cook and stir until cheese is melted. Pour over vegetables. Sprinkle with parsley and walnuts. Bake, uncovered, at 350° for 20-25 minutes, until sauce is bubbly. **Yield:** 2 servings.

LITTLE DIXIE POUND CAKE

Sometimes I dollop cake slices with whipped cream or top them with fresh berries.
—Ruby Williams, Bogalusa, Louisiana

3 tablespoons butter (no substitutes), softened
6 tablespoons sugar
1 egg
6 tablespoons all-purpose flour
Pinch baking soda
7 teaspoons buttermilk
1/4 teaspoon vanilla extract
1/8 teaspoon orange extract

In a small mixing bowl, cream the butter and sugar. Beat in egg. Combine flour and baking soda; add alternately with buttermilk to creamed mixture. Blend in extracts. Pour into a greased 5-3/4-in. x 3-in. x 2-in. loaf pan. Bake at 350° for 30-35 minutes or until cake tests done. Cool for 10 minutes; remove from the pan to cool on a wire rack. **Yield:** 1 mini loaf.

PORK GARDEN BEAN SOUP

(Not pictured)

This creamy soup is a great way to start a meal.
—Florence Schneidewend, Neenah, Wisconsin

1-3/4 cups water
1 bone-in pork chop (about 1/2 pound)
3/4 cup cut fresh green beans
3/4 cup cubed peeled potatoes
1 medium carrot, thinly sliced
1/2 teaspoon salt
1/4 teaspoon pepper
1/3 cup half-and-half cream

Place water and pork chop in a saucepan. Bring to a boil. Reduce heat; cover and simmer 15 minutes, just until pork is tender. Remove from water. Cool; cut into cubes.

Add the beans, potatoes, carrot, salt and pepper to cooking liquid. Return to a boil. Reduce heat; cover and simmer for 12 minutes or until vegetables are tender. Return pork to pan; stir in cream and heat through (do not boil). **Yield:** 2 servings.

GARLIC POTATO BALLS

I've used this recipe since I was married nearly 50 years ago. This is easy and quick to make on busy days.
—Alpha Wilson, Roswell, New Mexico

1 tablespoon butter *or* margarine
1 can (15 ounces) small whole
   potatoes, drained
1/4 teaspoon garlic salt
1/2 teaspoon minced fresh parsley

In a skillet, melt butter over medium heat. Add potatoes; sprinkle with garlic salt. Cook and stir for 15-18 minutes or until golden brown. Sprinkle with parsley. **Yield:** 2 servings.

APPLE SWISS CHICKEN

I'm always looking for new ways to serve chicken. My mother and I created this recipe.
—Lynne Glashoerster, Edmonton, Alberta

2 boneless skinless chicken breast
   halves
1/2 teaspoon dried rosemary, crushed
2 thin slices fully cooked ham
1 medium tart apple, peeled and
   thinly sliced, *divided*
1 tablespoon vegetable oil
2 thin slices Swiss cheese
1 tablespoon apple juice *or* chicken
   broth
Paprika

Flatten chicken breasts to 1/4-in. thickness; rub with rosemary. Top each with a ham slice and a few apple slices; roll up tightly. Secure with toothpicks. Place in a greased 1-qt. baking dish. Drizzle with oil.

Bake, uncovered, at 350° for 20 minutes. Top with cheese and remaining apple slices; drizzle with apple juice. Sprinkle with paprika. Bake 10-15 minutes longer, until chicken juices run clear and cheese is melted. Discard toothpicks. **Yield:** 2 servings.

HONEYED CARROT COINS

Carrots are frequently on my menu. They're so easy to work with and are usually on hand.
—Annie Hicks, Zephyrhills, Florida

1-1/2 cups sliced carrots
1/2 cup apple juice
1 tablespoon honey
1 teaspoon grated orange peel
1 teaspoon grated lemon peel
1 teaspoon butter *or* margarine
1/4 teaspoon salt, optional

In a small saucepan, combine carrots and apple juice. Cover and cook over medium heat for 10 minutes or until tender. Stir in the remaining ingredients. Serve with a slotted spoon. **Yield:** 2 servings. **Nutritional Analysis:** One 3/4-cup serving (prepared with margarine and without salt) equals 119 calories, 57 mg sodium, 0 cholesterol, 26 gm carbohydrate, 1 gm protein, 2 gm fat. **Diabetic Exchanges:** 2 vegetable, 1 fruit.

BREAD PUDDING FOR TWO

The best thing about this dessert is it satisfies a sweet tooth without being too rich.
—Jean Loomer, South Windsor, Connecticut

1 cup soft bread cubes
1 egg
2/3 cup milk
3 tablespoons brown sugar
1 tablespoon butter, melted
1/2 teaspoon ground cinnamon
1/4 teaspoon ground nutmeg
Dash salt
1/3 cup raisins
Vanilla ice cream

Place bread in a greased 1-qt. baking dish. In a bowl, whisk egg and milk. Stir in the brown sugar, butter, cinnamon, nutmeg and salt. Pour over bread; sprinkle with raisins. Bake, uncovered, at 350° for 30-35 minutes or until a knife inserted near the center comes out clean. Serve warm with ice cream. **Yield:** 2 servings.

HAM STEAK WITH LEMON

When you have a taste for ham but don't want leftovers, reach for this recipe.
Individual ham slices make just the right amount and take just minutes to cook.
—Lorraine Carr, Seattle, Washington

2 slices fully cooked ham (1/2 inch thick)
1 lemon, halved
3 tablespoons brown sugar
2 teaspoons prepared mustard

Broil ham slices 5 in. from the heat for 5 minutes. Meanwhile, slice one lemon half; set aside. Grate peel from the other half and squeeze 1 tablespoon juice into a bowl. Add peel, brown sugar and mustard to juice. Turn ham over; brush with the lemon mixture. Top with lemon slices. Broil 3-4 minutes more or until ham is heated through. **Yield:** 2 servings.

SMALL-BATCH POTATO SALAD

This salad conveniently calls for canned potatoes, so I can make it at a moment's notice.
—June Schwanz, Saukville, Wisconsin

4 bacon strips
1 tablespoon cornstarch
1/3 cup sugar
1/2 cup water
1/4 cup vinegar
1/2 teaspoon salt
1/4 teaspoon pepper
1 can (15 ounces) sliced potatoes, drained
Minced fresh parsley

In a skillet, cook bacon until crisp. Drain, reserving 2 tablespoons of drippings. Crumble bacon and set aside. Add cornstarch and sugar to drippings; stir until smooth. Add water, vinegar, salt and pepper; cook and stir over medium heat for 3-4 minutes or until thickened and bubbly. Stir in potatoes and bacon.

Cook for 2-3 minutes or until heated through. Serve warm or at room temperature. Garnish with parsley. **Yield:** 2 servings.

BISCUITS FOR TWO

A friend shared this recipe with me. I think the biscuits taste wonderful warm from the oven.
—Sylvia McCoy, Lees Summit, Missouri

1 cup all-purpose flour
2-1/2 teaspoons baking powder
1 teaspoon sugar
1/2 teaspoon salt
1/8 teaspoon cream of tartar
1/4 cup shortening
1/2 cup milk

In a bowl, combine dry ingredients. Cut in shortening until mixture resembles coarse crumbs. Stir in milk. Turn onto a floured surface; knead 1 minute. Roll or pat dough to 1/2-in. thickness. Cut with a floured 2-1/2-in. biscuit cutter. Place on a greased baking sheet. Bake at 450° for 10-12 minutes. **Yield:** 4 biscuits.

COZY HOT CHOCOLATE

(Not pictured)

The addition of vanilla extract makes this cocoa extra flavorful. It's especially good during the colder winter months. My husband and I often share a batch.
—Marie Hattrup, The Dalles, Oregon

2 tablespoons baking cocoa
2 tablespoons sugar
1/4 cup water
2 cups milk
1/2 teaspoon vanilla extract
Whipped cream
Ground cinnamon, optional

In a saucepan, mix the cocoa and sugar; add water. Bring to a boil, stirring constantly; boil for 1 minute. Reduce heat; add milk and heat through. Remove from the heat and stir in vanilla. Pour into 2 cups; top with whipped cream and sprinkle with cinnamon if desired. **Yield:** 2 servings.

Waldorf Salad for Two

The pear and hint of orange are a nice surprise in this salad. It always brings rave reviews.
—*Mildred Cummings, Cincinnati, Ohio*

1 small apple, diced
1 small pear, diced
1 celery rib, diced
2 tablespoons chopped walnuts
1/4 cup mayonnaise *or* salad dressing
1 tablespoon orange juice
2 lettuce leaves

In a small bowl, toss the apple, pear, celery and walnuts. Combine mayonnaise and orange juice; spoon over salad and toss to coat. Serve on lettuce. **Yield:** 2 servings.

SPECIAL SALMON STEAKS

After our children were married and gone, I prepared this entree often for my husband and me, especially on our anniversary. It was one of our favorites.
—Ruby Williams, Bogalusa, Louisiana

2 salmon *or* halibut steaks (8 ounces *each*)
2 tablespoons butter *or* margarine, melted
2 tablespoons lemon juice
1 green onion, sliced
1 tablespoon minced fresh parsley
1/4 teaspoon garlic salt
1/8 teaspoon lemon-pepper seasoning

Place salmon in a lightly greased 8-in. square baking dish. Top with butter and lemon juice. Combine onion, parsley, garlic salt and lemon pepper; sprinkle over salmon. Bake, uncovered, at 400° for 15-20 minutes or until fish flakes easily with a fork. **Yield:** 2 servings.

HERBED POTATO WEDGES

This recipe is simple and I've used it many times. Since it makes enough for two, I wrap half of the baked potato wedges in foil and freeze them for another time.
—R.V. Taibbi, Honolulu, Hawaii

3 tablespoons grated Parmesan cheese
1 tablespoon dried basil
1/4 teaspoon salt, optional
1/4 teaspoon pepper
1 large unpeeled baking potato, cut into wedges
2 teaspoons vegetable oil

In a shallow bowl, combine Parmesan cheese, basil, salt if desired and pepper. Brush cut sides of potato wedges with oil; dip into cheese mixture. Place in a greased 8-in. square pan. Bake, uncovered, at 400° for 20-25 minutes or until tender. **Yield:** 2 servings. **Nutritional Analysis:** One serving (prepared without salt) equals 190 calories, 183 mg sodium, 7 mg cholesterol, 25 gm carbohydrate, 6 gm protein, 8 gm fat. **Diabetic Exchanges:** 1-1/2 starch, 1-1/2 fat.

CHOCOLATE SHORTBREAD

Any chocolate lover will like these melt-in-your-mouth cookies.
—Sarah Bueckert, Austin, Manitoba

1/4 cup butter (no substitutes), softened
1/4 teaspoon vanilla extract
1/2 cup all-purpose flour
1/4 cup confectioners' sugar
1 to 2 tablespoons baking cocoa

In a mixing bowl, cream the butter. Add vanilla and mix well. Combine flour, sugar and cocoa; add to creamed mixture. Beat until dough holds together, about 3 minutes. Pat into a 9-in. x 4-in. rectangle. Cut into 2-in. x 1-1/2-in. strips. Place 1 in. apart on ungreased baking sheets. Prick with a fork. Bake at 300° for 20-25 minutes or until set. Cool for 5 minutes; remove to a wire rack to cool completely. **Yield:** 1 dozen.

PEACH MELBA DESSERT

This pretty dessert is an impressive end to any meal.
Refreshing and light, it's just right to satisfy a sweet tooth.
—Edna Christiansen, Edmore, Michigan

1 can (15-1/4 ounces) peach halves in syrup
2 individual round sponge cakes
2 scoops vanilla ice cream
1 tablespoon raspberry *or* strawberry jam
2 teaspoons chopped nuts, optional

Drain peaches, reserving syrup. Set aside two peaches and 1 tablespoon syrup (refrigerate remaining peaches and syrup for another use). Place each sponge cake on a plate; drizzle with reserved syrup. Top with ice cream and a peach half. In a small saucepan, heat jam until melted; drizzle over peaches. Top with nuts if desired. Serve immediately. **Yield:** 2 servings.

GROUND BEEF STROGANOFF

My mother-in-law gave me this economical yet tasty recipe 25 years ago.
—Marjorie Kriegh, Nampa, Idaho

1/2 pound lean ground beef
1/4 cup chopped onion
1 tablespoon butter *or* margarine
1/4 cup sliced fresh mushrooms
1 tablespoon all-purpose flour
1 garlic clove, minced
1/4 teaspoon salt
1/8 teaspoon pepper
2 tablespoons chili sauce
1/4 teaspoon Worcestershire sauce
1/3 cup sour cream
Hot cooked noodles

In a skillet, cook beef and onion in butter until meat is no longer pink. Stir in mushrooms, flour, garlic, salt and pepper. Cook and stir for 5 minutes. Add chili sauce and Worcestershire sauce. Reduce heat; cook, uncovered, for 10 minutes. Stir in sour cream just before serving; heat through (do not boil). Serve over noodles. **Yield:** 2 servings.

CARAWAY RYE MUFFINS

My family enjoys the distinctive taste of caraway, and it abounds in these muffins.
—Jean Tyner, Darlington, South Carolina

1 cup rye flour
3/4 cup all-purpose flour
1/4 cup sugar
2-1/2 teaspoons baking powder
1/2 teaspoon salt
1/2 teaspoon caraway seeds
3/4 cup shredded cheddar cheese
1 egg, beaten
3/4 cup milk
1/3 cup vegetable oil

In a large bowl, combine the first six ingredients. Stir in cheese. In another bowl, combine the egg, milk and oil; stir into the dry ingredients just until moistened. Fill greased or paper-lined muffin cups two-thirds full. Bake at 400° for 20-23 minutes or until golden brown. Serve warm. **Yield:** 10 muffins.

SALAD WITH HOT ITALIAN DRESSING

I created this recipe for a special dinner for our wedding anniversary.
—Bessie Hulett, Shively, Kentucky

2 cups torn leaf lettuce
4 green onions, sliced
2 radishes, sliced
1 medium tomato, cut into wedges
3 bacon strips, diced
1 teaspoon all-purpose flour
1/4 cup vinegar
2 tablespoons water
2 tablespoons sugar
3/4 teaspoon Italian salad dressing mix

Arrange first four ingredients in salad bowls; set aside. In a small skillet, cook bacon until crisp. Remove to paper towels to drain; reserve 1 tablespoon drippings. Add flour to drippings; stir until smooth. Cook over low heat for 3 minutes.

Combine vinegar, water, sugar and salad dressing mix; add to skillet. Bring to a boil over medium heat; cook and stir for 2 minutes. Pour over salads. Top with bacon. Serve immediately. Refrigerate leftover dressing for up to 2 weeks. **Yield:** 2 servings.

CRANBERRY CHICKEN

I made up this recipe myself because I love cranberries.
This dish is tangy and tart...an interesting combination of flavors.
—Angelina Lenhart, Concord, California

1/2 cup cranberry juice
2 tablespoons soy sauce
2 tablespoons Worcestershire sauce
2 garlic cloves, minced
2 bone-in chicken breast halves
Hot cooked rice, optional

In a resealable plastic bag, combine the first four ingredients. Add chicken and turn to coat. Seal bag and refrigerate 8 hours or overnight. Place chicken and marinade in a small ungreased baking pan. Bake, uncovered, at 350° for 1 hour or until the meat juices run clear. Serve over rice if desired. **Yield**: 2 servings.

CREAM OF BROCCOLI SOUP

When our two sons left home (in the same year) to build their own "nests", we had to make adjustments , especially in our menus. This recipe is easy, healthy and tasty.
—*Elsie Quance, Newark, New York*

1 cup water
2 chicken bouillon cubes
2 cups chopped fresh broccoli
2 tablespoons dried minced onion
1/4 teaspoon salt
1/8 teaspoon pepper
1/2 cup milk
2 teaspoons butter *or* margarine

In a saucepan, bring water and bouillon to a boil. Add broccoli, onion, salt and pepper. Reduce heat; simmer for 5-7 minutes or until broccoli is tender. Let cool for 10 minutes. Pour into a blender; cover and process until smooth. Return to pan; add milk and heat through. Top each serving with a teaspoon of butter. **Yield:** 2 servings.

FLUFFY BISCUIT MUFFINS

These biscuits are simple to make and have a wonderful aroma when baking. This particular recipe is one of my husband's favorites.
—*Virginia Foster, Paducah, Kentucky*

1 cup self-rising flour*
2 tablespoons mayonnaise (no substitutes)
1/2 cup milk

In a bowl, cut flour and mayonnaise together until mixture resembles coarse crumbs. Add milk; stir just until mixed. Spoon into four greased muffin cups. Bake at 425° for 14-16 minutes or until lightly browned. **Yield:** 4 biscuits.

*Editor's Note: As a substitute for self-rising flour, place 1-1/2 teaspoons of baking powder and 1/2 teaspoon salt in a measuring cup. Add all-purpose flour to equal 1 cup.

APPLE DESSERT

Delicious with ice cream or whipped topping, this dessert is always a welcome treat. We especially like it served warm.
—*Patricia Gross, Etna Green, Indiana*

2 large tart apples, peeled and sliced
1 tablespoon lemon juice
2 tablespoons brown sugar
2 tablespoons quick-cooking oats
2 tablespoons butter *or* margarine, melted
Dash ground cinnamon
Whipped cream *or* vanilla ice cream, optional

Place apples in an ungreased 2- or 3-cup baking dish; sprinkle with lemon juice. Combine brown sugar, oats, butter and cinnamon; sprinkle over apples. Cover and bake at 350° for 30 minutes. Uncover and bake 15 minutes longer or until apples are tender. Serve with whipped cream or ice cream if desired. **Yield:** 2 servings.

Au Gratin Cabbage

My heritage is Russian, and I have always loved cabbage. My husband didn't like it at all—
until I prepared it this way. Since we're health-conscious these days,
I scaled down the cheese and use low-fat milk, but it's still delicious.
—Katherine Stallwood, Kennewick, Washington

2 cups shredded cabbage
1/2 cup grated carrot
1/4 cup chopped green onions
1 egg
1/2 cup milk
3 tablespoons shredded Swiss cheese
1/4 teaspoon seasoned salt
1 tablespoon minced fresh parsley
1 tablespoon shredded Parmesan
cheese

In a skillet coated with nonstick cooking spray, saute the cabbage, carrot and onions until crisp-tender. Transfer to a greased shallow 1-qt. baking dish. In a bowl, combine the egg, milk, Swiss cheese and seasoned salt. Pour over the vegetables. Sprinkle with parsley and Parmesan cheese. Bake, uncovered, at 350° for 30-35 minutes or until a knife inserted near the center comes out clean. **Yield:** 2-3 servings.

BAVARIAN MEATBALLS

*Gingersnaps and mushrooms give these tender meatballs a special old-world flavor.
The recipe was handed down from my husband's family. I love to cook
and found that this was an easy recipe to double and share with friends.*
—Gusty Crum, Dover, Ohio

2 tablespoons chopped onion
1 teaspoon butter *or* margarine
3/4 cup soft bread crumbs
1 tablespoon milk
1/2 teaspoon prepared mustard
1/2 teaspoon salt
Dash pepper
1/2 pound ground beef
1 can (4 ounces) mushroom stems
   and pieces, undrained
2 gingersnaps, coarsely crushed
2 tablespoons water
1 tablespoon brown sugar
1/2 teaspoon beef bouillon granules

In a skillet, saute onion in butter until tender. Transfer to a bowl; add bread crumbs, milk, mustard, salt and pepper. Add beef and mix well. Shape into six meatballs; place in a greased 1-qt. baking dish. In a small saucepan, combine mushrooms, gingersnap crumbs, water, brown sugar and bouillon. Cook and stir over low heat for 2-3 minutes or until thickened. Pour over meatballs. Cover and bake at 350° for 25 minutes or until the meat is no longer pink. **Yield:** 2 servings.

CREAMY POTATO CASSEROLE

*Even though my family is grown and gone, I still like to
make mashed potatoes. I came up with this variation a long time ago.*
—Margaret Draughon, Clinton, North Carolina

1-1/2 cups hot mashed potatoes
   (prepared with milk and butter)
1/2 cup sour cream
1 to 2 tablespoons milk
1/8 teaspoon garlic powder
3/4 cup french-fried onions
1/2 cup shredded cheddar cheese

In a bowl, combine potatoes, sour cream, milk and garlic powder; mix well. Spoon half into a greased 1-qt. baking dish. Layer with half of the onions and cheese. Repeat layers. Bake, uncovered, at 350° for 30-35 minutes or until the cheese is melted. **Yield:** 2 servings.

APPLE PAN BETTY

*I found this recipe soon after I was married nearly 50 years ago. It uses few ingredients,
which are usually on hand, and takes little time to put together.*
—Shirley Leister, West Chester, Pennsylvania

1 medium apple, peeled and cubed
3 tablespoons butter *or* margarine
1 cup bread cubes
3 tablespoons sugar
1/4 teaspoon ground cinnamon

In a skillet over medium heat, saute apple in butter until tender, about 2-3 minutes. Add bread cubes. Sprinkle with sugar and cinnamon; mix well. Saute until bread is warm. Serve immediately. **Yield:** 2 servings.

Apple Ham Salad

This salad makes just the right amount for one and uses everyday ingredients.
The lively dressing makes it special.
—Ruth Stekert, Manheim, Pennsylvania

2 tablespoons mayonnaise
1/4 teaspoon prepared mustard
1/2 teaspoon honey
1/2 teaspoon lemon juice
Dash ground cloves
1/2 cup julienned fully cooked ham
1 small apple, diced
1 celery rib, sliced
Lettuce leaves, optional
1/4 teaspoon sesame seeds, toasted

In a bowl, blend the first five ingredients. Stir in ham, apple and celery. Cover and refrigerate for 1 hour. Serve on a bed of lettuce if desired. Sprinkle with sesame seeds. **Yield:** 1 serving. **Nutritional Analysis:** One serving (prepared with fat-free mayonnaise) equals 253 calories, 328 mg sodium, 48 mg cholesterol, 25 gm carbohydrate, 22 gm protein, 8 gm fat. **Diabetic Exchanges:** 3 lean meat, 1-1/2 fruit.

PEASANT SOUP FOR ONE

*In mere minutes this hearty soup simmers on the
stovetop to perfection, yet it tastes like it cooked for hours.*
—Kay Harris, Amarillo, Texas

1 boneless skinless chicken breast
   half (4 ounces), cubed
1/4 cup chopped onion
1 small potato, cubed
1 small carrot, sliced
1 cup chicken broth
1 garlic clove, minced
1/4 teaspoon dried tarragon, crushed
1/8 teaspoon salt, optional
Dash pepper
2 teaspoons chopped fresh parsley

Coat a saucepan with nonstick cooking spray; brown chicken over medium-high heat. Add the next eight ingredients; bring to a boil. Reduce heat. Cover and simmer for 20-25 minutes or until vegetables are tender. Sprinkle with parsley. **Yield:** 1 serving. **Nutritional Analysis:** One serving (prepared with fat-free low-sodium broth and without salt) equals 280 calories, 95 mg sodium, 73 mg cholesterol, 31 gm carbohydrate, 31 gm protein, 3 gm fat. **Diabetic Exchanges:** 3 lean meat, 2 vegetable, 1-1/2 starch.

SUNNY CORNMEAL MUFFINS

This pair of muffins is perfect alongside soup and a salad.
—Lethea Weber, Newport, Arkansas

1/4 cup biscuit/baking mix
1/4 cup yellow cornmeal
1 tablespoon sugar
1/4 cup milk
1 egg, beaten
2 teaspoons vegetable oil

In a small bowl, combine baking mix, cornmeal and sugar. Combine milk, egg and oil; stir into dry ingredients just until moistened (batter will be thin). Pour into two greased 6-oz. ovenproof custard cups. Bake at 400° for 15-18 minutes or until golden. **Yield:** 2 muffins.

   Editor's Note: Muffins may be baked in a muffin pan; fill empty cups halfway with water.

PECAN SANDIES

(Not pictured)

*Our grandchildren go through these cookies like locusts in a wheat field!
Sometimes I have to double or even triple the recipe.*
—Martha Crowe, La Plata, Maryland

1/2 cup butter *or* margarine, softened
1/4 cup sugar
1 teaspoon vanilla extract
1 cup cake flour
1/2 cup finely chopped pecans

In a mixing bowl, cream butter and sugar; stir in vanilla. Add flour; mix on low speed until well blended. Stir in pecans; mix well. Refrigerate for 30 minutes.

   Roll into 1-in. balls; place on a greased baking sheet. Bake at 350° for 15-18 minutes or until bottom edges are golden brown. Cool on a wire rack. **Yield:** about 1-1/2 dozen.

QUICK-STUFF PORK CHOPS

*This 15-minute entree is just right for a busy cook—it's delicious,
and the portions are perfect for two people.*
—Katie Koziolek, Hartland, Minnesota

1/4 **teaspoon dried thyme**
1/4 **teaspoon rubbed sage**
1/8 **teaspoon salt**
1/8 **teaspoon pepper**
　2 **boneless pork loin chops (3/4 inch thick)**
　1 **tablespoon butter *or* margarine**
　2 **tablespoons chopped celery**
　2 **tablespoons chopped onion**
1/4 **cup thinly sliced carrot**
1/2 **cup chicken broth**
3/4 **cup herb-seasoned stuffing**

Combine thyme, sage, salt and pepper; sprinkle on both sides of pork chops. In a skillet, cook chops in butter for about 5-6 minutes on each side or until juices run clear. Transfer to a serving platter and keep warm. In the pan drippings, saute celery, onion and carrot over medium heat until tender. Stir in broth and stuffing; heat through. Spoon over chops; serve immediately. **Yield:** 2 servings.

BACON CORN CHOWDER

*I've served this chowder for so many years that I don't remember where I got the recipe.
If there's some left over, I freeze it for another time.*
—Joan Baskin, Black Creek, British Columbia

6 bacon strips, diced
3/4 cup diced celery
1 small onion, diced
1 cup diced uncooked potato
1 cup water
1 can (14-3/4 ounces) cream-style corn
1 cup milk
1/2 teaspoon seasoned salt
1/2 teaspoon salt
1/4 teaspoon garlic powder
1/8 teaspoon pepper

In a saucepan, cook bacon, celery and onion over medium heat for 10-15 minutes or until bacon is cooked; drain. Add potato and water. Cover and simmer for 20 minutes or until potato is tender. Stir in remaining ingredients; heat through (do not boil). Refrigerate or freeze leftovers. **Yield:** 4 servings.

AUTUMN DESSERT

This instant dessert satisfies my craving for sweets in about 10 minutes!
—Lanny Lightner, Denver, Colorado

1 large ripe pear *or* tart apple, peeled and thinly sliced
1/2 cup water, *divided*
2 tablespoons sugar
1 tablespoon raisins, optional
1 teaspoon butter *or* margarine
1/8 teaspoon ground cinnamon
Dash ground nutmeg
1 tablespoon cornstarch
2 slices cinnamon bread, toasted
Ice cream *or* whipped cream, optional

In a small saucepan, combine pear, 1/4 cup water, sugar, raisins if desired, butter, cinnamon and nutmeg. Cook over medium heat for 8-10 minutes or until fruit is tender.

Combine cornstarch and remaining water until smooth; add to fruit mixture. Bring to a boil, stirring constantly. Cook and stir for 1-2 minutes or until thickened. Serve warm over cinnamon toast. Top with ice cream or whipped cream if desired. **Yield:** 2 servings.

SWEET POTATO PUFFS

(Not pictured)

Even children love this treat, though sweet potatoes may not be their favorite vegetable.
—Bernice Morris, Marshfield, Missouri

1 cup mashed sweet potato (without added milk *or* butter)
1 tablespoon brown sugar
1/4 teaspoon salt
1/8 teaspoon ground cinnamon
6 large marshmallows
1/3 to 1/2 cup graham cracker crumbs

Combine sweet potato, brown sugar, salt and cinnamon; shape a small amount around each marshmallow. Roll in crumbs. Place on a greased baking sheet. Bake at 350° for 6 minutes or until lightly puffed (do not overbake or marshmallows will melt). **Yield:** 2 servings.

MINI MEAT LOAF

This recipe is a nice and easy way to add vegetables to your diet.
They provide color, flavor and nutrition.
—Lethea Weber, Newport, Arkansas

1/2 slice bread, crumbled
  2 tablespoons finely shredded carrot
  1 tablespoon *each* chopped onion,
    celery and green pepper
1/4 teaspoon salt
Dash pepper
  2 tablespoons chili sauce *or* ketchup,
    divided
1/4 pound ground beef

In a bowl, combine bread, carrot, onion, celery, green pepper, salt, pepper and 1 tablespoon chili sauce. Add beef and mix well. Shape into a 3-in. x 2-1/2-in. loaf; place in an ungreased shallow baking dish. Top with remaining chili sauce. Bake, uncovered, at 350° for 35-40 minutes. **Yield:** 1 serving.

WILTED COLESLAW

I fix this snappy salad for myself whenever I have a taste for it. It's simple and delicious.
—Denise Albers, Belleville, Illinois

1 cup shredded cabbage
1 green onion, sliced
1/8 teaspoon celery seed
1/8 teaspoon salt
2 bacon strips
2 tablespoons sugar
4-1/2 teaspoons vinegar
Dash paprika

In a small bowl, combine the cabbage, onion, celery seed and salt; set aside. In a skillet, cook bacon until crisp. Drain, reserving 1 tablespoon drippings. Crumble bacon over cabbage mixture. To the drippings, add sugar, vinegar and paprika; heat until the sugar is dissolved. Pour over the cabbage mixture and toss to coat. Serve immediately. **Yield:** 1 serving.

MAC 'N' CHEESE FOR ONE

Here's a creamy, comforting casserole I enjoy. It goes well with any meat.
—Lucy Holland, Derby Line, Vermont

2 tablespoons butter, *divided*
1 tablespoon all-purpose flour
1/4 teaspoon salt
Pinch pepper
1/2 cup milk
1/3 cup diced cheddar cheese
1/4 teaspoon prepared mustard
1/4 teaspoon Worcestershire sauce
1/2 teaspoon chopped onion
3 tablespoons elbow macaroni,
    cooked and drained
2 saltines, crushed

In a saucepan, melt 1 tablespoon of butter; stir in flour, salt and pepper. Whisk in milk until smooth. Cook and stir for 2 minutes. Reduce heat to low. Add cheese, mustard, Worcestershire sauce and onion; stir until cheese is melted. Add macaroni. Transfer to a greased 1-cup baking dish. Sprinkle with saltines; dot with remaining butter. Bake, uncovered, at 350° for 15 minutes or until heated through. **Yield:** 1 serving.

MICROWAVE FRUIT CRISP

(Not pictured)

This dessert has lots of fruit and a golden oat topping. It's a treat I enjoy year-round.
—Luella Bogner, Attica, Ohio

1 medium apple *or* pear, peeled and
    thinly sliced
2 tablespoons brown sugar
2 tablespoons quick-cooking oats
1 tablespoon all-purpose flour
1/8 teaspoon ground cinnamon
1 tablespoon cold butter *or*
    margarine

Place fruit in a small microwave-safe dish. In another bowl, combine the dry ingredients; cut in butter until crumbly. Sprinkle over fruit. Microwave, uncovered, on high for 2-1/2 minutes or until fruit is tender. **Yield:** 1 serving. **Editor's Note:** This recipe was tested in a 700-watt microwave. It can also be baked in a small baking dish, uncovered, at 375° for 25-30 minutes.

STRAWBERRY BISCUIT SHORTCAKE

*I remember Mom was always making biscuits. She served them plain for breakfast and dinner,
especially when we had stew or baked beans. My favorite, though,
was when she topped them with strawberries to make shortcake.*
—Elaine Gagnon, Pawtucket, Rhode Island

1/2 cup all-purpose flour
1/4 cup sugar
3/4 teaspoon baking powder
1/8 teaspoon salt
1 tablespoon shortening
4 tablespoons milk, *divided*
Fresh strawberries and whipped cream

Combine flour, sugar, baking powder and salt; cut in shortening until mixture resembles coarse crumbs. Stir in 3 tablespoons of milk until a thick batter forms. Drop four mounds of batter onto a greased baking sheet. Brush with remaining milk. Bake at 375° for 14-16 minutes or until golden. Layer biscuits with berries and whipped cream. **Yield:** 2 servings.

ITALIAN BEEF SANDWICHES

My husband and I are retired ranchers, so beef is a favorite main dish.
Everyone enjoys these sandwiches, which can be made for two or any size group.
—Margery Bryan, Royal City, Washington

3 garlic cloves, *divided*
2 cups beef broth
1/2 teaspoon dried oregano, *divided*
1 small onion, sliced
1 small green pepper, cut into strips
1 tablespoon vegetable oil
2 beef tip *or* sandwich steaks (1/4 inch thick)
2 Italian rolls, split

Cut one garlic clove in half; place in a saucepan. Add broth and 1/4 teaspoon oregano; cook over medium-low heat for 10 minutes. Discard garlic clove. Remove broth from the heat and set aside. Mince remaining garlic; place in a skillet. Add the onion, green pepper, oil and remaining oregano; cook and stir over medium heat until crisp-tender. Remove vegetables and keep warm. Add meat to the skillet; cook over medium heat until browned on both sides. Add reserved broth; simmer for 10-12 minutes or until meat is tender. To serve, brush cut sides of rolls with some of the broth; top with meat and vegetables. **Yield:** 2 servings.

CRISP MARINATED CUKES

A dear friend shared this recipe with me. It's a wonderful side dish, compatible with any meal.
—Kathy Wallace, Madison, Tennessee

1/2 cup sugar
1/4 cup vinegar
1/2 teaspoon salt
1/4 teaspoon celery seed
2 cups sliced cucumbers
1/4 cup sliced onions

In a bowl, combine the sugar, vinegar, salt and celery seed; mix well. Stir in the cucumbers and onions. Cover and refrigerate for several hours or overnight. **Yield:** 2 servings. **Editor's Note:** This salad may be frozen for up to 2 months.

OLD-FASHIONED POTATO SALAD

The secret to the fine taste of this salad is adding the still-warm potatoes to the mayonnaise mixture. I'm frequently asked to share the recipe.
—Mary Elizabeth Martucci, South Bend, Indiana

3 medium red potatoes, peeled and cubed
1/2 cup mayonnaise
2 teaspoons sweet pickle relish
1/8 teaspoon salt
1/8 teaspoon pepper
2 tablespoons chopped carrots
2 tablespoons chopped celery
2 tablespoons chopped red onion
2 hard-cooked eggs, chopped
1/8 teaspoon paprika

Cook potatoes in boiling salted water for 10-15 minutes or until tender. Meanwhile, in a bowl, combine mayonnaise, relish, salt and pepper; add carrots, celery, onion and eggs. Drain the potatoes; gently stir into mayonnaise mixture. Sprinkle with paprika. Cover and refrigerate until serving. **Yield:** 2 servings.

BEEF & GROUND BEEF

You'll find 50 palate-pleasing
recipes featuring beef
and ground beef in this
indispensable chapter.
Whether you're making lunch
or planning a special dinner,
you'll have what you need.

LONDON BROIL (P. 143)

Cheese-Stuffed Flank Steak (p. 120)

CHEESE-STUFFED FLANK STEAK

(Pictured on page 119)

This pretty rolled steak never fails to impress. Pecans add crunch to the cheesy stuffing. Rosemary and thyme subtly flavor the meat.
—Evelyn Moll, Tulsa, Oklahoma

1 beef flank steak (3/4 pound)
1 can (6 ounces) pineapple juice
1 tablespoon Worcestershire sauce
1 small onion, chopped
1/2 teaspoon dried thyme
1/4 teaspoon dried rosemary, crushed
1/4 teaspoon salt
1/8 teaspoon pepper
STUFFING:
1/2 cup soft bread crumbs
1/2 cup shredded cheddar cheese
2 tablespoons chopped pecans
4-1/2 teaspoons finely chopped onion
4-1/2 teaspoons minced fresh parsley
1/4 teaspoon dried minced garlic
1 tablespoon vegetable oil

Flatten steak to 1/4-in. thickness. In a bowl, combine the pineapple juice, Worcestershire sauce, onion, thyme, rosemary, salt and pepper. Pour half of the marinade into a resealable plastic bag; add meat. Seal bag and turn to coat; refrigerate for 4-8 hours. Cover and refrigerate remaining pineapple juice mixture.

Drain and discard marinade from meat. For stuffing, in a bowl, combine the bread crumbs, cheese, pecans, onion, parsley and garlic. Sprinkle stuffing over meat. Roll up jelly-roll style, starting with a short side. Tie with kitchen string.

In a small skillet, brown meat in oil until browned on all sides. Pour reserved marinade into skillet. Bring to a boil. Reduce heat; cover and simmer for 30 minutes or until tender. Thicken pan juices if desired. **Yield:** 2 servings.

ITALIAN BEEF WITH MUSHROOMS

My husband, who is a mushroom lover, always smiles when I make this dish.
—Lynn Jachlewski, Schenectady, New York

1-1/2 cups sliced fresh mushrooms
2 tablespoons butter *or* margarine
1/3 cup thinly sliced green onions
1 garlic clove, minced
1/2 cup spaghetti sauce
2 tablespoons water
2 tablespoons dry red wine *or* beef broth
1/4 teaspoon dried basil
1/4 teaspoon dried thyme
1/8 teaspoon salt
Dash pepper

1 cup cubed cooked beef
Hot cooked noodles *or* mashed potatoes

In a saucepan, saute mushrooms in butter for 3 minutes. Add green onions and garlic; saute 2 minutes longer. Stir in the spaghetti sauce, water, wine or broth, basil, thyme, salt and pepper. Bring to a boil. Reduce heat; cover and simmer for 35 minutes. Stir in beef. Cover and simmer 10 minutes longer or until meat is heated through. Serve over noodles. **Yield:** 2 servings.

PEPPERED T-BONE STEAKS

(Pictured at right)

When I make these juicy steaks, I brush thin slices of potato with olive oil and grill them alongside the meat. I round out the meal with a spinach and red onion salad on the side and cheesecake for dessert.
—Diane Halferty, Corpus Christi, Texas

   3 tablespoons steak sauce
4-1/2 teaspoons minced fresh thyme
    ***or* 1 teaspoon dried thyme**
  1/4 teaspoon coarsely ground pepper
  1/4 teaspoon cayenne pepper
    2 beef T-bone steaks (about 3/4
     pound *each*)
  1/2 teaspoon salt

In a small bowl, combine steak sauce, thyme, pepper and cayenne. Sprinkle steaks on both sides with salt. Spoon about 2 teaspoons steak sauce mixture on one side of steaks.

Place on grill sauce side down. Grill, covered, over medium heat for 6 minutes.

Brush with remaining sauce and turn. Grill 4-6 minutes longer or until meat reaches desired doneness (for rare, a meat thermometer should read 140°; medium, 160°; well-done 170°). **Yield:** 2 servings.

CLASSIC POT ROAST

After our children grew up and left home, it was hard to cook for only two people. Now I've found a few tricks to make things easier. (Leftovers of this pot roast would be scrumptious in the Italian Beef with Mushrooms recipe at left.)
—Jan Roat, Grass Range, Montana

   1 boneless beef sirloin tip *or* bottom
    round roast (about 2 pounds)
   2 medium potatoes, cut into chunks
   2 medium carrots, cut into 2-inch
    chunks
   1 medium onion, cut into wedges
 1/4 teaspoon pepper
    1 can (14-1/2 ounces) Italian stewed
     tomatoes, undrained
    1 can (10-3/4 ounces) condensed
     cream of mushroom soup, undiluted
 1/2 cup water

Place meat in an ovenproof skillet or Dutch oven. Add the potatoes, carrots and onion. Sprinkle with pepper. Top with tomatoes. Spread soup over meat. Pour water around vegetables. Cover and bake at 325° for 1-1/2 hours or until meat and vegetables are tender. Thicken cooking liquid if desired. **Yield:** 6-8 servings.

SIRLOIN TIPS WITH MUSHROOMS

(Pictured at right)

My husband is an avid hunter, so I look for beef recipes that also work well using venison. This one fills the bill nicely.
—Nancy Zimmerman
Cape May Court House, New Jersey

3/4 pound boneless beef sirloin steak, cut into 1-inch cubes
4 teaspoons butter *or* margarine
2 teaspoons vegetable oil
1/2 pound fresh mushrooms, sliced
1 small onion, sliced and separated into rings
1 garlic clove, minced
1 teaspoon cornstarch
1/4 cup heavy whipping cream
3 tablespoons beef broth
3 tablespoons dry red wine *or* additional beef broth
1 teaspoon Dijon mustard
3/4 teaspoon soy sauce
Hot cooked noodles *or* rice

In a skillet, brown beef in butter; remove and set aside. To the same skillet, add the oil and mushrooms, onion and garlic; saute until tender. Add beef; transfer to a greased 1-qt. baking dish. Cover and bake at 325° for 1 hour or until beef is tender.

In a saucepan, combine the cornstarch, cream, broth, wine or additional broth, Dijon mustard and soy sauce until smooth. Bring to a boil; cook and stir for 1 minute or until thickened. Stir into meat mixture until blended. Serve over noodles. **Yield: 2 servings.**

TANGY MINI MEAT LOAVES

It's fun to make miniature meat loaves instead of one big loaf...and they cook up quickly in a skillet rather than in the oven. This recipe is one of my old standbys for a speedy supper.
—Paula Martin, Paxinos, Pennsylvania

1/2 pound ground beef
1/2 cup sliced onion
1/4 cup dark corn syrup
3 tablespoons steak sauce
2 teaspoons spicy brown mustard

Shape beef into four small loaves, 1/4 to 1/2 in. thick. Cook in a skillet over medium-high heat for 3-4 minutes on each side or until no longer pink. Remove to a serving plate and keep warm. Drain, reserving 1 table-spoon drippings; saute onion in drippings until tender. Add corn syrup, steak sauce and mustard; bring to a boil. Pour over meat loaves and serve immediately. **Yield: 2 servings.**

Nutritional Analysis: One serving (prepared with lean ground beef) equals 337 calories, 11 g fat (4 g saturated fat), 41 mg cholesterol, 552 mg sodium, 38 g carbohydrate, 1 g fiber, 24 g protein. **Diabetic Exchanges:** 2-1/2 starch, 2-1/2 lean meat.

OVEN-FRIED RANCH STEAK

I've made this recipe with chicken instead of beef, and the results were equally good. The combination of ranch salad dressing and cajun seasoning also is great as a dip for fresh veggies.
—LaDonna Reed, Ponca City, Oklahoma

1 cup ranch salad dressing
1 teaspoon Cajun seasoning
3/4 pound boneless beef sirloin steak
1/3 cup cornmeal
1/3 cup dry bread crumbs
1/2 teaspoon garlic powder

In a large resealable plastic bag, combine salad dressing and seasoning; add the beef. Seal bag and turn to coat; refrigerate for at least 8 hours or overnight. Drain and discard marinade. In a shallow plate, combine the cornmeal, bread crumbs and garlic powder. Coat both sides of beef in cornmeal mixture.

Place in a greased 13-in. x 9-in. x 2-in. baking dish. Bake at 350° for 30-35 minutes or until meat reaches desired doneness (for rare, a meat thermometer should read 140°; medium, 160°; well-done, 170°). **Yield: 2 servings.**

CHILI CON CARNE

(Pictured at right)

I love to cook, but meals at my house have to be ready in a hurry because we're always on the go. I found this recipe in a magazine almost 30 years ago.
—Karleen Warkentin, McAllen, Texas

1/2 pound ground beef
1/2 cup chopped onion
1 garlic clove, minced
1 can (10 ounces) diced tomatoes and green chilies, undrained
1 can (8 ounces) tomato sauce
3/4 cup canned pinto beans, rinsed and drained
2-1/2 teaspoons chili powder
1/2 teaspoon dried oregano
1/4 teaspoon salt, optional
1/4 teaspoon ground cumin
1/4 teaspoon pepper

In a large saucepan, cook the beef, onion and garlic over medium heat until meat is no longer pink; drain. Stir in the tomatoes, tomato sauce, beans, chili powder, oregano, salt if desired, cumin and pepper. Bring to a boil. Reduce heat; cover and simmer for 1 hour. **Yield: 2 servings.**

Nutritional Analysis: One 1-1/3-cup serving (prepared with lean ground beef and without salt) equals 357 calories, 12 g fat (4 g saturated fat), 41 mg cholesterol, 1,247 mg sodium, 34 g carbohydrate, 10 g fiber, 31 g protein. **Diabetic Exchanges:** 3-1/2 lean meat, 2 starch.

MEXICAN SPAGHETTI

(Pictured at right)

Everyone who tries this recipe is pleasantly surprised by the combination of flavors.
—Melissa Tarbox, Allen, Texas

1/4 pound ground beef
  1 can (14-1/2 ounces) diced tomatoes
1/3 cup salsa
  2 tablespoons tomato paste
1/2 teaspoon ground cumin
1/4 teaspoon garlic salt *or* garlic
    powder
1/4 teaspoon salt
1/4 teaspoon dried oregano
Hot cooked spaghetti
Minced fresh cilantro *or* parsley

In a saucepan, cook beef over medium heat until no longer pink; drain. Stir in the tomatoes, salsa, tomato paste, cumin, garlic salt, salt and oregano. Bring to a boil. Reduce heat; simmer, uncovered, for 15 minutes. Serve over pasta. Sprinkle with cilantro. **Yield:** 2 servings.

HAMBURGER STEW

(Pictured at right)

My grandmother gave me this recipe, so it always brings back warm memories.
—Julie Kretchman, Meyersdale, Pennsylvania

1/2 pound ground beef
1/4 cup chopped onion
1/4 cup chopped celery
3/4 cup beef broth
  1 cup canned diced tomatoes with
    juice
3/4 cup cubed peeled potato
1/4 cup thinly sliced carrot
  2 tablespoons uncooked long grain
    rice

1/2 teaspoon salt, optional
1/8 teaspoon pepper

In a large saucepan, cook the beef, onion and celery over medium heat until meat is no longer pink; drain. Stir in broth, tomatoes, potato, carrot, rice, salt if desired and pepper. Bring to a boil. Reduce heat; cover and simmer 40-45 minutes, until rice and vegetables are tender. **Yield:** 2 servings.

BACON SWISS BURGERS

(Pictured at right)

I came up with this when we wanted something other than regular hamburgers.
—Tammy Fortney, Spokane, Washington

1/2 pound ground beef
  1 teaspoon chopped jarred jalapeno
    pepper
  1 bacon strip, cooked and crumbled
1/4 teaspoon salt
1/8 teaspoon coarsely ground pepper
  2 slices Swiss cheese
Mayonnaise
  2 sourdough rolls, split
Tomato slices, optional

In a bowl, combine the beef, jalapeno pepper, bacon, salt and pepper. Shape into two patties. Grill, covered, over medium heat or broil 4 in. from heat for 6 minutes on each side or until a meat thermometer reads 160° and meat is no longer pink. Top with cheese. Spread mayonnaise on rolls. Serve hamburgers on rolls with tomato slices if desired. **Yield:** 2 servings.

MEXICAN SPAGHETTI
HAMBURGER STEW
BACON SWISS BURGERS

ITALIAN GREEN BEAN STEW

This stew recipe from my daughter warms the heart on a cold winter day.
—Lois Schulheis, St. James, Missouri

1/2 **pound beef stew meat, cut into**
3/4-inch cubes
2 **tablespoons butter** *or* **margarine,**
divided
1 **celery rib, chopped**
1/3 **cup chopped onion**
1 **garlic clove, minced**
1 **can (14-1/2 ounces) diced tomatoes,**
undrained
1 **cup water,** *divided*
1/2 **teaspoon salt**
1/2 **teaspoon dried oregano**
1/8 **teaspoon pepper**
1 **cup frozen cut green beans**
1/4 **teaspoon minced fresh parsley**
1 **to 2 tablespoons cornstarch**

In a large saucepan, cook meat in 1 tablespoon butter until browned; drain and set meat aside. In same saucepan, saute the celery, onion and garlic with remaining butter until tender. Stir in the tomatoes, 3/4 cup water, salt, oregano, pepper and reserved meat. Bring to a boil. Reduce heat; cover and simmer for 1 hour.

Stir in beans and parsley. Return to a boil. Reduce heat; cover and simmer for about 30 minutes longer or until meat and beans are tender. Combine cornstarch and remaining water until smooth. Gradually stir into stew. Bring to a boil; cook and stir for 1-2 minutes or until thickened. **Yield:** 2 servings.

SAUCY BROCCOLI BEEF BAKE

(Pictured below)

This is one of those casseroles that tastes even better when reheated the next day.
—Joan Cooper, McComb, Mississippi

1/2 **pound ground beef**
1/4 **cup chopped onion**
1 **cup frozen broccoli cuts, thawed**
1 **block (4 ounces) process cheese**
(Velveeta), cubed
3/4 **cup cooked rice**
1/4 **cup chopped green pepper**
1/4 **cup canned mushroom stems and**
pieces
3 **tablespoons Homemade**
Cream-Style Soup Mix (page 75)
2/3 **cup water**

In a skillet, cook beef and onion over medium heat until meat is no longer pink; drain. Remove from the heat. Add the broccoli, cheese, rice, green pepper and mushrooms; set aside. In a microwave-safe bowl, whisk together the soup mix and water. Microwave, uncovered, on high for 2 minutes, whisking occasionally. Pour over beef mixture and stir until combined.

Transfer to a greased 1-qt. baking dish. Bake, uncovered, at 350° for 30-35 minutes or until heated through. **Yield:** 2 servings.

SAVORY BEEF BRISKET

(Pictured at right)

There's nothing like seeing my husband's eyes light up when he comes through the door and sees I've prepared this meal for him. The recipe is tried and true.
—Michelle Harley, Hoisington, Kansas

  1 fresh beef brisket* (1-1/4 to 1-1/2 pounds)
  2 teaspoons Creole *or* Cajun seasoning
  1 teaspoon garlic salt
  1 teaspoon lemon-pepper seasoning
  1 teaspoon dried parsley flakes
  1 bay leaf
2/3 cup tomato sauce
1/4 cup sugar
1/4 cup packed brown sugar
  1 to 2 teaspoons liquid smoke, optional
1/8 teaspoon hot pepper sauce

Place meat, fat side up, in a greased 11-in. x 7-in. x 2-in. baking dish. In a bowl, combine the Creole seasoning, garlic salt, lemon-pepper and parsley. Rub over meat. Add bay leaf. Cover and bake at 350° for about 2-1/2 hours or until meat is just tender. Drain and discard juices. Discard bay leaf.

In a saucepan, combine the tomato sauce, sugar, brown sugar, liquid smoke if desired and hot pepper sauce. Bring to a boil over medium heat. Pour over meat. Cover and bake 30 minutes longer or until the meat is tender and sauce is heated through. **Yield:** 2-3 servings.

*Editor's Note: This is a fresh beef brisket, not corned beef.

CHICKEN-FRIED STEAK STRIPS

My husband and I were dating when I first made him this dish, which is an old favorite of mine. I would swear it was this entree that made him decide to marry me. Today, our kids eat them as fast as I can make 'em.
—Jeanine Adams, Silverdale, Washington

    1 egg, lightly beaten
  1/4 cup milk
    1 cup all-purpose flour
    1 tablespoon onion powder
1-1/2 teaspoons garlic powder
    1 teaspoon seasoned salt
    1 teaspoon paprika
  1/2 teaspoon dried parsley flakes
  1/2 pound boneless beef round steak, cut into thin strips
Oil for frying

In a shallow bowl, combine egg and milk. In another shallow bowl, combine flour and seasonings. Dip beef in egg mixture, then in flour mixture. Dip again in egg mixture and coat with flour mixture. Let stand for 5 minutes.

In a skillet, heat 1/4 in. of oil over medium heat. Place a few pieces of meat in the skillet at a time. Fry until golden brown, about 4 minutes. Drain on paper towels. **Yield:** 2 servings.

MARINATED CHUCK ROAST

This marinade makes the toughest cuts of meat tender. I'm frequently asked for the recipe. It's also good with venison and elk meat.
—Marte Schoening, Superior, Montana

2 tablespoons ketchup
2 tablespoons red wine vinegar *or* cider vinegar
2 teaspoons vegetable oil
2 teaspoons soy sauce
1 teaspoon Worcestershire sauce
1/4 teaspoon prepared mustard
1/4 teaspoon garlic powder
1/4 teaspoon salt
1/4 teaspoon pepper
1 boneless beef chuck steak (about 3/4 pound and 3/4 inch thick)

In a resealable plastic bag, combine the ketchup, vinegar, oil, soy sauce, Worcestershire sauce, mustard, garlic powder, salt and pepper; add meat. Seal bag and turn to coat; refrigerate 8 hours or overnight.

Drain and discard marinade. Grill, covered, over medium heat or broil 4 in. from heat for 6-8 minutes on each side or until meat reaches desired doneness (for rare, a meat thermometer should read 140°; medium, 160°; well-done 170°). **Yield:** 2 servings.

SWISS CHEESE MEAT LOAF

(Pictured at right)

I saw this recipe on a TV show on Amish cooking in the 1980s, and I've adapted it to suit our tastes. The Swiss cheese and bacon make it very satisfying on cold fall and winter evenings.
—Terri Olson, Capitola, California

1 bacon strip, cut into thirds
1 egg, lightly beaten
1/3 cup crushed butter-flavored crackers (about 8 crackers)
5 tablespoons shredded Swiss cheese, *divided*
4-1/2 teaspoons chopped onion
1 garlic clove, minced
1/4 teaspoon salt
1/4 teaspoon rubbed sage
1/8 teaspoon pepper
1/2 pound lean ground beef

In a skillet, cook bacon over medium heat for 2 minutes on each side or until cooked but not crisp. Drain on a paper towel; set aside.

In a bowl, combine the egg, crackers, 4 tablespoons cheese, onion, garlic, salt, sage and pepper. Crumble beef over mixture and mix well. Shape into a loaf and place in a greased 5-3/4-in. x 3-in. x 2-in. loaf pan. Place bacon pieces over top. Bake, uncovered, at 350° for 30 minutes. Sprinkle with remaining cheese; bake 2-4 minutes longer or until a meat thermometer reads 160° and cheese is melted. **Yield:** 2 servings.

STEAK 'N' ONION PIE

(Pictured at right)

When I was growing up, Mom let us pick our birthday meals. This one was a frequent choice. I made sure to copy down the recipe to use in my own home years later.
—Dorcas Yoder, Weyers Cave, Virginia

    2 tablespoons all-purpose flour
    1 teaspoon salt
 1/2 teaspoon pepper
 1/2 teaspoon paprika
 1/2 pound boneless beef round steak,
       cut into 1/2-inch cubes
    1 small onion, sliced and separated
       into rings
    2 tablespoons vegetable oil
1-1/2 cups beef broth
    1 cup cubed cooked potatoes
CRUST:
    1 cup all-purpose flour
 1/4 teaspoon salt
    3 tablespoons cold butter *or*
       margarine
    3 tablespoons shortening
    2 to 3 tablespoons cold water
    1 teaspoon milk

In a large resealable plastic bag, combine the flour, salt, pepper and paprika; mix well. Add beef, a few pieces at a time, and shake to coat.

In a skillet, cook beef and onion in oil until beef is browned and onion is tender. Add broth to the skillet. Bring to a boil. Reduce heat; cover and simmer for 45 minutes. Uncover; stir in the potatoes. Cook until heated through. Spoon meat mixture into a greased 6-1/2-in. pie plate or 2-cup baking dish.

For the crust, in a bowl, combine the flour and salt; cut in the butter and shortening until crumbly. Gradually add water, tossing with a fork until dough forms a ball. Roll out pastry to fit baking dish. Use a small cookie cutter to cut a shape in the center of the pastry; place pastry over meat mixture. Trim pastry to 1/2 in. beyond edge of dish; flute edges. Brush with milk. Bake at 375° for 35-40 minutes or until pastry is lightly browned on edges. **Yield:** 2 servings.

TIMELY TIP

Italian sausage links come portion controlled. Before freezing a package, separate the links and wrap each in plastic wrap. Place all in a resealable freezer bag. (Don't forget to label and date the bag.) When you need 1/4 pound of Italian sausage just use 1 link, for 1/2 pound use 2 links. To easily remove the casing from Italian sausage, make a slit down the length of the sausage with a sharp knife. Then just peel away the casing. When browning the loose sausage, crumble into skillet, then cook over medium heat until no longer pink.

SWEET 'N' SOUR POT ROAST

(Pictured at right)

This has been a favorite in our family for years. I can still remember how the aroma filled the house and made everyone's mouths water before Sunday dinner. Here, the recipe is sized for two people.
—Denise Skinner, Mercerburg, Pennsylvania

1/2 teaspoon salt
1/4 teaspoon dried thyme
1/4 teaspoon dried marjoram
1/8 teaspoon ground nutmeg
1/8 teaspoon pepper
  1 boneless beef chuck steak (3/4 pound and 3/4 inch thick)
  1 tablespoon vegetable oil
1-1/2 cups water, *divided*
  2 tablespoons white vinegar
  2 tablespoons molasses
  2 small carrots, cut into chunks
  1 large red potato, cut into chunks
  1 medium onion, cut into eight wedges
  1 tablespoon all-purpose flour

In a small bowl, combine the salt, thyme, marjoram, nutmeg and pepper. Rub over meat. In a skillet, cook meat in oil until browned on both sides; drain. Combine 1-1/4 cups water, vinegar and molasses. Stir into skillet. Bring to a boil. Reduce heat; cover and simmer for 1-1/4 hours.

Stir in the carrots, potato and onion. Return to a boil. Reduce heat; cover and simmer for 30-40 minutes or until vegetables and meat are tender. Remove meat and vegetables to a serving platter; keep warm. Combine flour and remaining water until smooth. Gradually stir into pan juices. Bring to a boil; cook and stir for 1-2 minutes or until thickened. Serve with pot roast and vegetables. **Yield:** 2 servings.

MUSHROOM-ONION BEEF STEW

(Pictured at right)

I've noticed that when I make this dish for friends, they always ask me when I'm going to invite them back for more.
—Ronald Schmeling, Brookfield, Wisconsin

3/4 pound beef stew meat, cut into 3/4-inch cubes
  2 tablespoons vegetable oil, *divided*
  1 garlic clove, minced
1/4 cup beef broth
1/2 cup red wine *or* additional beef broth
  2 thin strips orange peel (about 3 inches x 1/4 inch *each*)
1/4 teaspoon salt
1/4 teaspoon dried thyme
1/4 pound small fresh mushrooms
  1 cup frozen pearl onions, thawed
1/2 cup frozen peas, thawed
  2 teaspoons cornstarch
  2 tablespoons water

In a large saucepan, brown meat in 1 tablespoon oil. Add garlic; cook and stir for 1 minute. Stir in the broth, wine or additional broth, orange peel, salt and thyme. Bring to a boil. Reduce heat; cover and simmer for 1-1/4 to 1-1/2 hours or until meat is tender. Discard orange peel.

Remove stems from mushrooms. In a saucepan, cook mushroom caps and stems in remaining oil until tender. Add onions; cook until lightly browned. Stir into meat mixture; add peas. In a bowl, combine cornstarch and water until smooth. Gradually stir into stew. Bring to a boil; cook and stir for 1-2 minutes or until thickened. **Yield:** 2 servings.

Sweet 'n' Sour Pot Roast
Mushroom-Onion Beef Stew

MEAT LOAF PATTIE

With this recipe, we can have a hearty meat loaf dinner without leftovers. That delights both my husband and me. He never liked the creative ways I used up leftover meat loaf!
—Dorothy Hunt, Waltham, Massachusetts

1/3 cup seasoned bread crumbs
3 tablespoons milk
1 teaspoon Worcestershire sauce
1 teaspoon finely chopped onion
1/4 teaspoon salt, optional
1/2 pound lean ground beef

In a bowl, combine the bread crumbs, milk, Worcestershire, onion and salt if desired. Crumble beef over mixture and mix well. Shape into a large pattie. Place in a shallow microwave-safe dish. Microwave, uncovered, on high for 3-4 minutes. Let stand for 3 minutes or until a meat thermometer reads 160°. **Yield:** 2 servings.

Editor's Note: This recipe was tested in an 850-watt microwave oven. Meat loaf may also be baked at 350° for 20 minutes or until a meat thermometer reads 160°.

HEARTY BEEF STEW

(Pictured below)

A few years ago, we served this beef stew at a fund-raising dinner at church. It received lots of compliments. This mini version serves two perfectly.
—Carin Illig, Arlington, Texas

1 tablespoon all-purpose flour
1/4 teaspoon salt
1/8 teaspoon pepper
1/2 pound beef stew meat, cut into 3/4-inch cubes
1 tablespoon vegetable oil
1/3 cup chopped onion
1 garlic clove, minced
1-1/4 cups beef broth
1/3 cup white wine *or* additional beef broth
1 medium potato, cut into large chunks
2 medium carrots, cut into chunks
1/4 pound fresh mushrooms, halved
1 bay leaf
4-1/2 teaspoons quick-cooking tapioca
1/2 teaspoon dried thyme

In a large resealable plastic bag, combine the flour, salt and pepper; add beef and shake to coat. In a large saucepan, brown beef in oil. Add onion and garlic; cook and stir 2 minutes longer. Stir in broth and wine or additional broth, scraping brown bits from pan. Transfer to a greased 5-cup baking dish. Stir in potato, carrots, mushrooms, bay leaf, tapioca and thyme. Let stand for 15 minutes. Cover and bake at 350° for 1 hour. Uncover; bake 1 to 1-1/2 hours longer until meat and vegetables are tender, stirring every 30 minutes. Discard bay leaf. **Yield:** 2 servings.

GROUND BEEF WELLINGTON

(Pictured at right)

Trying new recipes is one of my favorite hobbies. It's also the most gratifying. What could beat the smiles and compliments of the ones you love? This recipe is easy enough for family yet fancy enough for company.
—Julie Frankamp, Nicollet, Minnesota

1/2 cup chopped fresh mushrooms
1 tablespoon butter *or* margarine
2 teaspoons all-purpose flour
1/4 teaspoon pepper, *divided*
1/2 cup half-and-half cream
1 egg yolk
2 tablespoons finely chopped onion
1/4 teaspoon salt
1/2 pound ground beef
1 tube (4 ounces) refrigerated crescent rolls
1 teaspoon dried parsley flakes

In a saucepan, saute mushrooms in butter until softened. Stir in flour and 1/8 teaspoon pepper until blended. Gradually add the cream. Bring to a boil; cook and stir for 2 minutes or until thickened. Remove from the heat and set aside.

In a bowl, combine the egg yolk, onion, 2 tablespoons mushroom sauce, salt and remaining pepper. Crumble beef over mixture and mix well. Shape into two loaves. Separate crescent dough into two rectangles on a baking sheet. Seal perforations. Place a meat loaf on each rectangle. Bring edges together and pinch to seal. Bake at 350° for 24-28 minutes or until a meat thermometer inserted into meat loaf reads 160°.

Meanwhile, warm remaining sauce over low heat; stir in parsley. Serve sauce with Wellingtons. **Yield:** 2 servings.

SKILLET SAUERBRATEN

I've used this recipe successfully with steak, antelope and venison. I generally serve it with red cabbage and egg noodles that have been sprinkled with poppy seeds.
—Nancy Adams, Hancock, New Hampshire

3/4 pound boneless beef sirloin steak, cut into thin strips
1 medium onion, chopped
2 tablespoons olive *or* vegetable oil
1/4 cup finely crushed gingersnaps (about 6 cookies)
1/2 teaspoon ground allspice
2 cups beef broth
2 tablespoons red wine vinegar *or* cider vinegar
Hot cooked egg noodles

In a large skillet, saute beef and onion in oil until beef is browned and onion is tender. Add gingersnaps and allspice to the skillet. Slowly stir in beef broth. Bring to a boil. Reduce heat; cover and simmer until mixture is thickened, about 45 minutes. Remove from the heat. Stir in the vinegar; mix well. Serve over noodles. **Yield:** 2 servings.

Grilled Orange Flank Steak

I've been experimenting with marinades for years. This recipe is the result of the combined efforts of several friends and a few cookbook recipes.
—Sue Miller, Goochland, Virginia

1/2 cup orange marmalade
1/4 cup water
1/4 cup prepared Italian *or* Italian salad dressing
1/4 cup soy sauce
2 tablespoons brown sugar
2 tablespoons orange juice
1-1/2 teaspoons grated orange peel
1 teaspoon ground ginger
1/4 teaspoon garlic powder
1 beef flank steak (3/4 pound)

In a mixing bowl, combine the first nine ingredients; mix well. Pour 1 cup marinade into a large resealable plastic bag; Cover and refrigerate remaining marinade. Add beef to the bag. Seal and turn to coat; refrigerate for at least 8 hours or overnight, turning occasionally.

Drain and discard marinade from beef. Grill, uncovered, over medium heat or broil 4 in. from heat for 10-12 minutes on each side or until beef reaches desired doneness (for rare, a meat thermometer should read 140°; medium, 160°; well-done 170°), basting frequently with reserved marinade and turning once. **Yield:** 2 servings.

Stuffed Manicotti

When I bought a 25-year-old cookbook at an auction, I found this gem inside. I think you'll make it again and again, as I do.
—Pam Goodlet, Washington Island, Wisconsin

4 uncooked manicotti shells
1/2 pound ground beef
1 small onion, finely chopped
1/2 medium green pepper, finely chopped
1 can (15 ounces) tomato sauce
1 to 1-1/2 teaspoons dried oregano
1 teaspoon dried thyme
1 cup (4 ounces) shredded mozzarella cheese, *divided*

Cook manicotti according to package directions; drain. In a skillet, cook the beef, onion and green pepper over medium heat until meat is no longer pink; drain. Stir in the tomato sauce, oregano and thyme; bring to a boil. Reduce heat; simmer, uncovered, for 10 minutes. Add 1/2 cup cheese; stir until melted.

Stuff half meat mixture into manicotti shells; arrange in a greased 8-in. square baking dish. Spoon remaining meat mixture over shells. Bake, uncovered, at 325° for 20 minutes. Sprinkle with remaining cheese; bake 5-10 minutes longer or until heated through and cheese is melted. **Yield:** 2 servings.

PRIME RIB AND POTATOES

(Pictured below)

I've discovered a variety of small roasts that work well for two, without creating leftovers for the rest of the week. This prime rib is perfect for a holiday meal when company isn't coming. The portion for each is generous, and the flavor is unsurpassed.
—Richard Fairchild, Tustin, California

1 tablespoon olive *or* vegetable oil
1 small garlic clove, minced
1 standing beef rib roast (about 3 pounds and 2 ribs)
2 large baking potatoes

Combine the oil and garlic; rub evenly over roast. Place roast, fat side up, in a small roasting pan. Place a potato on each side of roast. Bake, uncovered, at 325° for 2 to 2-1/2 hours until meat reaches desired doneness (for rare, a meat thermometer should read 140°; medium, 160°; well-done, 170°). Let stand for 10 minutes before carving. **Yield:** 2 servings.

MEXICAN SPOON BREAD CASSEROLE

*This casserole really hits the spot when it's cold outside.
It's tasty and filling. It will warm you right up.*
—Paula Lock, Glenwood, Arkansas

1/2 pound ground beef
1 small onion, chopped
2 tablespoons chopped green pepper
1 garlic clove, minced
2/3 cup tomato sauce
1/2 cup frozen corn, thawed
2 tablespoons sliced ripe olives
3/4 teaspoon chili powder
1/2 teaspoon salt
Dash pepper
TOPPING:
3 tablespoons cornmeal
1/2 cup milk
1/8 teaspoon salt
1/4 cup shredded cheddar cheese
1 egg, lightly beaten

In a skillet, cook the beef, onion, green pepper and garlic over medium heat until meat is no longer pink; drain. Add the tomato sauce, corn, olives, chili powder, salt and pepper; bring to a boil. Reduce heat; simmer, uncovered, for 10 minutes.

Meanwhile, in a saucepan, combine the cornmeal, milk and salt; bring to a boil, stirring frequently. Remove from the heat. Stir in cheese and egg. Spoon meat mixture into an ungreased 1-qt. baking dish. Pour topping over meat mixture. Bake, uncovered, at 375° for 22-26 minutes or until a knife inserted near the center comes out clean. **Yield:** 2 servings.

FILET MIGNON WITH GARLIC CHEESE BUTTER

Cooking is something I've enjoyed since I was a girl. I'm always looking for new and exciting recipes to make. My dream is to start up a catering service.
—Donna Mahoney, Milford, Connecticut

1 large whole garlic bulb
1/4 teaspoon olive *or* vegetable oil
3/4 teaspoon minced fresh thyme
    ***or* 1/4 teaspoon dried thyme**
1/4 cup butter *or* margarine, softened
4-1/2 teaspoons crumbled blue cheese
2 beef tenderloin steaks (6 ounces *each*)
1/2 teaspoon pepper
2 bacon strips

Remove papery outer skin from garlic (do not peel or separate cloves). Cut top off of garlic bulb. Brush with oil. Sprinkle with thyme. Wrap the bulb in heavy-duty foil.

Bake at 425° for 30-35 minutes or until softened. Cool for 10-15 minutes. Squeeze softened garlic into a mixer or food processor. Add butter; process until smooth. Transfer mixture to a small bowl. Stir in cheese. Cover and refrigerate for at least 1 hour.

Rub both sides of steaks with pepper. Wrap a bacon strip around each steak; secure with a toothpick. Broil 4-6 in. from the heat for 8-12 minutes on each side or until meat reaches desired doneness (for rare a meat thermometer reads 140°; medium, 160°; well-done, 170°), basting with butter mixture. Serve with any remaining butter mixture. **Yield:** 2 servings.

CABBAGE ROLLS

(Pictured below)

These cabbage rolls make a hearty meal when accompanied by old-fashioned rye bread.
—Lucille Proctor, Panguitch, Utah

4 large cabbage leaves
1/4 pound ground beef
1/4 pound bulk pork sausage
1/4 cup chopped onion
1/2 cup cooked rice
1 teaspoon Worcestershire sauce
1/2 teaspoon Dijon mustard
1 egg
1 cup tomato juice
2 tablespoons brown sugar, optional

In a large saucepan, cook the cabbage leaves in boiling water for 5 minutes; drain and set aside. In a medium skillet, cook beef, sausage and onion over medium heat until meat is no longer pink; drain. Stir in the rice, Worcestershire sauce, mustard and egg; mix well. Spoon about 1/3 cup onto each cabbage leaf. Fold in sides and roll up leaf.

Place seam side down in a greased 11-in. x 7-in. x 2-in. baking dish. Pour juice over rolls; sprinkle with brown sugar if desired. Cover and bake at 350° for 50 minutes. Uncover; bake 10 minutes longer. **Yield:** 2 servings.

Beef Chow Mein

(Pictured at right)

*This is my basic recipe for stir-fry.
I've tried others but always come back to
this one. I have also substituted chicken and
chicken broth for the beef and beef
broth and found it just as good.*
—*Margery Bryan, Royal City, Washington*

　4 teaspoons cornstarch
　1 teaspoon sugar
　4 teaspoons soy sauce
　1 garlic clove, minced
1/2 pound beef tenderloin, cut into
　　thin strips
　1 tablespoon canola *or* vegetable oil
　2 cups uncooked vegetables (carrots,
　　green pepper, broccoli, celery,
　　cauliflower *and/or* green onions)
1/3 cup beef broth
Chow mein noodles *or* hot cooked rice

In a bowl, combine the first four ingredients. Add beef and toss to coat. In a large skillet or wok, stir-fry beef in oil until no longer pink; remove and keep warm. Reduce heat to medium. Add vegetables and broth; stir-fry for 4 minutes. Return beef to the pan; cook and stir for 2 minutes or until heated through. Serve over chow mein noodles or rice. **Yield:** 2 servings.

Nutritional Analysis: One serving (prepared with reduced-sodium soy sauce and calculated without chow mein noodles or rice) equals 296 calories, 16 g fat (4 g saturated fat), 70 mg cholesterol, 643 mg sodium, 12 g carbohydrate, 1 g fiber, 26 g protein. **Diabetic Exchanges:** 3 lean meat, 2 vegetables, 2 fat.

Beef Fajitas

*My husband never tires of Mexican food.
I usually serve these fajitas with Mexican rice and pinto beans.*
—*O. Dell Cook, Yarnell, Arizona*

1/4 cup vegetable oil
1/4 cup lemon juice
　3 garlic cloves, minced
1-1/2 teaspoons grated lemon peel
1/4 to 1/2 teaspoon chili powder
1/4 teaspoon pepper
　1 beef flank steak (about 3/4 pound),
　　cut into thin strips
　3 green onions, thinly sliced
　4 flour tortillas (8 inches)
Salsa, optional

In a bowl, combine the oil, lemon juice, garlic, lemon peel, chili powder and pepper. Place half in a resealable plastic bag; cover and refrigerate remaining marinade. Add meat to bag. Seal and turn to coat; refrigerate for 4-8 hours.

Drain and discard marinade. In a skillet, heat reserved marinade. Add meat and green onions. Cook and stir until meat reaches desired doneness. Using a slotted spoon, place about 1/2 cup meat mixture down the center of each tortilla. Top with salsa if desired. Fold sides over meat mixture. **Yield:** 2 servings.

SLOPPY JOE SANDWICHES

(Pictured at right)

This is one of those recipes that cooks love because it's quick, easy and inexpensive. Brown sugar adds a touch of sweetness. In addition to rolls, the beef mixture is tasty over rice, biscuits or baked potatoes.
—Laurie Hauser, Rochester, New York

1/2 pound ground beef
1/2 cup ketchup
  2 tablespoons water
  1 tablespoon brown sugar
  1 teaspoon Worcestershire sauce
  1 teaspoon prepared mustard
1/4 teaspoon garlic powder
1/4 teaspoon onion powder
1/4 teaspoon salt
  2 hamburger buns, split

In a saucepan, cook beef over medium heat until no longer pink; drain. Stir in the ketchup, water, brown sugar, Worcestershire sauce, mustard, garlic powder, onion powder and salt. Bring to a boil. Reduce heat; cover and simmer for 30-40 minutes. Serve on buns. **Yield:** 2 servings.

    Nutritional Analysis: One sandwich (prepared with lean ground beef) equals 409 calories, 13 g fat (5 g saturated fat), 41 mg cholesterol, 1,391 mg sodium, 46 g carbohydrate, 2 g fiber, 28 g protein. **Diabetic Exchanges:** 3 lean meat, 2 starch, 2 fat, 1 fruit.

TEXAS-STYLE STEAK SANDWICHES

(Pictured at right)

I love the bold flavor of these hearty sandwiches. They cook quickly on the grill and taste great whether they're topped with salsa or guacamole.
—Linda Stinson, New London, Missouri

  1 beef flank steak (about 1/2 pound)
1/3 cup finely chopped onion
1/4 cup olive *or* vegetable oil
  2 tablespoons lime juice
  2 tablespoons red wine vinegar *or* cider vinegar
  1 garlic clove, minced
1/2 to 3/4 teaspoon chili powder
1/4 to 1/2 teaspoon salt
1/8 to 1/4 teaspoon ground cumin
  2 French rolls, split and toasted
1/2 cup salsa *or* guacamole

Pound steak to 1/4-in. thickness. In a resealable plastic bag, combine the onion, oil, lime juice, vinegar, garlic, chili powder, salt and cumin; add meat. Seal bag and turn to coat; refrigerate for 8 hours or overnight.

    Drain and discard marinade. Grill steak, uncovered, over medium heat or broil 4 in. from heat for 3-5 minutes on each side or until meat reaches desired doneness (for rare, a meat thermometer should read 140°; medium, 160°; well-done 170°). Slice meat against the grain. Serve on rolls. Top with salsa or guacamole if desired. **Yield:** 2 servings.

SLOPPY JOE SANDWICHES
TEXAS-STYLE STEAK SANDWICHES

BEEF ROULADEN

It took me years to work up the nerve to try a recipe that called for meat to be wrapped around pickles and cooked. Once I did, though, it became a favorite. My husband and boys request this for Christmas dinner.
—Janet Crooks, Jackson, Wyoming

2 tablespoons Dijon mustard, *divided*
2 beef cube steaks (about 6 ounces *each*)
1 medium dill pickle, cut lengthwise into eight pieces
1 small onion, thinly sliced, *divided*
1 bacon strip, halved
2 tablespoons butter *or* margarine
1 bay leaf
2 teaspoons beef bouillon granules
1/2 teaspoon dried rosemary, crushed
1/8 teaspoon salt
1-1/2 cups water, *divided*
1 tablespoon all-purpose flour
1 teaspoon browning sauce, optional

Spread 1 tablespoon mustard over one side of each piece of meat. Top each piece with four pickle pieces, a fourth of onion and a piece of bacon. Roll up jelly-roll style and secure with toothpicks. In a skillet, cook meat in butter on all sides until browned. Add the bay leaf, bouillon, rosemary, salt and remaining onion. Stir in 1-1/4 cups water; bring to a boil. Reduce heat; cover and simmer for 1-1/2 to 1-3/4 hours or until meat is tender.

Remove meat and keep warm. Combine flour and remaining water until smooth. Gradually stir into juices in skillet. Bring to a boil; cook and stir for 1-2 minutes or until thickened. Discard bay leaf. Stir in browning sauce if desired. Remove toothpicks before serving. **Yield:** 2 servings.

SPICY BEANLESS CHILI

My father came up with this recipe when I lived at home. He always added the optional cayenne pepper, and we four kids would mop up the chili with slices of bread. I don't use the cayenne for my family, but it still warms you up on cold days.
—Kathy Wittig, Loveland, Ohio

1/2 pound ground beef
1/3 cup chopped green pepper
2 tablespoons chopped onion
1 garlic clove, minced
1 can (8 ounces) tomato sauce
1 can (5-1/2 ounces) tomato juice
1/2 cup water
2 tablespoons chili powder
1/2 teaspoon dried oregano
1/2 teaspoon paprika
1/4 teaspoon ground cumin
1/4 teaspoon cayenne pepper, optional
1/8 teaspoon salt, optional

In a large saucepan, cook beef, green pepper, onion and garlic over medium heat until meat is no longer pink; drain. Stir in the tomato sauce, tomato juice, water, chili powder, oregano, paprika, cumin and cayenne and salt if desired. Bring to a boil. Reduce heat; simmer, uncovered, for 45 minutes or to desired thickness. **Yield:** 2 servings.

Nutritional Analysis: One serving (prepared with lean ground beef and reduced-sodium tomato juice and without additional salt) equals 282 calories, 12 g fat (4 g saturated fat), 41 mg cholesterol, 894 mg sodium, 19 g carbohydrate, 6 g fiber, 27 g protein. **Diabetic Exchanges:** 3 lean meat, 1 starch, 1 fat.

BAKED SWISS STEAK

(Pictured at right)

This dish is one of my husband's favorites, so I make it often. The meat becomes very tender, and the vegetables add delicious flavor.
—Dolores Wynne, Clearwater, Florida

1/2 to 3/4 pound boneless round steak
2 tablespoons all-purpose flour, *divided*
1/2 teaspoon salt
2 tablespoons vegetable oil
1 can (14-1/2 ounces) stewed tomatoes
1/2 cup chopped carrot
1/4 cup chopped celery
1 tablepoon chopped onion
1/4 teaspoon Worcestershire sauce
2 tablespoons sharp cheddar cheese

Cut meat into two portions; pound to 1/4-in. thickness. Combine 1 tablespoon flour and salt; coat meat on both sides. In a skillet, brown meat in oil. Transfer meat to a greased shallow 2-qt. baking dish; set aside. To pan drippings, add tomatoes, carrot, celery, onion, Worcestershire sauce and remaining flour. Bring to a boil over medium heat; cook and stir for 2 minutes.

Pour over the meat. Cover and bake at 350° for 1-1/2 hours or until the meat is tender. Sprinkle with cheese; return to the oven until cheese is melted. **Yield: 2 servings.**

ORIENTAL BEEF RIBBONS

A fellow nurse who also happens to be a fabulous cook shared this recipe with me. We like it served with steamed rice and stir-fried vegetables.
—Dianne Livingston, Woodland, California

1 beef flank steak (3/4 pound)
2 tablespoons teriyaki sauce
1-1/2 teaspoons vegetable oil
1 garlic clove, minced
1/4 teaspoon ground ginger
   ***or* 1 teaspoon minced fresh gingerroot**
1/8 teaspoon crushed red pepper flakes
1/2 teaspoon sesame seeds, toasted

Slice meat across the grain into 1/4-in. strips. In a resealable plastic bag, combine the teriyaki sauce, oil, garlic, ginger and red pepper flakes; add meat. Seal bag and turn to coat; refrigerate for 8 hours or overnight, turning several times.

Drain and discard marinade. Weave meat onto metal or soaked wooden skewers. Grill, covered, over medium heat or broil 4 in. from heat for 2-4 minutes on each side or until desired doneness. Remove from grill or boiler and sprinkle with sesame seeds. **Yield: 2 servings.**

APPLE-GLAZED BEEF BRISKET

My mother-in-law shared this wonderful recipe with me.
Of all the recipes I give out, this is the most requested.
—Jennifer Stephens, Tacoma, Washington

1 fresh beef brisket* (1 to 1-1/4 pounds)
1 tablespoon vegetable oil
1 small onion, quartered
1 garlic clove, halved
2 whole cloves
1-1/2 cups water
1/3 cup apple jelly
2 tablespoons white wine *or* white grape juice
1 teaspoon minced green onion
3/4 teaspoon Dijon mustard
1/4 teaspoon salt
1/8 teaspoon pepper
1/8 teaspoon curry powder

In a large skillet, brown meat in oil on both sides; drain. Add the onion, garlic, whole cloves and water. Bring to a boil. Reduce heat; cover and simmer for 2-1/2 hours or until meat is tender. Drain and discard pan juices. Cover and refrigerate meat for at least 2 hours.

In a saucepan, combine the apple jelly, wine or juice, green onion, mustard, salt, pepper and curry powder. Cook and stir until jelly is melted. Place meat in a greased foil-lined 11-in. x 7-in. x 2-in. baking dish. Pour half of sauce over meat. Bake, uncovered, at 325° for 25-30 minutes or until meat is heated through and glazed, basting several times. Serve with remaining sauce. **Yield:** 3-4 servings.

*Editor's Note: This is a fresh beef brisket, not corned beef.

CARROT-TOPPED SWISS CUBE STEAK

Serve this dish with mashed potatoes, and you have a whole meal.
You get plenty of veggies in the tasty topping.
—Nila Grahl, Des Plaines, Illinois

3 tablespoons all-purpose flour
1 teaspoon ground mustard
1/4 teaspoon salt
1/8 teaspoon pepper
2 beef cube steaks (about 6 ounces *each*)
1 to 2 tablespoons vegetable oil
1/3 cup chopped onion
2 tablespoons finely chopped celery
1 garlic clove, minced
1 cup canned diced tomatoes with juice
2 tablespoons shredded carrots
2-1/4 teaspoons Worcestershire sauce
1-1/2 teaspoons honey

In a shallow bowl, combine the flour, mustard, salt and pepper; coat meat with flour mixture. In a skillet, brown meat in oil for 2 minutes on each side. Remove meat and keep warm.

Saute the onion, celery and garlic in pan drippings for 1-2 minutes. Stir in tomatoes, scraping browned bits from bottom of pan. Stir in the carrots, Worcestershire sauce and honey. Return meat to skillet, Bring to a boil. Reduce heat; cover and simmer 6-10 minutes or until meat and vegetables are tender. **Yield:** 2 servings.

LONDON BROIL

(Pictured on page 118)

I was bored making the usual London broil, so I got a little creative and sparked up the flavor with crushed red pepper flakes, garlic and Worcestershire sauce.
—Dan Wright, San Jose, California

1 beef flank steak (about 3/4 pound)
1 garlic clove, minced
1/2 teaspoon seasoned salt
1/8 teaspoon crushed red pepper flakes
1/4 cup Worcestershire sauce

With a meat fork, poke holes in both sides of meat. Make a paste with garlic, seasoned salt and red pepper flakes; rub over both sides of meat. Place the steak in a large re-sealable plastic bag. Add Worcestershire sauce. Seal bag and turn to coat. Refrigerate for at least 4 hours, turning once.

Drain and discard marinade. Grill, uncovered over hot heat or broil 4 in. from the heat for 4-5 minutes on each side or until meat reaches desired doneness (for rare a meat thermometer should read 140°; medium, 160°; well-done, 170°). To serve, thinly slice across the grain. **Yield:** 2 servings.

FLASH-IN-THE-PAN PEPPER STEAK

(Pictured below)

My husband and I are big stir-fry fans, and this simple recipe is one we turn to often.
—Rochelle Higgins, Woodbridge, Virginia

3/4 pound boneless beef round steak, cut into thin strips
1/2 medium onion, cut into thin wedges
1/2 small green pepper, julienned
2 garlic cloves, minced
1 tablespoon butter *or* margarine
3/4 cup beef broth
1 tablespoon soy sauce
1 tablespoon cornstarch
2 tablespoons cold water
1/2 medium tomato, cut into wedges
1/4 cup fresh *or* frozen snow peas
1 teaspoon paprika
Hot cooked rice

In a large skillet, cook the beef, onion, green pepper and garlic in butter over medium heat for 5-7 minutes or until vegetables are tender and meat is no longer pink. Add the broth and soy sauce; bring mixture to a boil. Reduce heat; simmer, uncovered, for 1-2 minutes.

In a small bowl, combine cornstarch and water until smooth; stir into skillet. Bring to a boil; cook and stir for 2 minutes or until thickened. Stir in the tomato, snow peas and paprika; cook 30 seconds longer. Serve over rice. **Yield:** 2 servings.

STIR-FRY FOR ONE

(Pictured below)

Whenever I ask my husband what he'd like for dinner, this is what he requests.
—Margery Bryan, Royal City, Washington

1 tablespoon soy sauce
2 teaspoons cider *or* red wine vinegar
1 garlic clove, minced
1/2 teaspoon sugar
1/4 pound beef sirloin steak, cut into
   1/4-inch strips
1/4 cup broccoli florets
1/4 cup cauliflowerets
1/2 teaspoon canola *or* vegetable oil
1/4 cup diced green *or* sweet red pepper
1/4 cup diced cabbage
1/4 cup sliced water chestnuts
2 green onions, sliced
1 teaspoon cornstarch
3 tablespoons beef broth
Hot cooked rice

In a large resealable plastic bag, combine the first four ingredients; add beef. Seal bag and turn to coat. Refrigerate for at least 10 minutes.

In a skillet or wok, stir-fry broccoli and cauliflower in oil until vegetables begin to soften. Add beef and marinade; cook on medium-high for 3 minutes. Add the green pepper, cabbage and water chestnuts; stir-fry for 2-3 minutes or until the vegetables are crisp-tender. Add onions. Combine cornstarch and broth until smooth; stir into skillet. Bring to a boil; cook and stir for 2 minutes or until thickened. Serve over rice. **Yield:** 1 serving.

MUSTARD GRILLED STEAKS

For a meal that's hearty in a hurry, I grill these yummy steaks.
—Sharon Kraeger, Plattsmouth, Nebraska

1/3 cup Dijon mustard
1 tablespoon minced fresh parsley
2 tablespoons honey
1 tablespoon cider vinegar
1 tablespoon water
1/4 teaspoon hot pepper sauce
1/8 teaspoon coarsely ground pepper
2 beef top loin steaks (1 inch thick)
1 large onion, cut into 4 thick slices

In a bowl, combine the first seven ingredients. Brush over both sides of the steaks and onion slices. Grill over hot heat for 15-20 minutes or until steaks reach desired doneness (for rare a meat thermometer should read 140°; medium, 160°; well-done, 170°) and onion is tender, turning once. Brush occasionally with sauce. Serve onion slices with steak. **Yield:** 2 servings.

BEEF RAGOUT

My mother used to serve this to our family as a one-dish meal by adding sliced potatoes with the carrots. I've updated it by substituting mushrooms for the potatoes and adding chili sauce. It's also good over rice or mashed potatoes.
—Peggy Blomquist, Newfield, New York

2 tablespoons all-purpose flour
1 teaspoon salt
1/2 teaspoon pepper, *divided*
3/4 pound boneless beef round steak, cut into thin strips
1 large onion, sliced and separated into rings
1 tablespoon vegetable oil
3/4 cup water
3/4 cup red wine *or* beef broth
1 to 2 tablespoons chili sauce
2 bacon strips, cooked and crumbled
1 garlic clove, minced
1/4 teaspoon dried oregano
Dash dried thyme
3/4 cup sliced carrots
3/4 cup sliced fresh mushrooms
Hot cooked noodles

In a large resealable plastic bag, combine the flour, salt and 1/4 teaspoon pepper. Add beef, a few pieces at a time, and shake to coat.

In a large skillet, saute beef and onion in oil over medium heat until meat is browned and onion is tender. Add the water, wine or broth, chili sauce, bacon, garlic, oregano, thyme and remaining pepper; mix well. Bring to a boil. Reduce heat; cover and simmer for 2 hours, stirring occasionally. Add carrots and mushrooms; cover and simmer for 30 minutes or until carrots and meat are tender. Serve over noodles. **Yield:** 2 servings.

BEEF STUFFED PEPPERS

I used to bake for a restaurant, so I have lots of experience and enjoy being in the kitchen. Raisins add a touch of sweetness to the mild cheese sauce over these stuffed peppers.
—Janice Napper, Sedgwick, Kansas

2 medium sweet red *or* green peppers
1/2 pound ground beef
2 thin slices onion
1/4 cup raisins
1/4 teaspoon salt
1/8 teaspoon pepper
2 tablespoons butter *or* margarine
2 tablespoons all-purpose flour
1 cup milk
1/2 cup shredded cheddar cheese

Cut peppers in half lengthwise; remove seeds. In a large saucepan, cook peppers in boiling water for 3-5 minutes. Drain and rinse in cold water; set aside. In a skillet, cook beef and onion over medium heat until meat is no longer pink; drain. Stir in the raisins, salt and pepper. Place pepper halves in a greased 8-in. square baking dish. Spoon meat mixture into peppers.

In a saucepan, melt butter. Stir in flour until blended. Gradually stir in milk. Bring to a boil; cook and stir for 1 minute or until thickened. Reduce heat; add cheese. Cook and stir until cheese is melted. Pour over peppers. Bake, uncovered, at 350° for 25-30 minutes or until heated through. **Yield:** 2 servings.

CALIFORNIA KABOBS

My aunt gave me this recipe years ago. When my boys were young,
they weren't very fond of beef, but this was a sure way to entice them to eat.
—Bet Brown, Granville, Ohio

1/3 cup lemon juice
2 tablespoons vegetable oil
2 teaspoons white vinegar
2 teaspoons Worcestershire sauce
1 teaspoon paprika
1 garlic clove, minced
1/2 teaspoon sugar
1/2 teaspoon salt
1/8 to 1/4 teaspoon hot pepper sauce
3/4 pound boneless beef sirloin steak, cut into 1-inch cubes
8 large fresh whole mushrooms
1 medium onion, cut into chunks
1 medium green pepper, cut into chunks

In a bowl, combine the first nine ingredients; mix well. Pour 1/4 cup marinade into a large resealable plastic bag; cover and refrigerate remaining marinade. Add beef to the bag. Seal and turn to coat; refrigerate for at least 2 hours or overnight, turning occasionally.

Drain and discard marinade. On metal or soaked wooden skewers, alternately thread beef and vegetables. Grill, uncovered, over medium heat or broil 4 in. from heat for 6-8 minutes on each side or until beef reaches desired doneness, basting frequently with reserved marinade and turning once. **Yield:** 2 servings.

CURRIED BEEF WITH RICE

This time-tested recipe is a natural outgrowth of raising our own beef and
cooking for a family of mostly men who love meat and gravy.
—Marion Brogortti, Joseph, Oregon

1-1/3 cups water, *divided*
2 tablespoons uncooked wild rice
1/3 cup uncooked long grain rice
1/4 teaspoon vegetable oil
1/2 teaspoon salt, *divided*
1/4 pound ground beef
2 tablespoons chopped onion
1 tablespoon all-purpose flour
3/4 teaspoon curry powder
1/8 teaspoon pepper
1 cup milk
Optional toppings: toasted slivered almonds, minced fresh parsley, sliced green onions, chopped sweet red pepper *and/or* golden raisins

In a saucepan, combine 2/3 cup water and wild rice; bring to a boil. Reduce heat; cover and simmer for 40 minutes. Add the long grain rice, oil, 1/4 teaspoon salt and remaining water; return to a boil. Reduce heat; cover and simmer 15 minutes longer. Remove from heat; let stand for 5 minutes.

Meanwhile, in a skillet, cook beef and onion over medium heat until meat is no longer pink; drain. Stir in the flour, curry powder, pepper and remaining salt until blended. Gradually add milk. Bring to a boil; cook and stir for 1-2 minutes or until thickened. Serve over rice. Sprinkle with toppings if desired. **Yield:** 2 servings.

SPAGHETTI AND MEATBALLS FOR TWO

(Pictured below)

Through the years, I've modified my spaghetti recipe from serving four people to two. This one's a keeper.
—David Stierheim, Pittsburgh, Pennsylvania

1 egg
3 tablespoons seasoned bread crumbs
2 tablespoons chopped onion
1 tablespoon grated Parmesan cheese
1/8 teaspoon pepper
1/4 pound ground beef
1/4 pound bulk Italian sausage
1 jar (14 ounces) spaghetti sauce
   or 1-1/2 cups homemade sauce
Hot cooked spaghetti
Additional Parmesan cheese, optional

In a bowl, combine the first five ingredients. Crumble beef and sausage over mixture and mix well. Shape into 2-in. meatballs. Brown in a skillet over medium heat; drain. Stir in the spaghetti sauce. Simmer, uncovered, for 20-30 minutes or until the meatballs are no longer pink. Serve over spaghetti; sprinkle with Parmesan cheese if desired. **Yield:** 2 servings

GREEK-STYLE RIB EYE STEAKS

Because our children are grown, I often cook for just my husband and me. When I want to serve something special, this is the entree I usually reach for. Seasonings, black olives and feta cheese give steak great flavor.
—Ruby Williams, Bogalusa, Louisiana

1-1/2 teaspoons garlic powder
1-1/2 teaspoons dried oregano
1-1/2 teaspoons dried basil
1/2 teaspoon salt
1/8 teaspoon pepper
2 beef rib eye steaks (1-1/2 inches thick)
1 tablespoon olive *or* vegetable oil
1 tablespoon lemon juice
2 tablespoons crumbled feta *or* blue cheese
1 tablespoon sliced ripe olives

In a small bowl, combine the first five ingredients; rub onto both sides of steaks. In a large skillet, cook steaks in oil for 7-9 minutes on each side or until meat reaches desired doneness (for rare a meat thermometer should read 140°; medium, 160°; well-done, 170°). Sprinkle with lemon juice, cheese and olives. Serve immediately. **Yield:** 2 servings.

CHICKEN & TURKEY

If poultry is a staple on your dinner table, you'll appreciate the variety in this useful chapter. Select your favorite cut of chicken or turkey, then choose from 58 mouth-watering recipes.

APRICOT CHICKEN AND SNOW PEAS (P. 164)

CHICKEN MARINARA (P. 150)
GRILLED TARRAGON MUSTARD TURKEY (P. 150)

CHICKEN MARINARA

(Pictured on page 149)

*If some people in your family prefer dark-meat chicken and others prefer light,
this recipe is a good choice. It offers both with a delightful marinara sauce.*
—Vikki Rebholz, Westchester, Ohio

2 tablespoons chopped onion
1 garlic clove, minced
1-1/2 teaspoons olive *or* vegetable oil
1 can (8 ounces) tomato sauce
1-1/2 teaspoons minced fresh parsley
1/4 teaspoon salt
1/4 teaspoon dried oregano
1/8 teaspoon dried basil
1/8 teaspoon pepper
1/4 cup all-purpose flour
1 to 1-1/4 pounds meaty bone-in chicken pieces
2 tablespoons butter *or* margarine, melted
2 tablespoons grated Parmesan cheese

In a skillet, saute onion and garlic in oil until crisp-tender. Stir in the tomato sauce, parsley, salt, oregano, basil and pepper. Bring to a boil. Reduce heat; simmer, uncovered, for 10 minutes.

Place flour in a resealable plastic bag. Add chicken, one piece at a time, and shake to coat. In a skillet, cook chicken in butter until lightly browned on all sides. Place skin side up in a greased shallow 1-1/2-qt. baking dish. Pour sauce over chicken. Cover and bake at 350° for 35 minutes. Uncover; sprinkle with Parmesan. Bake 5-15 minutes longer or until chicken juices run clear. **Yield:** 2 servings.

GRILLED TARRAGON MUSTARD TURKEY

(Pictured on page 149)

*I adapted a chicken recipe for turkey breasts instead. It quickly
became one of my husband's favorites for the grill.*
—Ann Greene, Dowagiac, Michigan

2 tablespoons lemon juice
2 tablespoons vegetable oil
1/4 teaspoon pepper
1 turkey breast tenderloin (1/2 pound)
4-1/2 teaspoons tarragon vinegar *or* cider vinegar
2 tablespoons dry white wine *or* chicken broth
1 teaspoon dried tarragon
1/4 cup butter *or* margarine, cubed
2 tablespoons Dijon mustard

In a resealable plastic bag, combine the lemon juice, oil and pepper; add turkey. Seal bag and turn to coat; refrigerate for up to 2 hours.

In a small saucepan, combine the vinegar, wine or broth and tarragon. Bring to a boil; cook until reduced by half. Reduce heat; add butter and mustard. Stir until butter is melted; set aside and keep warm.

Drain and discard marinade. Grill turkey, uncovered, over medium heat for 5 minutes; turn and baste with mustard sauce. Cook 10-15 minutes longer or until juices run clear, basting frequently. **Yield:** 2 servings.

TURKEY SPAGHETTI PIE

(Pictured at right)

*This pie is practically a meal in itself.
I usually put a green salad and crusty
French rolls on the table with it.
—Colleen Sherman, Bakersfield, California*

   2 ounces uncooked spaghetti,
     broken in half
   1 egg, lightly beaten
   2 tablespoons grated Parmesan
     cheese
   3 tablespoons sour cream
 1/2 pound ground turkey
 1/4 cup chopped green pepper
   2 tablespoons chopped onion
   1 teaspoon butter *or* margarine
 1/3 cup tomato sauce
 1/4 teaspoon garlic salt
 1/4 teaspoon dried oregano
Salt and pepper to taste
 1/3 cup shredded mozzarella cheese

Cook spaghetti according to package directions; drain. In a bowl, combine the egg, Parmesan cheese and spaghetti. Press spaghetti mixture onto the bottom and up sides of a greased shallow 2-cup baking dish or 6-1/2-in. pie plate. Spread with sour cream.

Crumble turkey into a skillet; add the pepper, onion and butter. Cook over medium heat until meat is no longer pink; drain. Stir in the tomato sauce, garlic salt, oregano, salt and pepper. Spoon into spaghetti crust. Sprinkle with mozzarella cheese. Cover edges loosely with foil. Bake at 350° for 15-20 minutes or until heated through and cheese is melted. Serve immediately. **Yield:** 2 servings.

GARLIC CHICKEN

*This time-tested recipe was given to me by my sister. The garlic is sweet and tender.
—Martha Banks, Houston, Texas*

   2 boneless skinless chicken breast
     halves (4 ounces *each*)
 1/8 teaspoon salt
 1/8 teaspoon pepper
  10 garlic cloves, peeled
1-1/2 teaspoons canola *or* vegetable oil
   5 tablespoons chicken broth, *divided*
 1/4 cup dry white wine *or* additional
     chicken broth
   1 teaspoon lemon juice
 1/2 teaspoon dried basil
 1/4 teaspoon dried oregano
1-1/2 teaspoons cornstarch

Season chicken with salt and pepper. In a skillet, cook chicken with garlic in oil for 4-6 minutes. Add 4 tablespoons broth, wine or additional broth, lemon juice, basil and oregano. Reduce heat; cover and simmer for 6-8 minutes or until chicken juices run clear.

Transfer chicken to a serving platter and keep warm. In a small bowl, combine cornstarch and remaining broth until smooth. Stir into skillet. Bring to a boil; cook and stir for 1 minute or until thickened. Spoon sauce over chicken. **Yield:** 2 servings.

CORNISH HEN WITH ORANGE STUFFING

(Pictured below)

*A delicate orange flavor makes this stuffing memorable. I serve potatoes
and coin carrots alongside the hen for a satisfying meal.*
—Amy Mueller Hoening, Yukon, Oklahoma

1 medium navel orange
1/4 cup sliced green onions
1/4 cup chopped celery
1 tablespoon vegetable oil
1-1/2 cups seasoned stuffing mix
1/4 teaspoon grated orange peel
4 to 5 tablespoons orange juice
1 Cornish game hen (20 ounces), halved
1 tablespoon honey, warmed
1 tablespoon water

Peel and section orange; cut each section into quarters and set aside. In a skillet, saute onions and celery in oil until crisp-tender. In a bowl, combine the onion mixture, stuffing mix, orange peel and reserved orange sections. Stir in enough orange juice to just moisten stuffing mixture.

Arrange stuffing in two mounds in a greased shallow 2-qt. baking dish. Place Cornish hen halves skin side up over stuffing. Cover and bake at 375° for 30 minutes. Uncover; bake for 15 minutes. Combine honey and water. Brush over hens. Bake 10-15 minutes longer or until juices run clear. **Yield:** 2 servings.

CHICKEN FRICASSEE

This is one of our all-time favorites. When you have guests over, just double the recipe.
—Carol Hemker, Phenix City, Alabama

4-1/2 teaspoons all-purpose flour, *divided*
1/4 teaspoon salt
1/8 teaspoon pepper
1/8 teaspoon dried thyme
2 chicken thighs (about 6 ounces *each*), skin removed
2 tablespoons butter *or* margarine
3/4 cup sliced fresh mushrooms
1/2 cup diced onion
1/4 cup diced celery
3/4 cup water
1 small bay leaf
1/4 cup milk
2 teaspoons minced fresh parsley

In a resealable plastic bag, combine 2-1/4 teaspoons flour, salt, pepper and thyme. Add chicken and shake to coat. In a small skillet, brown chicken in butter. Remove chicken and set aside. In same skillet, saute the mushrooms, onion and celery until crisp-tender. Return chicken to the pan. Add water and bay leaf. Bring to a boil. Reduce heat; cover and simmer for 30-35 minutes or until chicken juices run clear, turning occasionally.

Place remaining flour mixture in a bowl; stir in milk until smooth. Stir into pan juices. Bring to a boil; cook and stir for 2 minutes or until thickened. Discard bay leaf. Sprinkle with parsley. **Yield:** 2 servings.

APRICOT-GLAZED TURKEY DRUMSTICKS

*My wife likes apricots, so I revised a recipe for orange-glazed ham
to be used with turkey. My family says it's tops.*
—Joseph Atkinson, Tacoma, Washington

2 turkey drumsticks (about 3/4 pound
   each)
2 tablespoons vegetable oil
1 celery rib, halved
1 small onion, halved
1/2 teaspoon salt
1/4 teaspoon whole peppercorns
1/3 cup apricot preserves, warmed
1 can (8-3/4 ounces) apricot halves,
   drained

In a Dutch oven, brown turkey in oil. Add
the celery, onion, salt, peppercorns and
enough water to cover drumsticks. Bring
to a boil. Reduce heat; cover and simmer
for 20 minutes or until meat is tender. Remove drumsticks from broth; drain well.
(Discard broth or strain and reserve for another use.)

Place drumsticks in a greased shallow
roasting pan. Brush with half the preserves.
Top with apricot halves; brush apricots with
remaining preserves. Bake, uncovered, at
400° for 8-10 minutes or until glaze is set.
Yield: 2 servings.

SPINACH TURKEY PENNE

(Pictured below)

*A friend served this recipe to me as a vegetarian dish. I enjoyed it, but my husband
and three sons love meat, so I added turkey Italian sausage.*
—Sharon MacLean, Laguna Niguel, California

3 ounces uncooked penne *or* medium
   tube pasta
2 turkey Italian sausage links (about
   1/2 pound), casings removed
1 garlic clove, minced
1 tablespoon olive *or* vegetable oil
4 cups packed torn fresh spinach
1/4 cup golden raisins, optional
1/2 teaspoon chicken bouillon granules
2 plum tomatoes, seeded and chopped
1/4 cup sliced almonds, toasted
2 tablespoons shredded Parmesan
   cheese

Cook pasta according to package directions.
Crumble sausage into a skillet. Cook over
medium heat until no longer pink; drain
and set aside. In same skillet, cook garlic in
oil for 1-2 minutes. Add the spinach, raisins
if desired and bouillon. Cook and stir until
spinach is wilted. Stir in tomatoes and
sausage. Drain pasta; transfer to a serving
bowl. Add spinach mixture; toss gently. Garnish with almonds and Parmesan cheese.
Yield: 2 servings.

CHICKEN 'N' BISCUIT BAKE

(Pictured at right)

My mother used to make this dish years ago, and everyone in the family enjoyed it.
—Shireen Rancier, Killam, Alberta

2 cups chicken broth
1 pound meaty bone-in chicken pieces
1 medium onion, chopped
1 celery rib, cut into 1/2-inch pieces
1 teaspoon salt
1 bay leaf
CREAM SAUCE:
   3 tablespoons plus 1-1/2 teaspoons
     butter *or* margarine, melted
   3 tablespoons plus 1-1/2 teaspoons
     all-purpose flour
Salt and pepper to taste
Dash ground mace
   1/3 cup milk
   1/8 teaspoon Worcestershire sauce
BISCUITS:
   2/3 cup plus 1 tablespoon all-purpose
     flour
1-1/4 teaspoons baking powder
   1/8 teaspoon salt
   2 tablespoons shortening
   1/3 cup milk

In a large saucepan, combine the broth, chicken, onion, celery, salt and bay leaf.

Bring to a boil. Reduce heat; cover and simmer for 20 minutes or until chicken juices run clear. Remove chicken from broth; cool. When cool enough to handle, remove skin and meat from bones. Discard skin and bones. Cut up meat. Strain broth. Reserve vegetables and 1 cup broth; discard bay leaf. (Discard or save remaining broth for another use.) Arrange chicken and vegetables in a greased 3-cup dish.

For sauce, melt butter in a saucepan. Stir in the flour, salt, mace and pepper until smooth. Gradually add the milk and Worcestershire sauce and reserved broth. Bring to a boil; cook and stir for 2 minutes or until thickened. Pour over chicken.

For biscuits, in a bowl, combine the flour, baking powder and salt; cut in shortening until the mixture resembles coarse crumbs. Stir in milk. On a floured surface, knead 8-10 times. Pat into a 1/2-in.-thick square and cut into quarters. Arrange biscuits over sauce. Bake, uncovered, at 450° for 17-20 minutes or until biscuits are golden brown. **Yield:** 2 servings.

TURKEY LO MEIN

(Pictured at right)

When I have only 20 minutes to get dinner on the table, this is the recipe I reach for.
—Fran Schellman, Rockville, Missouri

2 cups frozen stir-fry vegetables
3/4 cup chicken broth
2 tablespoons soy sauce
1/2 teaspoon ground ginger
1/4 teaspoon sugar
1/4 teaspoon garlic powder
1/8 teaspoon crushed red pepper flakes
   2 ounces uncooked angel hair pasta *or*
     vermicelli, broken into 2-inch pieces
1 teaspoon cornstarch
1 tablespoon water
1 cup julienned cooked turkey breast

In a large saucepan, combine the vegetables, broth, soy sauce, ginger, sugar, garlic powder and red pepper flakes. Bring to a boil. Add pasta. Reduce heat; cover and simmer for 8-10 minutes or until pasta is tender. In a bowl, combine cornstarch and water until smooth. Stir into pasta mixture; add turkey. Bring to a boil; cook and stir 3 minutes, until thickened. **Yield:** 2 servings.

CHICKEN 'N' BISCUIT BAKE
TURKEY LO MEIN

HOME-STYLE CHICKEN AND SAUSAGE

This great entree is perfect for a busy day because it's made with only simple ingredients.
—*Charla Domina, Shortsville, New York*

1 Italian sausage link (about 1/4 pound)
2 medium potatoes, cut into 1/2-inch cubes
2 tablespoons olive *or* vegetable oil, *divided*
2 chicken thighs (about 6 ounces *each*)
1/2 cup sweet red *or* green pepper chunks (1 inch)
1 small onion, quartered
2 tablespoons water
1/2 teaspoon salt
1/2 teaspoon dried oregano
1/4 teaspoon pepper
3/4 cup frozen cut green beans

In a skillet, cook sausage link over medium heat until no longer pink; cut into 1/2-in. pieces and set aside. Place potatoes in a 8-in. square baking dish; drizzle with 1 tablespoon oil. Bake, uncovered, at 425° for 15 minutes.

Meanwhile, in a skillet, brown the chicken in remaining oil. Add the chicken, reserved sausage, sweet pepper, onion, water, salt, oregano and pepper to the potatoes. Bake, uncovered, for 15 minutes. Add beans. Bake 10-15 minutes longer or until chicken juices run clear and vegetables are tender, stirring occasionally. **Yield:** 2 servings.

ITALIAN CHICKEN CASSEROLE

My aunt created this recipe, and the whole family has been enjoying it for years now.
It's equally good with Polish or Italian sausage.
—*Angela Jencks, Pinon Hills, California*

1 turkey Italian sausage link (about 1/4 pound), casing removed
1 small onion, chopped
1/3 cup chopped celery
2 boneless skinless chicken breast halves (4 ounces *each*)
1/2 teaspoon paprika
2 teaspoons canola *or* vegetable oil
3/4 cup water
1/4 cup sherry *or* chicken broth
1/4 teaspoon chicken bouillon granules
2 garlic cloves, minced
1/4 cup uncooked long grain rice
1/8 teaspoon salt
1/8 teaspoon pepper
1/2 cup sliced fresh mushrooms

Crumble sausage into a skillet; add onion and celery. Cook over medium heat until meat is no longer pink; drain and set aside. Sprinkle chicken with paprika. In the same skillet, cook chicken in oil for 2-3 minutes on each side or until chicken juices run clear; remove and set aside.

Return sausage mixture to the skillet. Add the broth, bouillon, garlic, rice, salt and pepper. Bring to a boil. Reduce heat; cover and simmer for 15 minutes. Add chicken and mushrooms; cook 5 minutes longer or until rice is done and chicken is heated through. **Yield:** 2 servings.

Nutritional Analysis: One serving equals 378 calories, 11 g fat (2 g saturated fat), 89 mg cholesterol, 650 mg sodium, 27 g carbohydrate, 1 g fiber, 37 g protein. **Diabetic Exchanges:** 4 lean meat, 2 vegetable, 1 starch.

CHICKEN 'N' CARROT DUMPLING STEW

(Pictured at right)

It's been many years since I clipped this recipe from a magazine. It's always welcome at a family get-together.
—Ruth Haight, Markham, Ontario

1/2 **pound boneless skinless chicken breasts**
1 **cup chicken broth**
1 **small onion, chopped**
1 **celery rib, sliced**
1/8 **to 1/4 teaspoon salt**
Dash dried thyme
Dash pepper
4-1/2 **teaspoons all-purpose flour**
3 **tablespoons water**
DUMPLINGS:
1/2 **cup all-purpose flour**
1 **teaspoon baking powder**
1/4 **teaspoon salt**
2 **tablespoons shortening**
1/4 **cup milk**
2 **tablespoons finely grated carrot**
1/2 **teaspoon minced fresh parsley**

In a large saucepan, combine the chicken, broth, onion, celery, salt, thyme and pepper. Bring to a boil. Reduce heat; cover and simmer for 15 minutes or until chicken juices run clear and vegetables are tender. Combine flour and water until smooth. Stir into broth. Bring to a boil; cook and stir for 1 minute or until thickened.

For dumplings, in a bowl, combine the flour, baking powder and salt; cut in shortening until mixture resembles coarse crumbs. Stir in the milk, carrot and parsley. Drop by rounded tablespoonfuls into simmering broth. Cover and simmer for 20 minutes or until a toothpick inserted in a dumpling comes out clean (do not lift the cover while simmering). **Yield:** 2 servings.

CHICKEN-FETA PHYLLO BUNDLES

Making these delicious bundles requires just a few ingredients. I put the remaining pastry back in the freezer to use another time.
—Kathryn Acreman, Carstairs, Alberta

6 **sheets phyllo dough (18 inches x 14 inches)**
1/4 **cup butter** *or* **margarine, melted**
2 **boneless skinless chicken breast halves**
Lemon-pepper seasoning
1/2 **cup crumbled feta** *or* **shredded mozzarella cheese**

Place one sheet of phyllo dough on a work surface; brush with melted butter. Repeat with 2 more sheets of phyllo, brushing each layer. (Keep remaining phyllo dough covered with waxed paper to avoid drying out.) Season chicken with lemon-pepper. Place 1 chicken breast along one short edge of pastry. Top with 1/4 cup cheese. Fold sides over chicken, then roll up. Brush with melted butter. Place on an ungreased baking sheet. Repeat with remaining ingredients. Bake, uncovered, at 350° for 30-35 minutes or until phyllo dough is golden brown. **Yield:** 2 servings.

ASPARAGUS-TURKEY PASTA TOSS

(Pictured below)

Since turkey is economical, we enjoy it in many different ways year-round.
This springtime favorite started out as a seafood recipe, but I adapted it.
—Lori Lytton, State Center, Iowa

4 ounces uncooked angel hair pasta
1 tablespoon butter *or* margarine
1 tablespoon all-purpose flour
1/2 teaspoon chicken bouillon granules
1/4 teaspoon pepper
1/8 teaspoon salt
3/4 cup milk
1/4 cup shredded Swiss cheese
3 tablespoons shredded Parmesan cheese
1 cup diced cooked turkey
10 fresh asparagus spears, cut into 1-inch pieces
1/2 cup sliced fresh mushrooms

Cook pasta according to package directions. In a saucepan, melt butter. Stir in the flour, bouillon, pepper and salt until smooth; gradually add milk. Bring to a boil; cook and stir 2 minutes or until thickened. Reduce heat; add cheeses and stir until smooth. Stir in the turkey, asparagus and mushrooms. Cook until heated through. Drain pasta and place in a serving bowl. Pour sauce mixture over pasta; toss gently to coat. **Yield:** 2 servings.

LEMON-THYME CORNISH HENS

Now that I've retired from nursing, I have more time to cook and read.
My husband loves Cornish hens made this way.
—Deborah Jackson, Rutland, Vermont

1/4 cup butter *or* margarine, melted
1/4 cup lemon juice
2 garlic cloves, minced
2 teaspoons dried thyme
1/2 teaspoon salt
1/2 teaspoon pepper
1/8 teaspoon paprika
2 Cornish game hens (20 ounces *each*)

In a bowl, combine the first seven ingredients. Place hens on a rack in a shallow baking pan. Tuck wings under hen. Spoon half of butter sauce over hens. Bake, uncovered, at 425° for 40-45 minutes or until juices run clear and a meat thermometer reads 180°, basting occasionally with remaining sauce. **Yield:** 2 servings.

HERB-ROASTED TURKEY BREAST

(Pictured at right)

Whenever we're in the mood for turkey, this is the recipe I use. It always wins me compliments. (Leftovers would be great in the Asparagus-Turkey Pasta Toss recipe at left.)
—Cheryl King, West Lafayette, Indiana

6 tablespoons butter *or* margarine
2 tablespoons lemon juice
1 tablespoon soy sauce
1 tablespoon chopped green onion
1/2 teaspoon dried thyme
1/2 teaspoon dried marjoram
1/4 to 1/2 teaspoon rubbed sage
1/4 teaspoon salt, optional
1/8 teaspoon pepper
1 boneless skinless turkey breast half (2 pounds)

In a small saucepan, combine the first nine ingredients. Bring to a boil; remove from the heat and set aside to cool. Place turkey breast on a rack in a greased shallow roasting pan. Spoon some of the butter mixture over the top. Cover and bake at 325° for 1-1/4 to 1-3/4 hours or until juices run clear and a thermometer reads 170°; basting often with butter mixture. Let stand for 10-15 minutes before slicing. **Yield:** 6 servings.

STUFFING CHICKEN CASSEROLE

This recipe was quite a hit at my son's engagement party a few years ago.
—Jacqueline Stefanik, Chicopee, Massachusetts

4-2/3 cups water, *divided*
2 boneless skinless chicken breast halves
1 small onion, quartered
1 celery rib, cut into 1-inch pieces
1 large carrot, cut into 1-inch pieces
Salt and pepper to taste
2 cups herb stuffing mix
1/4 cup butter *or* margarine, melted
3 tablespoons Homemade Cream-Style Soup Mix (page 75)
1/2 cup sour cream
1/2 cup frozen peas

In a large saucepan, combine 4 cups water, chicken, onion, celery, carrot, salt and pepper. Bring to a boil. Reduce heat; cover and simmer for 15-20 minutes or until chicken juices run clear and vegetables are tender. Remove and set aside chicken and carrot. Strain broth, discarding remaining vegetables. Set aside 1/2 cup chicken broth. (Discard or save remaining broth for another use.)

In a bowl, combine stuffing mix and margarine. In a microwave-safe bowl, whisk together the soup mix and the remaining water. Microwave, uncovered, on high for 2 to 2-1/2 minutes, whisking occasionally. Add sour cream and reserved broth. Stir soup mixture into stuffing mixture. Place half the stuffing mix in a greased shallow 5-cup baking dish; top with reserved chicken and carrots, then peas. Cover with remaining stuffing mix. Cover and bake at 350° for 20-30 minutes or until heated through. **Yield:** 2 servings.

LIME JALAPENO TURKEY WRAPS

(Pictured at right)

This recipe came about years ago when I was a child. My grandfather enjoyed burritos filled with leftover turkey, lime and chiles. I've tweaked the recipe a little to better suit our tastes.
—Mary Jo Amos, Noel, Missouri

3 lettuce leaves
1 cup shredded cooked turkey breast (6 ounces)
2 tablespoons chopped seeded tomato
1 green onion, thinly sliced
1 teaspoon lime juice
1-1/2 teaspoons finely chopped jalapeno pepper*
1/8 teaspoon sugar
1/8 teaspoon salt
1/8 teaspoon garlic powder
1/8 teaspoon pepper
2 flour tortillas (8 inches), warmed
2 red onion rings (1/4 to 1/2 inch thick)
2 pitted ripe *or* stuffed olives, optional

Chop one lettuce leaf; set aside remaining leaves. In a medium bowl, combine the turkey, chopped lettuce, tomato, green onion, lime juice, jalapeno, sugar, salt, garlic powder and pepper; set aside.

Place one lettuce leaf on each tortilla. Spoon half the filling off center on each. Fold one end over filling and roll up. Slide each wrap through the middle of an onion ring. Secure roll-up with a toothpick near the onion ring; top each with an olive if desired. **Yield:** 2 servings.

Nutritional Analysis: One tortilla equals 291 calories, 4 g fat (1 g saturated fat), 71 mg cholesterol, 483 mg sodium, 31 g carbohydrate, 1 g fiber, 31 g protein. **Diabetic Exchanges:** 4 very lean meat, 2 starch.

*Editor's Note: When cutting or seeding hot peppers, use rubber or plastic gloves to protect your hands. Avoid touching your face.

CITRUS TURKEY

(Pictured at right)

My sister Sandra shared this recipe with me, so around my house we call it "Sandi's Citrus Turkey".
—Diane Baker, Bothell, Washington

1 garlic clove, minced
1 turkey tenderloin (about 1/2 pound)
1/3 cup orange juice
1/4 cup plus 1 tablespoon chicken broth, *divided*
1 tablespoon lemon juice
1 teaspoon minced fresh thyme *or* 1/4 teaspoon dried thyme
Salt to taste, optional
Pepper to taste
2 teaspoons cornstarch

Rub garlic over all sides of tenderloin. Place in a greased shallow 5-cup baking dish. Pour the orange juice, 1/4 cup broth and lemon juice over turkey. Sprinkle with the thyme, salt if desired and pepper. Cover and bake at 325° for 20 minutes. Uncover; bake 10-20 minutes longer or until meat juices run clear and a meat thermometer reads 170°, basting occasionally. Remove turkey to a serving platter and keep warm.

For sauce, pour drippings and loosened browned bits into a measuring cup. Skim fat; pour drippings into a saucepan. Combine cornstarch and remaining broth until smooth. Stir into drippings. Bring to a boil; cook and stir for 1-2 minutes or until thickened. Serve with turkey. **Yield:** 2 servings.

LIME JALAPENO TURKEY WRAPS
CITRUS TURKEY

SOUTHWESTERN SAUSAGE STEW

I created this healthy, low-fat recipe to feed my family. Here, it's sized just right for two people. We like that it's delicious, economical and fast to prepare.
—Amie Jaramillo, Interlaken, New York

1 cup cubed peeled potato
1/2 cup chicken broth
1 turkey Italian sausage link (about 1/4 pound), casings removed
1 small onion, chopped
3/4 cup canned kidney beans, rinsed and drained
3/4 cup canned diced tomatoes with juice
3/4 cup frozen corn, thawed
1/4 cup salsa
1 tablespoon canned green chilies
1/2 teaspoon ground cumin
1/4 teaspoon salt, optional
1/8 teaspoon cayenne pepper

In a saucepan, combine potato and broth; bring to a boil. Reduce heat; cover and simmer for 15-20 minutes or until potato is tender. Crumble sausage into a small skillet. Add onion and cook over medium heat until meat is no longer pink; drain and set aside.

Add sausage mixture to potatoes. Stir in the remaining ingredients. Cook, uncovered, for 8-10 minutes or until heated through. **Yield:** 2 servings.

Nutritional Analysis: One 1-1/4-cup serving (prepared with reduced-sodium chicken broth and without salt) equals 318 calories, 5 g fat (1 g saturated fat), 23 mg cholesterol, 1,047 mg sodium, 54 g carbohydrate, 9 g fiber, 18 g protein.

WHITE CHILI

This dish goes over especially well on a cool night. We're racing fans, and I'm frequently asked to bring this dish to the races. I'm happy to do so, because I enjoy it, too. I just double or triple the recipe.
—Carol Swainston, Sheridan, Michigan

2 green onions, chopped
1 to 2 tablespoons chopped seeded jalapeno pepper*
2 garlic cloves, minced
1-1/2 teaspoons plus 1 tablespoon butter or margarine, *divided*
1/4 teaspoon rubbed sage
1/4 teaspoon ground cumin
1/8 teaspoon ground ginger
1/2 pound boneless skinless chicken breast, cut into 1-inch cubes
1 tablespoon all-purpose flour
1-1/4 cups chicken broth
2 tablespoons milk
1 can (15-1/2 ounces) great northern beans, rinsed and drained
Shredded cheddar cheese

In a skillet, saute the onions, jalapeno and garlic in 1-1/2 teaspoons butter until crisp-tender. Add the sage, cumin and ginger; cook for 1 minute. Add chicken; cook and stir until lightly browned.

In a small saucepan, melt remaining butter. Stir in flour until smooth; gradually add the broth and milk. Bring to a boil; cook and stir 2 minutes or until thickened. Add beans. Pour over chicken mixture. Cook over medium heat until heated through. Sprinkle cheese on each serving. **Yield:** 2 servings.

***Editor's Note:** When cutting or seeding hot peppers, use rubber or plastic gloves to protect your hands. Avoid touching your face.

TURKEY PICCATA

This alternative to veal piccata is wonderfully tasty and much more economical.
—Sue Stephen McWhorter, Madison, Alabama

1/2 pound turkey cutlets *or* breast slices
1/4 cup all-purpose flour
1/2 teaspoon salt
1/4 teaspoon pepper
4-1/2 teaspoons vegetable oil
1/3 cup dry white wine *or* chicken broth
2 tablespoons butter *or* margarine
2 teaspoons lemon juice
1-1/2 teaspoons grated lemon peel

Flatten turkey cutlets to 1/4-in. thickness. In a resealable plastic bag, combine the flour, salt and pepper. Add turkey cutlets, one at a time, and shake to coat. In a skillet, cook cutlets in oil for 2-3 minutes on each side or until lightly browned; remove cutlets to a serving platter and keep warm.

In a small saucepan, bring wine to a boil; cook until liquid is reduced by half. Stir in butter and lemon juice. Remove from the heat and pour over cutlets. Sprinkle with lemon peel. **Yield:** 2 servings.

GREEK CHICKEN DINNER

(Pictured below and on front cover)

I received this wonderful recipe from our daughter-in-law, who is from Athens, Greece.
—Mary Anne Janzen, Manitoba, Canada

1 to 1-1/4 pounds meaty bone-in chicken pieces
2 to 3 tablespoons olive *or* vegetable oil, *divided*
2 medium carrots, cut into 1-inch pieces
1 medium potato, cut into 1/2-inch cubes
1 small onion, quartered
1 teaspoon minced fresh parsley
1 teaspoon dried basil
1/4 teaspoon dried oregano
1/8 teaspoon garlic powder
Salt and pepper to taste
1 to 2 tablespoons lemon juice

In a skillet, brown chicken in 1 tablespoon oil. In a greased 9-in. square baking dish, place the carrots, potato and onion. Drizzle with remaining oil and toss to coat. Top with chicken.

In a small bowl, combine the parsley, basil, oregano, garlic powder, salt and pepper. Sprinkle over chicken and vegetables, then sprinkle with lemon juice. Cover and bake at 375° for 40 minutes. Uncover; bake 15-20 minutes longer or until chicken juices run clear and vegetables are tender. **Yield:** 2-3 servings.

APRICOT CHICKEN AND SNOW PEAS

(Pictured on page 148)

I adore this dish. It's simple and fast to make, plus it tastes great.
—Lori Lockrey, West Hill, Ontario

1 small garlic clove, minced
1/2 teaspoon vegetable oil
1/4 pound boneless skinless chicken breast, cut into thin strips
1/2 cup fresh snow peas
3 tablespoons apricot preserves
2 tablespoons water
3/4 teaspoon sesame oil
1/2 teaspoon sesame seeds, toasted
1/2 teaspoon soy sauce
1/8 teaspoon Dijon mustard
1/8 teaspoon ground ginger
Hot cooked rice *or* pasta

In a skillet, saute garlic in oil for 30 seconds. Add chicken; stir-fry for 3 minutes. Stir in the snow peas, preserves, water, sesame oil, sesame seeds, soy sauce, mustard and ginger. Bring to a boil. Reduce heat; simmer, uncovered, for 5-7 minutes or until chicken juices run clear and vegetables are tender. Serve over rice. **Yield:** 1 serving.

CHICKEN ROLL-UPS

I made this recipe when I was visiting my family on the Mainland. It's fast and delicious.
—Debra Santos, Kapaa, Hawaii

1/2 teaspoon cornstarch
2 teaspoons soy sauce
3 tablespoons plum jam
1/2 teaspoon cider vinegar
1/4 teaspoon ground ginger
1/8 teaspoon garlic powder
1/8 teaspoon ground mustard
1/2 pound boneless skinless chicken breasts, cut into strips
2 teaspoons olive *or* vegetable oil
3 cups (6 ounces) coleslaw mix
4 flour tortillas (8 inches), warmed

In a bowl, combine cornstarch and soy sauce until smooth. Stir in jam, vinegar, ginger, garlic powder and mustard. Mix well; set aside. In a skillet, cook chicken in oil until no longer pink. Add jam mixture and coleslaw mix; cook until coleslaw is crisp-tender. Spoon into tortilla; roll up. **Yield:** 2 servings.

CHICKEN WELLINGTON CASSEROLE

A friend shared this recipe after I got married, and it's been my husband's favorite ever since.
—Jennifer Hassen, Tecumseh, Oklahoma

2 boneless skinless chicken breast halves
2 teaspoons butter *or* margarine
1 package (3 ounces) cream cheese, softened
1/2 cup sliced fresh mushrooms
1 tablespoon chopped green onion
1/8 teaspoon salt
Dash pepper
1 tube (4 ounces) refrigerated crescent rolls

In a skillet, cook chicken in butter 3-4 minutes on each side. Place chicken in a greased 3-cup baking dish. In a bowl, combine cream cheese, mushrooms, onion, salt and pepper. Spoon over chicken. Unroll dough into one long rectangle; seal seams and perforations. If necessary, trim dough to fit top of dish and patch together by overlapping edges. Pinch edges to seal. Place over filling. Bake, uncovered, at 350° for 20 minutes or until heated through. **Yield:** 2 servings.

HERBED CITRUS CHICKEN

This recipe is to die for! Even folks who don't care for chicken always ask for seconds.
—Victoria Newman, Sonora, California

1/4 cup lime *or* lemon juice
2 tablespoons olive *or* canola oil
3/4 teaspoon seasoned salt
1/2 teaspoon garlic powder
1/2 teaspoon paprika
1/2 teaspoon dried basil
1/4 teaspoon dried thyme
2 boneless skinless chicken breast halves (4 ounces *each*)

In a bowl, combine the first seven ingredients; mix well. Pour 3 tablespoons marinade into a resealable plastic bag. Cover and refrigerate remaining marinade; add chicken to the bag. Seal bag and turn to coat; refrigerate for at least 3 hours or overnight.

Drain and discard marinade. Grill, uncovered, over medium heat or broil 6 in. from heat for 5-7 minutes on each side or until juices run clear; basting occasionally with reserved marinade. **Yield:** 2 servings.

Nutritional Analysis: One 1-1/4-cup serving equals 191 calories, 8 g fat (1 g saturated fat), 66 mg cholesterol, 359 mg sodium, 2 g carbohydrate, trace fiber, 26 g protein. **Diabetic Exchange:** 3-1/2 lean meat.

BARBECUED CHICKEN

(Pictured below right)

When I was a young girl, I went with my parents to visit one of their friends. When I married, I wrote to that friend and asked her to share her recipe. Lucky for me, she said yes.
—Margaret Hanson-Maddox, Montpelier, Indiana

1/3 cup all-purpose flour
3/4 teaspoon salt
1 to 1-1/4 pounds meaty bone-in chicken pieces
1 tablespoon plus 1 teaspoon butter *or* margarine, *divided*
1/4 cup chopped onion
1/4 cup chopped celery
2 tablespoons chopped green pepper
1/3 cup water
1/3 cup ketchup
2 teaspoons brown sugar
2 teaspoons Worcestershire sauce
Dash pepper

In a large resealable plastic bag, combine flour and salt. Add chicken, one piece at a time, and shake to coat. In a skillet, brown chicken in 1 tablespoon butter. Transfer chicken to a greased 2-qt. baking dish.

In the same skillet, saute onion, celery and green pepper in remaining butter until crisp-tender. Add the water, ketchup, brown sugar, Worcestershire sauce and pepper. Bring to a boil. Reduce heat; simmer, uncovered, for 10-15 minutes or until thickened. Remove from the heat; pour over chicken. Bake, uncovered, at 350° for 35-50 minutes or until chicken juices run clear. **Yield:** 2-3 servings.

EASY LEMON CHICKEN AND RICE

I can throw this together quickly after work and still serve a satisfying dinner.
—Dixie Terry, Marion, Illinois

1-1/2 teaspoons cornstarch
1/4 teaspoon garlic powder
1/4 teaspoon grated lemon peel
3/4 cup chicken broth
4 to 4-1/2 teaspoons lemon juice
1/2 cup julienned sweet red pepper
1/2 cup thinly sliced zucchini
1 tablespoon butter *or* margarine
3/4 cup uncooked instant rice
3/4 cup cubed cooked chicken breast

In a bowl, combine cornstarch, garlic powder and lemon peel. Stir in broth and lemon juice until smooth; set aside. In a 3-cup microwave-safe dish, cook pepper and zucchini in butter until crisp-tender. Stir in broth mixture and rice. Cover; microwave on high for 4 minutes. Stir in chicken. Cover and let stand for 5 minutes; fluff rice. Cook 30-45 seconds, until heated through. **Yield:** 2 servings.
   Editor's Note: This recipe was tested in an 850-watt microwave.

CHICKEN A LA KING

We serve this saucy chicken over hot cooked noodles, rice or toast.
—Rebecca Knox, Liberal, Missouri

1/2 cup quartered fresh mushrooms
1/4 cup chopped green pepper
1/4 cup butter *or* margarine
1/4 cup all-purpose flour
3/4 teaspoon chicken bouillon granules
1/4 teaspoon pepper
1/8 teaspoon salt, optional
3/4 cup milk
1/4 cup water

1 cup cubed cooked chicken

In a skillet, saute the mushrooms and green pepper in butter until crisp-tender. Add in the flour, bouillon, pepper and salt; stir until smooth. Gradually add milk and water. Bring to a boil; cook and stir 1-2 minutes or until thickened. Stir in chicken; cook until heated through. **Yield:** 2 servings.

VEGETABLE CHICKEN PIE

This delicious dish is a longtime favorite that's just right for two.
—Ruth Walker, Ruffin, North Carolina

1 cup cubed cooked chicken
1 can (10-3/4 ounces) condensed
   cream of celery soup, undiluted
1/2 cup frozen pea and carrot mix
1/4 cup chopped onion
1/4 cup chopped green pepper
3 tablespoons chicken broth
2 tablespoons butter, melted
TOPPING:
1/3 cup self-rising flour*
1/3 cup buttermilk
1/4 cup butter *or* margarine, softened
1/8 teaspoon pepper
Refrigerated butter-flavored spray
Paprika

In a bowl, combine the first seven ingredients. Transfer into two greased 12-oz. baking dishes. For topping, in a bowl, combine the flour, buttermilk, butter and pepper (batter will be thin). Spoon evenly over each dish; spread to cover top. Spritz each casserole with butter-flavored spray; sprinkle with paprika. Bake, uncovered, at 350° for 30-35 minutes or until bubbly and top is firm. **Yield:** 2 servings.
   ***Editor's Note:** As a substitute for 1/3 cup self-rising flour, place 1/2 teaspoon baking powder and 1/8 teaspoon salt in a 1/3 cup measuring cup. Add all-purpose flour to measure 1/3 cup.

TURKEY CUTLETS WITH TOMATO SAUCE

(Pictured below)

I'm the mother of two todders, so I depend on easy-to-prepare recipes like this.
—Nancy Sibenaller, Lonsdale, Minnesota

2 tablespoons all-purpose flour
1/8 teaspoon salt, optional
1/8 teaspoon pepper
4 turkey cutlets *or* breast slices (1/2 pound)
2 teaspoons butter *or* margarine
MUSHROOM TOMATO SAUCE:
1 cup sliced fresh mushrooms
1-1/2 teaspoons olive *or* canola oil
2 garlic cloves, minced
1/4 teaspoon dried rosemary, crushed
2 medium tomatoes, peeled, seeded and chopped
2 tablespoons dry white wine *or* chicken broth
1 teaspoon brown sugar
Salt and pepper to taste, optional
1 teaspoon butter *or* margarine
1 tablespoon minced fresh basil *or* 1 teaspoon dried basil
1-1/2 teaspoons lemon juice
2 tablespoons minced fresh parsley

In a large resealable plastic bag, combine the flour, salt if desired and pepper. Add the cutlets, two at a time and shake to coat. In a skillet, cook cutlets in butter for 2-3 minutes on each side or until lightly browned.

Meanwhile, in a skillet, saute mushrooms in oil until tender. Add garlic and rosemary; cook and stir for 1 minute. Add the tomatoes, wine or broth, brown sugar, salt if desired and pepper; cook and stir for 5 minutes. Stir in butter and basil. Serve cutlets with sauce. Sprinkle with lemon juice and parsley. **Yield:** 2 servings.

Nutritional Analysis: One serving (calculated without salt) equals 306 calories, 11 g fat (4 g saturated fat), 86 mg cholesterol, 125 mg sodium, 19 g carbohydrate, 2 g fiber, 31 g protein. **Diabetic Exchanges:** 4 very lean meat, 2 fat, 1 starch.

TURKEY QUESADILLAS

With only five ingredients, this recipe goes together in a flash yet tastes great.
—Edie Farm, Farmington, New Mexico

1 flour tortilla (10 inches)
1-1/2 teaspoons butter *or* margarine, softened
1/4 cup shredded Monterey Jack cheese
2 slices deli smoked turkey
Salsa, optional

Spread one side of tortilla with butter. Place tortilla greased side down on griddle. Sprinkle with cheese, then top with turkey. Fold tortilla in half. Cook over low heat for 2-3 minutes on each side or until golden brown and cheese is melted. Serve with salsa if desired. **Yield:** 1 serving.

WHITE BEAN TURKEY CHILI

My husband came home from a sales trip to the East Coast raving about white bean chili. This is our version.
—Mary Tauber, Brookings, South Dakota

1/2 pound turkey tenderloin
1/2 cup chopped onion
  1 garlic clove, minced
  1 to 1-1/2 teaspoons butter *or* margarine
  1 cup chicken broth
3/4 cup canned great northern beans, rinsed and drained
  1 cup canned diced tomatoes with juice
  2 tablespoons salsa
  1 teaspoon dried parsley flakes
1/8 to 1/4 teaspoon cayenne pepper
Shredded cheddar cheese *or* sour cream, optional

Cut turkey tenderloin lengthwise into quarters. In a skillet, cook the turkey, onion and garlic in butter until turkey is no longer pink and vegetables are crisp-tender. Remove turkey and let stand until cool enough to handle. Cut into cubes. Transfer vegetables to a saucepan. Add the turkey, broth, beans, tomatoes, salsa, parsley and cayenne. Bring to a boil. Reduce heat; simmer, uncovered, for 12-16 minutes or until slightly thickened. Top each serving with cheese or sour cream if desired. **Yield:** 2 servings.

Nutritional Analysis: One 1-1/2-cup serving (prepared with 1 teaspoon butter, reduced-sodium chicken broth and without cheese or sour cream) equals 305 calories, 3 g fat (2 g saturated fat), 75 mg cholesterol, 621 mg sodium, 31 g carbohydrate, 8 g fiber, 38 g protein. **Diabetic Exchanges:** 4 very lean meat, 2 starch.

MUSHROOM TURKEY CASSEROLE

To change up the flavor, I sometimes substitute leftover cooked chicken for the turkey and stir 1/2 cup of seedless white grapes into the mixture just before adding the topping.
—Nella Parker, Hersey, Michigan

1-1/2 cups cubed cooked turkey
1-1/2 cups sliced fresh mushrooms
  1 cup condensed cream of chicken soup, undiluted
  1 small celery rib, chopped
  1 small carrot, grated
  1 teaspoon minced fresh parsley
1/8 teaspoon pepper
1/4 cup soft bread crumbs
  1 teaspoon butter *or* margarine, melted
1/2 teaspoon paprika

In a bowl, combine the turkey, mushrooms, soup, celery, carrot, parsley and pepper. Divide the mixture into two greased 2-cup baking dishes. In a small bowl, toss bread crumbs with butter. Sprinkle half over each dish. Sprinkle with paprika. Bake, uncovered, at 350° for 15-20 minutes or until golden brown and bubbly. **Yield:** 2 servings.

Nutritional Analysis: One 1-1/2-cup serving (prepared with reduced-fat reduced-sodium soup) equals 326 calories, 10 g fat (4 g saturated fat), 95 mg cholesterol, 643 mg sodium, 22 g carbohydrate, 2 g fiber, 36 g protein. **Diabetic Exchanges:** 3-1/2 lean meat, 1-1/2 starch.

GARLIC ROASTED CHICKEN

(Pictured at right)

This recipe is deceptively simple, yet it never fails to get rave reviews from family and friends alike. Any leftovers can be reheated for another night's meal.
—Jane Allen, Ennismore, Ontario

1 broiler/fryer chicken (3 pounds)
1/2 cup white wine *or* chicken broth, *divided*
1 to 2 lime wedges
2 garlic cloves, peeled
1 bay leaf
Thyme sprig, optional
1/4 teaspoon paprika
1 tablespoon cornstarch
1 teaspoon chicken bouillon granules
2 tablespoons sherry *or* apple juice

Place chicken breast side up on a rack in a roasting pan. In a bowl, combine 1/4 cup wine or broth, lime wedges, garlic, bay leaf and thyme. Pour into cavity of chicken. Pour remaining wine or broth in roasting pan. Sprinkle chicken with paprika. Loosely tent with foil. Bake at 375° for 45 minutes, basting occasionally. Remove foil; bake 40-45 minutes longer or until juices run clear and a meat thermometer reads 180°, basting occasionally. Add additional wine or broth to pan if liquid evaporates.

Discard bay leaf and lime wedges. Remove chicken to a serving platter and let stand for 10 minutes before carving. Pour drippings and loosened brown bits into a measuring cup. Skim fat. In a saucepan, combine the cornstarch, bouillon and sherry or juice until smooth. Gradually stir in drippings. Bring to a boil; cook and stir for 2 minutes or until thickened. Serve gravy with chicken. **Yield:** 3-4 servings.

MUSTARD DRUMSTICKS FOR TWO

I come from a large family and learned to cook when I was very young. This perfectly portioned dish comes in handy now that I'm cooking for just the two of us.
—Virginia LeJeune, Agassiz, British Columbia

2 tablespoons *each* mayonnaise, vegetable oil and prepared mustard
1/2 cup crushed butter-flavored crackers
1 teaspoon chili powder
4 chicken legs, skin removed

In a small bowl, combine the mayonnaise, oil and mustard. In a plastic bag, combine crackers and chili powder. Dip chicken legs in mustard mixture, then shake in crumbs. Place in a greased 8-in. square baking dish. Bake, uncovered, at 400° for 35-40 minutes or until juices run clear. **Yield:** 2 servings.

CHICKEN JAMBALAYA

(Pictured at right)

This is one of my husband's favorites, and he's a picky eater, so you know it's good! Some folks are surprised how well chicken and shrimp complement each other.
—Laurie Henderson, Fort Wayne, Indiana

1 small onion, chopped
1 garlic clove, minced
1 tablespoon butter *or* margarine
1/4 pound fully cooked smoked sausage, cut into 1/2-inch slices
1/2 cup chicken broth
1/2 cup canned diced tomatoes with juice
1/4 cup chopped green pepper
1 bay leaf
1/8 teaspoon dried thyme
Dash cayenne
1/4 cup uncooked long grain rice
1/2 cup cubed cooked chicken breast
1/4 pound uncooked medium shrimp, peeled and deveined

In a skillet, saute onion and garlic in butter until crisp-tender. Add the sausage, broth, tomatoes, green pepper, bay leaf, thyme and cayenne. Bring to a boil; add rice. Reduce heat; cover and simmer for 15 minutes. Add chicken and shrimp; cook 5-10 minutes longer or until shrimp turn pink and rice is tender. Discard bay leaf before serving. **Yield:** 2 servings.

Nutritional Analysis: One 1-1/4-cup serving (prepared with turkey sausage) equals 386 calories, 12 g fat (5 g saturated fat), 158 mg cholesterol, 986 mg sodium, 34 g carbohydrate, 2 g fiber, 33 g protein. **Diabetic Exchanges:** 4 very lean meat, 2 starch, 1-1/2 fat, 1 vegetable.

ROASTED CHICKEN WITH BASIL-RICE STUFFING

(Pictured at right)

This stuffing, with its pleasant herb flavor, is a nice change of pace from traditional bread stuffing. The crunch comes from sunflower kernels. (Leftovers would be great in the Chicken Jambalaya recipe above.)
—Edna Hoffman, Hebron, Indiana

1/4 cup chopped celery
1-1/2 teaspoons butter *or* margarine
1 cup cooked long grain rice
2 tablespoons minced fresh parsley
1 tablespoon sliced green onion
1 tablespoon minced fresh basil *or* 1 teaspoon dried basil
2-1/4 teaspoons sunflower kernels *or* chopped almonds
1/8 teaspoon salt
Dash pepper
1 broiler/fryer chicken (3 pounds)

In a small skillet, saute celery in butter until crisp-tender. In a bowl, combine the celery, rice, parsley, green onion, basil, sunflower kernels, salt and pepper. Stuff chicken. Tie drumsticks together with kitchen string if desired. Place breast side up on a rack in a roasting pan.

Bake, uncovered, at 375° for 1-1/4 to 1-1/2 hours or until juices run clear and a meat thermometer reads 180° for chicken and 165° for stuffing. Cover and let stand for 10 minutes before removing stuffing and slicing. **Yield:** 3-4 servings.

CHICKEN JAMBALAYA
ROASTED CHICKEN WITH BASIL-RICE STUFFING
POPPY SEED CREAMED CHICKEN (P. 172)

POPPY SEED CREAMED CHICKEN

(Pictured on page 171)

A dear friend gave me this recipe. It's been such a hit with family that I'm happy to share it. A few years back, it won a blue ribbon in a chicken recipe contest.
—*June Sheaffer, Fredericksburg, Pennsylvania*

2 cups cubed cooked chicken
1 can (10-3/4 ounces) condensed cream of chicken soup, undiluted
1/2 cup sour cream
1 teaspoon poppy seeds
3/4 cup crushed butter-flavored crackers (about 18 crackers)
2 tablespoons butter *or* margarine, melted
Hot cooked noodles

In a bowl, combine the chicken, soup, sour cream and poppy seeds. Pour mixture into a greased shallow 3-cup baking dish. In a bowl, combine cracker crumbs and butter; sprinkle over top. Bake, uncovered, at 350° for 30-35 minutes or until bubbly. Serve over noodles. **Yield:** 2 servings.

WESTERN DRUMSTICKS

With beans, corn and green pepper, these drumsticks are practically a meal by themselves.
—*Doris Heath, Bryson City, North Carolina*

1 can (16 ounces) barbecue-flavored baked beans, undrained
1 can (8 ounces) whole kernel corn, drained
1-1/2 cups chopped green pepper
1 tablespoon ketchup
4 chicken legs, skin removed

In a 2-qt. saucepan, combine the beans, corn, green pepper and ketchup; add chicken legs. Bring to a boil. Reduce heat; cover and simmer for 40 minutes or until chicken juices run clear, stirring occasionally. **Yield:** 2 servings.

ALFREDO CHICKEN SUPPER

I'm always impressed when something so easy tastes so good. This dish is one of those.
—*Gloria Wentland, Williamsburg, Virginia*

12 frozen cheese *or* mushroom ravioli
2 boneless skinless chicken breast halves
2 teaspoons olive *or* vegetable oil
1-1/2 cups Alfredo sauce
1/2 cup sliced fresh mushrooms
1 cup diced plum tomatoes
2 slices mozzarella cheese
1/4 cup seasoned bread crumbs

Cook ravioli according to package directions. Drain; set aside. In a skillet, saute chicken breasts in oil until lightly browned on both sides. In a bowl, combine the Alfredo sauce, mushrooms and tomatoes. Add ravioli; toss to coat.

Transfer to a greased shallow 5-cup baking dish. Place chicken breasts on top of ravioli. Place a slice of cheese on each chicken breast. Sprinkle with bread crumbs. Bake, uncovered, at 425° for 15-20 minutes or until cheese is melted and top is golden brown. **Yield:** 2 servings.

TERIYAKI TURKEY MEATBALLS

(Pictured at right)

We raise turkeys, so I'm always on the lookout for tasty recipes. These meatballs are great as hors d'oeuvres or as a main dish over noodles or rice.
—Vicki Olthoff, Stanhope, Iowa

1 egg
1/4 cup dry bread crumbs
2 tablespoons chopped celery
2 teaspoons dried minced onion
Dash ground ginger
Salt and pepper to taste
1/2 pound ground turkey
SAUCE:
1 tablespoon cornstarch
1 teaspoon ground ginger
1 cup chicken broth
2 tablespoons soy sauce
2 tablespoons sherry *or* additional chicken broth
2 tablespoons pineapple juice
Hot cooked rice *or* noodles

In a bowl, combine the egg, bread crumbs, celery, onion, ginger, salt and pepper. Crumble turkey over mixture and mix well. Shape into 1-in. balls. Place 1 in. apart on a greased 15-in. x 10-in. x 1-in. baking pan. Bake, uncovered, at 400° for 12-18 minutes or until no longer pink; drain.

For sauce, in a saucepan, combine the cornstarch, ginger and broth until smooth. Stir in the soy sauce, sherry or additional broth and juice. Bring to a boil; cook and stir for 2 minutes or until slightly thickened. Add meatballs and cook until heated through. Serve over rice or noodles. **Yield:** 2 servings.

CRISPY PARMESAN CHICKEN

I can't make this dish often enough for my husband. This chicken is delicious; in fact, it's one of our favorite meals.
—Marian Platt, Sequim, Washington

2 boneless skinless chicken breast halves (about 6 ounces *each*)
1 egg
3 tablespoons grated Parmesan cheese
3 tablespoons finely crushed saltine *or* butter-flavored cracker crumbs
1 tablespoon vegetable oil

Flatten chicken breasts to 1/4-in. thickness. Beat egg in a shallow bowl. In another shallow bowl, combine Parmesan cheese and cracker crumbs. Dip chicken in egg, then coat with the crumb mixture. Let stand for 5 minutes. In a skillet, cook chicken in oil for 2-3 minutes on each side or until juices run clear. **Yield:** 2 servings.

PINEAPPLE MACADAMIA CHICKEN

(Pictured below)

My family enjoys this summertime entree. It's quick, easy and oh-so-good served with cantaloupe wedges and iced tea. Each spicy-sweet bite reminds us of our trip to Hawaii.
—Kimberlie Smith, Coeur d'Alene, Idaho

2 boneless skinless chicken breast halves
3/4 cup finely chopped macadamia nuts
1/4 teaspoon seasoned salt
1/4 teaspoon Caribbean jerk seasoning
1/8 teaspoon dried minced onion
1/8 teaspoon onion powder
1/8 teaspoon pepper
1 egg, lightly beaten
2 tablespoons vegetable oil
1/4 cup crushed pineapple
1 tablespoon apricot preserves, warmed
Lettuce leaves

Flatten chicken to 1/4-in. thickness. In a shallow bowl, combine the nuts, seasoned salt, jerk seasoning, minced onion, onion powder and pepper. Place egg in another shallow bowl. Dip chicken in egg; coat with nut mixture. Let stand for 5 minutes.

In a skillet, cook chicken in oil for 3-4 minutes on each side or until chicken juices run clear. In a small bowl, combine pineapple and apricot preserves. Place lettuce on each plate; top with chicken and pineapple mixture. **Yield:** 2 servings.

CHICKEN QUESADILLAS

I've always loved going out for quesadillas. Then one day I came up with a recipe for making them in my oven. They cook in about 10 minutes.
—Carol Hemker, Phenix City, Alabama

1 cup shredded cooked chicken
1/2 cup chopped onion
1/2 cup shredded mozzarella cheese
1/2 cup shredded cheddar cheese
2 to 3 flour tortillas (8 to 10 inches)
Ranch salad dressing *or* salsa

In a bowl, combine chicken, onion, mozzarella and cheddar; set aside. Spray one side of each tortilla with nonstick cooking spray. Place tortilla greased side down on hot griddle. Place chicken on half of each tortilla. Fold over and cook over low for 1-2 minutes on each side or until tortilla is golden brown. Cut into wedges. Serve with dressing. **Yield:** 2 servings.

HONEYED CHICKEN

*My mother first tried this fast and easy recipe more than 20 years ago,
and we've been enjoying it ever since.*
—Joy Davis, Waterloo, Ontario

2 tablespoons butter *or* margarine,
    melted
2 tablespoons honey, warmed
1 tablespoon Dijon mustard
1/2 to 3/4 teaspoon curry powder
1 to 1-1/4 pounds meaty bone-in
    chicken pieces

In a bowl, combine the butter, honey, mustard and curry powder; set aside. Place chicken skin side down in a greased 8-in. baking dish; brush with sauce. Turn chicken skin side up; brush with sauce. Bake, uncovered, at 375° for 35-40 minutes or until chicken juices run clear, basting often. **Yield:** 2 servings.

SPICY TURKEY TENDERLOIN

(Pictured below)

Here's a full-flavored dish that will really wake up your taste buds.
—Sharon Skildum, Maple Grove, Minnesota

1/2 teaspoon chili powder
1/2 teaspoon ground cumin
1/4 to 1/2 teaspoon salt
1/8 teaspoon cayenne pepper
1 turkey tenderloin (1/2 pound)
3 teaspoons olive *or* canola oil, *divided*
1/4 cup chicken broth
2 tablespoons lime juice
3 tablespoons chopped onion
2 tablespoons chopped jalapeno
    pepper*
1 cup canned black beans, rinsed and
    drained
1/2 cup frozen corn, thawed
3 tablespoons chopped fresh tomato
4 teaspoons picante sauce
1 tablespoon minced fresh cilantro *or*
    parsley
2 lime wedges

In a small bowl, combine the chili powder, cumin, salt and cayenne. Sprinkle half the spice mixture over turkey. In a skillet, brown turkey in 2 teaspoons oil for 3-4 minutes on each side. Add broth and lime juice to skillet. Reduce heat; cover and simmer for 15-18 minutes or until turkey juices run clear and thermometer reads 170°, turning once.

In a small skillet, saute the onion and jalapeno in remaining oil until crisp-tender. Transfer to a bowl. Add the beans, corn, tomato, picante sauce, cilantro and remaining spice mixture. Serve turkey with salsa and lime wedges. **Yield:** 2 servings.

*Editor's Note: When cutting or seeding hot peppers, use rubber or plastic gloves to protect your hands. Avoid touching your face.

ROASTED TURKEY DRUMSTICKS

Of all the turkey recipes I've tried, I like this one best. The tender drumsticks have just a bit of zip.
—Ross Njaa, Salinas, California

1/4 cup all-purpose flour
1/8 teaspoon white pepper
  2 turkey drumsticks, skin removed
    (about 3/4 pound *each*)
  2 tablespoons vegetable oil
  1 can (8 ounces) tomato sauce
3/4 cup chicken broth
3/4 cup red wine *or* additional chicken
    broth
  5 teaspoons onion soup mix
1-1/2 teaspoons paprika
1-1/2 teaspoons Worcestershire sauce
  2 garlic cloves, minced
3/4 teaspoon sugar
1/4 teaspoon salt
  1 bay leaf

In a large resealable plastic bag, combine flour and white pepper. Add drumsticks, one at a time, and shake to coat. In a skillet, brown drumsticks on all sides in oil. Transfer to a greased 11-in. x 7-in. x 2-in. baking dish; set aside. In a saucepan, combine the tomato sauce, broth, wine or additional broth, soup mix, paprika, Worcestershire sauce, garlic, sugar and salt. Bring to a boil. Reduce heat; simmer, uncovered, for 3 minutes or until flavors are blended. Add bay leaf.

Pour the sauce over the drumsticks. Cover and bake at 350° for 30 minutes. Turn drumsticks over; cover and bake 30-40 minutes longer or until juices run clear and thermometer reads 180°. Discard bay leaf before serving. **Yield:** 2 servings.

STUFFED CORNISH GAME HENS

This entree makes an ordinary day special. Whenever I cook Cornish hens for my husband and me, it stirs up warm memories of family times around the holiday dinner table.
—Nancy Aubrey, Ruidoso, New Mexico

1/2 cup chopped celery
1/4 cup chopped onion
1/2 cup butter *or* margarine, *divided*
  3 cups crumbled corn bread
  3 cups soft bread crumbs
  1 jar (2 ounces) diced pimientos,
    drained
  1 cup chicken broth
  1 egg
1/2 teaspoon poultry seasoning
  1 teaspoon salt, *divided*
1/2 teaspoon pepper, *divided*
  2 Cornish game hens (about 20
    ounces *each*)
  1 garlic clove, minced
  1 teaspoon grated lemon peel
3/4 teaspoon chopped fresh mint *or* 1/4
    teaspoon dried mint flakes

In a large skillet or saucepan, saute celery and onion in 2 tablespoons butter until tender. Remove from the heat. Stir in corn bread, bread crumbs, pimientos, broth, egg, poultry seasoning, 1/2 teaspoon salt and 1/4 teaspoon pepper; mix well.

Stuff each hen with 3/4 cup stuffing. Place extra stuffing in a greased 1-qt. baking dish; refrigerate. Place hens breast side up on a rack in a greased 13-in. x 9-in. x 2-in. baking dish. Cover loosely with foil; bake at 375° for 45 minutes. Meanwhile, in a small saucepan, melt the remaining butter; add garlic, lemon peel, mint and remaining salt and pepper. Brush over hens. Bake 15-30 minutes longer or until a meat thermometer reads 180° for hens and 165° for stuffing. Bake the extra stuffing, covered, for 30 minutes. **Yield:** 2 servings.

BROCCOLI-STUFFED CHICKEN

(Pictured at right)

Mother served fried chicken every Sunday, but sometimes she surprised us with this creation.
—*Donald Laugherty, Connellsville, Pennsylvania*

  2 boneless skinless chicken breast
    halves (about 6 ounces *each*)
  1 teaspoon poultry seasoning
1/2 teaspoon white pepper
1/2 teaspoon garlic powder
1/2 teaspoon curry powder
1/4 teaspoon salt
  1 cup finely chopped fresh broccoli
1/2 cup shredded cheddar cheese
1/2 cup chicken broth
Hot cooked rice, optional

Flatten chicken to 1/4-in. thickness. Combine the poultry seasoning, pepper, garlic powder, curry powder and salt; sprinkle over chicken. Combine broccoli and cheese; place half in the center of each chicken breast. Fold long sides over filling; fold ends up and secure with a toothpick.

Place, seam side down, in an 8-in. square baking dish. Add broth. Cover loosely and bake at 350° for 30 minutes. Uncover; baste chicken with pan juices. Bake 10 minutes longer or until meat juices run clear. Remove toothpicks before serving. Thicken pan juices for gravy if desired. Serve with rice if desired. **Yield:** 2 servings.

Nutritional Analysis: One serving (prepared with garlic powder, reduced-fat cheese, reduced-sodium chicken broth and calculated without rice) equals 289 calories, 8 g fat (5 g saturated fat), 119 mg cholesterol, 569 mg sodium, 5 g carbohydrate, 2 g fiber, 48 g protein. **Diabetic Exchanges:** 6 very lean meat, 1 vegetable, 1 fat.

CHICKEN 'N' NOODLES FOR TWO

I discovered this recipe quite a few years ago. It's a fast and flavorful supper that's just the right size for us empty nesters. But it can be easily doubled for guests.
—*Verna Keinath, Millington, Michigan*

1/2 cup cottage cheese
1/4 cup chopped onion
1/4 cup mayonnaise *or* salad dressing
  2 tablespoons chopped green pepper
  1 tablespoon chopped pimientos
  1 teaspoon Dijon mustard
1/2 teaspoon chopped fresh chives
1/2 teaspoon Worcestershire sauce
  2 drops hot pepper sauce
  1 cup cubed cooked chicken

  1 cup cooked egg noodles
1/2 cup frozen peas, thawed
1/8 teaspoon ground paprika

In a large bowl, combine first nine ingredients. Add the chicken, noodles and peas; gently toss to coat. Spoon into a greased 1-qt. baking dish; sprinkle with paprika. Bake, uncovered, at 350° for 25-30 minutes or until bubbly. **Yield:** 2 servings.

CHICKEN VEGETABLE POTPIE

*I actually created this recipe when I was a girl. Since then, I've found
it's a good way to use up the second pastry when I make a one-crust pie.*
—Marva Vandivier, Battle Ground, Washington

2 medium carrots, sliced
1 medium potato, peeled and cubed
1 small onion, chopped
1 celery rib, chopped
1 cup water
1/2 cup frozen peas, thawed
1 cup cubed cooked chicken
1 can (10-3/4 ounces) condensed
  cream of chicken soup, undiluted
Pastry for single-crust pie (9 inches)

In a saucepan, cook the carrots, potato, onion and celery in water for 10 minutes or until tender; drain. Stir in the peas, chicken and soup. Pour into a greased 1-1/2-qt. deep baking dish. Roll out pastry to fit top of dish; place over filling. Trim, seal and flute edges. Cut slits in pastry. Bake at 350° for 50 minutes or until crust is golden and filling is bubbly. **Yield:** 2 servings.

CHICKEN AND CASHEWS

*My husband and I enjoy Thai food, and we count this recipe
among our favorites. It's tasty without being spicy.*
—Laura Manning, Lilburn, Georgia

1 tablespoon sugar
1 teaspoon cornstarch
1/3 cup water
2 tablespoons soy sauce
1 small onion, cut into wedges
1 tablespoon vegetable oil
1 boneless skinless chicken breast,
  cut into 1/2-inch cubes
1/2 cup salted cashew halves
Hot cooked rice

In a bowl, combine the sugar, cornstarch, water and soy sauce until smooth; set aside. In a skillet, saute onion in oil until crisp-tender. Add chicken and cook until no longer pink. Stir in soy sauce mixture. Bring to a boil; cook and stir for 2 minutes or until thickened. Stir in cashews. Serve over rice. **Yield:** 1-2 servings.

CHICKEN CAESAR SALAD

This main-dish salad may sound fancy, but in reality it couldn't be easier to make.
—Kay Andersen, Bear, Delaware

2 boneless skinless chicken breast
  halves (1/2 pound)
2 teaspoons olive *or* vegetable oil
1/8 teaspoon dried basil
1/8 teaspoon dried oregano
1/4 teaspoon garlic salt, optional
1/4 teaspoon pepper
1/4 teaspoon paprika
4 cups torn romaine
1 small tomato, thinly sliced
Caesar salad dressing
Caesar salad croutons, optional

Brush chicken with oil. Combine the basil, oregano, garlic salt if desired, pepper and paprika; sprinkle over chicken. Grill, uncovered, over medium-low heat for 12-15 minutes or until juices run clear, turning several times. Arrange romaine and tomato on plates. Cut chicken into strips; place on top. Drizzle with dressing. Sprinkle with croutons if desired. **Yield:** 2 servings.

BACON-WRAPPED CHICKEN

(Pictured below)

One of the things my family likes about this recipe, which I created, is that you can adjust the "heat index" by using green chilies or jalapeno peppers.
—LaDonna Reed, Ponca City, Oklahoma

4 bacon strips
2 boneless skinless chicken breast halves
1/4 teaspoon seasoned salt
2 ounces cream cheese, softened
1 can (4 ounces) chopped green chilies, drained
2 garlic cloves, minced

In a skillet, cook bacon over medium heat until cooked but not crisp. Remove to paper towels to drain; keep warm. Flatten chicken to 1/4-in. thickness. Sprinkle chicken breasts with seasoned salt. In a bowl, combine the cream cheese, chilies and garlic. Spread half of the mixture on each chicken breast. Roll up chicken and wrap with two bacon strips; secure with toothpicks.

Place chicken in a greased shallow 4-1/2-cup baking dish. Bake, uncovered, at 375° for 45 minutes. Cover and bake 10-15 minutes longer or until chicken juices run clear. Discard toothpicks before serving. **Yield:** 2 servings.

TURKEY CURRY

Shortly before we married, I tried this recipe out on my husband.
I've been making it regularly ever since.
—Jennifer Pageler, Mahnomen, Minnesota

1 medium tart apple, peeled and cut into pieces
1 small onion, chopped
2 tablespoons chopped celery
1 tablespoon butter *or* margarine
2 teaspoons all-purpose flour
1 to 1-1/2 teaspoons curry powder
1/4 teaspoon salt
1/4 teaspoon chicken bouillon granules
1/8 teaspoon cayenne pepper
3/4 cup milk
1 cup cubed cooked turkey
1/4 cup peanuts
Hot cooked rice
Minced fresh parsley

In a saucepan, saute the apple, onion and celery in butter until crisp-tender. Stir in the flour, curry powder, salt, bouillon and cayenne. Gradually stir in milk until smooth. Bring to a boil; cook 1-2 minutes or until thickened. Stir in turkey and peanuts; cook until turkey is heated through. Serve over rice and garnish with parsley. **Yield:** 2 servings.

PORK & LAMB

When you want a main dish
that's sure to satisfy, pork is
the perfect pick. Turn here for
50 recipe choices, ranging
from casual and filling fare to
dressed up and delicious.
Plan on serving second helpings!

LAMB SHEPHERD'S PIE (P. 201)

PORK TENDERLOIN WITH ROASTED POATOES (P. 182)
PORK CHOPS WITH HERBED GRAVY (P. 182)

PORK TENDERLOIN WITH ROASTED POTATOES

(Pictured on page 181)

My mother found this delicious recipe many years ago, when I was a teenager.
Now I make it for my husband, Bob, who adores it.
—Kim Wilson, Plainfield, Illinois

1/4 cup olive *or* vegetable oil
2 garlic cloves, minced
1-1/2 teaspoons dried rosemary, crushed
1/2 teaspoon salt
1/4 teaspoon pepper
1 pork tenderloin (about 3/4 pound)
2 medium red potatoes, cut into chunks

In a bowl, combine the oil, garlic, rosemary, salt and pepper. Place half of the marinade in each of two resealable plastic bags.

Add pork to one bag and potatoes to the other bag. Seal bags and turn to coat; refrigerate for 8 hours or overnight.

Drain and discard marinades. Place meat and potatoes in a greased 11-in. x 7-in. x 2-in. baking dish. Bake, uncovered, at 425° for 20-25 minutes or until potatoes are almost tender. Broil 5 in. from heat for 4-5 minutes or until potatoes are tender and a meat thermometer inserted in the pork reads 160°. Let stand for 5 minutes before slicing. **Yield:** 2 servings.

PORK CHOPS WITH HERBED GRAVY

(Pictured on page 181)

These chops fill the kitchen with a wonderful aroma. The meat comes out fork-tender.
—Chris Snyder, Boulder, Colorado

2 tablespoons all-purpose flour
1/8 teaspoon paprika
Dash garlic powder
2 boneless pork loin chops (6 ounces *each* and 3/4 inch thick)
1 tablespoon canola *or* vegetable oil
2 tablespoons chopped onion
3/4 cup water
1 teaspoon chicken bouillon granules
1/4 teaspoon dried basil
1/4 teaspoon dried thyme
1 plum tomato, chopped

In a resealable plastic bag, combine the flour, paprika and garlic powder. Set aside 2 teaspoons flour mixture for gravy. Add chops to remaining flour mixture; shake to coat.

In a skillet, brown pork chops in oil for 4 minutes on each side. Transfer to a greased shallow 1-qt. baking dish. Add onion to skillet; cook and stir until tender. Stir in reserved flour mixture until blended; cook and stir for 1 minute or until lightly browned. Gradually stir in water. Add the bouillon, basil and thyme. Bring to a boil; cook and stir for 1-2 minutes or until thickened. Pour over pork.

Cover and bake at 350° for 25 minutes. Uncover; sprinkle with tomato. Bake 5-10 minutes longer or until a meat thermometer inserted in pork reads 160° and tomato is heated through. **Yield:** 2 servings.

Nutritional Analysis: One serving with 1/3 cup gravy equals 324 calories, 15 g fat (3 g saturated fat), 107 mg cholesterol, 666 mg sodium, 9 g carbohydrate, 1 g fiber, 37 g protein. **Diabetic Exchanges:** 5 lean meat, 1/2 starch.

KIELBASA CABBAGE SKILLET

(Pictured at right)

This easy, quick-to-fix recipe has long been a staple at my house because it tastes so good.
—Sue Engle, Irving, Texas

1/2 cup chopped onion
1/2 cup chopped green pepper
  1 to 2 teaspoons butter *or* margarine
1/2 pound fully cooked kielbasa *or* Polish sausage, cut into 1/2-inch slices
1/2 small head cabbage, coarsely chopped (about 3 cups)
1/4 cup chicken broth *or* water
Salt to taste, optional
Pepper to taste

In a skillet, saute onion and green pepper in butter until crisp-tender. Add sausage; cook and stir until browned. Add the cabbage, broth, salt if desired and pepper. Cover and cook 10-12 minutes or until cabbage is tender. **Yield:** 2 servings.

Nutritional Analysis: One 1-1/2-cup serving (prepared with 1 teaspoon butter, turkey sausage, reduced-sodium chicken broth and without salt) equals 269 calories, 13 g fat (6 g saturated fat), 66 mg cholesterol, 1,201 mg sodium, 19 g carbohydrate, 5 g fiber, 22 g protein. **Diabetic Exchanges:** 2 lean meat, 1 starch, 1 vegetable, 1 fat.

CHEESY HAM CASSEROLE

I've often increased this recipe for big family events. It's a hearty dish that goes over well with a couple or a crowd.
—Mary Shetler, Carrollton, Ohio

1/4 cup cubed process cheese (Velveeta)
3/4 cup cubed fully cooked ham
1/3 cup condensed cream of mushroom soup, undiluted
1-1/2 teaspoons butter *or* margarine, melted
  1 tablespoon chopped onion
1/8 teaspoon pepper
3/4 cup mashed potatoes (without added milk and butter)
1/4 cup sour cream
  1 bacon strip, cooked and crumbled
  3 slices process cheese, halved

In a bowl, combine the cubed cheese, ham, soup, butter, onion and pepper. Transfer into a greased shallow 3-cup baking dish. In a bowl, combine mashed potatoes and sour cream. Spread over ham mixture. Arrange cheese slices over top of potato mixture. Bake, uncovered, at 350° for 15-20 minutes or until heated through. **Yield:** 2 servings.

Dijon Pork Ragout

(Pictured at right)

I've collected cookbooks since I was a little girl. This recipe always makes my family happy.
—Nancy Shirvani, Terryville, Connecticut

      3/4 **pound boneless pork loin, cut into**
           1/2-inch cubes *or* **3/4 pound pork**
           chop suey meat
        2 **tablespoons Dijon mustard**
        3 **tablespoons all-purpose flour**
        3 **tablespoons brown sugar**
  4-1/2 **teaspoons vegetable oil**
        1 **small onion, chopped**
        1 **garlic clove, minced**
      1/2 **cup chicken broth**
      1/4 **cup white wine** *or* **additional**
           chicken broth
        4 **small red potatoes, peeled and cut**
           into cubes
        1 **medium carrot, thinly sliced**
      1/2 **teaspoon salt**
      1/8 **teaspoon pepper**
        2 **tablespoons minced fresh parsley**

In a bowl, combine pork and mustard until evenly coated. In a resealable plastic bag, combine flour and brown sugar. Add pork in batches and shake to coat. In a skillet, brown pork in oil over medium heat. Remove from the pan and keep warm.

In the same skillet, cook onion and garlic until tender. Gradually stir in broth and wine or additional broth, stirring to loosen brown bits from pan. Bring to a boil; cook and stir for 1-2 minutes or until mixture is slightly thickened. Stir in the potatoes, carrot, salt, pepper and pork.

Transfer to a greased 1-qt. baking dish. Cover and bake at 350° for 45-55 minutes or until pork and vegetables are tender. Sprinkle with parsley. **Yield:** 2 servings.

Greek Feta Casserole

Cinnamon and feta cheese give this hot dish a special taste.
—Joyce Hill, Quesnel, British Columbia

      1/2 **cup uncooked elbow macaroni**
        1 **egg, lightly beaten**
        2 **tablespoons milk**
      1/2 **cup crumbled feta cheese** *or*
           shredded mozzarella cheese,
           divided
      1/2 **pound ground pork**
        2 **tablespoons chopped onion**
      1/2 **cup tomato sauce**
      1/8 **to 1/4 teaspoon ground cinnamon**

Cook macaroni according to package directions; drain. In a bowl, combine the egg, milk and 1/4 cup cheese. Stir in macaroni. Transfer to a greased 3-cup baking dish. In a skillet, cook pork and onion over medium heat until meat is no longer pink; drain. Stir in tomato sauce and cinnamon.

Pour over macaroni mixture. Sprinkle with remaining cheese. Cover and bake at 375° for 20 minutes. Uncover; bake 12-16 minutes longer or until bubbly and heated through. **Yield:** 2 servings.

PORK MEDALLIONS

My wife always raves about dinner when I make this recipe, but that may just be her way of getting me to do more of the cooking!
—Donald Wolter, Oshkosh, Wisconsin

1 pork tenderloin (about 1/2 pound)
1 tablespoon olive *or* canola oil
1-1/2 teaspoons butter *or* margarine
1 small onion, sliced
1/4 cup sliced fresh mushrooms
1 garlic clove, minced
2 teaspoons all-purpose flour
1/2 cup chicken broth
1/4 teaspoon dried rosemary, crushed
1/4 teaspoon dried savory
1/4 teaspoon salt
1/8 teaspoon pepper
Minced fresh parsley, optional

Slice tenderloin into 1/2-in.-thick medallions. In a skillet, brown pork in oil for about 2 minutes on each side. Remove from skillet and set aside. In same skillet melt butter. Add the onion, mushrooms and garlic; saute for 1 minute. Stir in flour until blended. Gradually stir in the broth, rosemary, savory, salt and pepper. Bring to a boil; cook and stir for 1 minute or until thickened.

Lay pork medallions over mixture. Reduce heat; cover and simmer for 15 minutes or until meat juices run clear. Garnish with parsley if desired. **Yield:** 2 servings.

Nutritional Analysis: One serving equals 206 calories, 15 g fat (4 g saturated fat), 83 mg cholesterol, 631 mg sodium, 6 g carbohydrate, 1 g fiber, 25 g protein. **Diabetic Exchanges:** 3 lean meat, 1 fat, 1/2 starch.

PORK OLÉ

(Pictured at right)

This recipe was given to me by a fellow I used to work with. We both enjoyed trying new recipes. The pork mixture is also great over rice.
—Sandy High, Globe, Arizona

1/4 to 1/3 pound chop suey meat *or* boneless pork loin, cut into 1/2-inch cubes
1 tablespoon taco seasoning mix
1 tablespoon olive *or* vegetable oil
1/4 cup chunky salsa
1 tablespoon peach preserves
Flour tortillas

In a resealable plastic bag, combine pork and taco seasoning; toss to coat. In a saucepan, brown pork in oil over medium heat. Stir in salsa and peach preserves. Bring to a boil. Reduce heat; cover and simmer for 10-15 minutes or until pork is tender. Serve with tortillas. **Yield:** 1 serving.

LEMON-PLUM PORK ROAST

(Pictured at right)

My mother often served this recipe for Sunday dinner. The drippings make a delicious gravy.
(Leftovers would be wonderful in the recipe below.)
—Jane Paschke, Duluth, Minnesota

  1 boneless pork loin roast (2 pounds)
1/4 teaspoon garlic salt
1/4 teaspoon pepper
1/4 cup chopped onion
  2 teaspoons butter *or* margarine
1/4 cup plum jam
  3 tablespoons lemonade concentrate
  2 tablespoons chili sauce
3/4 teaspoon soy sauce
1/2 teaspoon prepared mustard
1/4 teaspoon ground ginger
GRAVY:
  1 tablespoon all-purpose flour
1/4 cup water

Sprinkle roast with garlic salt and pepper. Place roast fat side up in a shallow roasting pan. In a skillet, saute onion in butter until tender; stir in the remaining ingredients. Stir until heated. Pour over roast.

Bake, uncovered, at 350° for 1 hour or until a meat thermometer reads 160°. Remove roast to a serving platter and keep warm. Let stand for 10 minutes.

Pour drippings and loosed brown bits into a bowl. Skim fat. In a small saucepan, combine flour and water until smooth. Gradually stir in drippings. Bring to a boil; cook and stir for 2 minutes or until thickened. Slice roast and serve with gravy. **Yield:** 6 servings.

Nutritional Analysis: One 3-ounce cooked portion with 1/3 cup gravy (prepared with reduced-sodium soy sauce) equals 296 calories, 9 g fat (4 g saturated fat), 87 mg cholesterol, 368 mg sodium, 16 g carbohydrate, trace fiber, 33 g protein. **Diabetic Exchanges:** 4 lean meat, 1 fruit.

LEFTOVER PORK AND VEGETABLES

(Pictured at right)

When I buy a pork roast that's too much for two people, I have this second-day dish in mind.
It's a family favorite that doesn't taste like leftovers.
—Shirley Tower, Southwick, Massachusetts

1/3 cup chopped red onion
1/2 cup chopped sweet red *or* green
    pepper
  1 celery rib, chopped
  1 tablespoon olive *or* vegetable oil
  1 cup cubed cooked pork (1/2-inch
    cubes)
3/4 cup frozen sliced carrots, thawed
  1 jar (4-1/2 ounces) sliced
    mushrooms, drained
1/2 cup canned pork gravy
1/3 cup chicken broth
  2 tablespoons soy sauce
1/8 teaspoon pepper
Hot cooked rice

In a skillet, saute the onion, red pepper and celery in oil until crisp-tender. Add the pork, carrots, mushrooms, gravy, broth, soy sauce and pepper. Bring to a boil. Reduce heat; cover and simmer for 20-25 minutes or until carrots are tender. Serve over rice. **Yield:** 2 servings.

LEMON-PLUM PORK ROAST
LEFTOVER PORK AND VEGETABLES

SAUCY BARBECUED SPARERIBS

*Everyone who has tasted these ribs has asked for the recipe. It's a family recipe
handed down from my mother-in-law.*
—Ruth Weatherford, Huntington Beach, California

1-1/2 to 2 pounds pork spareribs
1/2 cup chopped onion
1/2 cup molasses
1/2 cup ketchup
1/4 cup orange juice
1 tablespoon butter *or* margarine
1 tablespoon vegetable oil
1 tablespoon steak sauce
1-1/2 teaspoons cider vinegar
3 whole cloves
1 garlic clove, minced
1/2 teaspoon chopped orange peel
1/2 teaspoon prepared mustard
1/2 teaspoon Worcestershire sauce
1/4 teaspoon salt
1/4 teaspoon pepper
1/4 teaspoon hot pepper sauce

Cut ribs into serving size pieces. Line a 11-in. x 7-in. x 2-in. baking dish with foil; grease the foil. Place ribs meat side up in prepared pan. Bake, uncovered, at 350° for 1 hour; drain.

Meanwhile, in a saucepan, bring remaining ingredients to a boil. Reduce heat; simmer, uncovered, for 15 minutes. Discard cloves. Baste ribs with sauce. Bake, uncovered, 40-45 minutes longer or until ribs are tender, basting several times. Serve with remaining sauce. **Yield:** 2 servings.

SHREDDED PORK TACOS

*I used to make a similar recipe with beef, but I switched to pork when
we lived in Singapore for 3 years. Beef was expensive and not very good there.
We like it so much with pork, we never switched back.*
—Mary McKay, Pleasant Hill, California

1 pork tenderloin (3/4 pound), cut
    into 1-inch pieces
1 teaspoon vegetable oil
1 small onion, chopped
2 garlic cloves, minced
1 can (8 ounces) tomato sauce
1 can (4 ounces) chopped green chilies
1 teaspoon chili powder
1/2 teaspoon salt
1/2 teaspoon dried oregano
1/2 teaspoon ground cumin
1/4 teaspoon pepper
2 to 4 flour tortillas (7 inches),
    warmed
Shredded lettuce and chopped tomato,
    optional

In a skillet, brown pork in oil. Remove from pan and keep warm. In same skillet, saute onion and garlic in drippings until tender. Stir in the tomato sauce, chilies, chili powder, salt, oregano, cumin and pepper. Add pork; bring to a boil. Reduce heat; cover and simmer for 20 minutes or until pork is tender.

Cool slightly; shred with two forks. Return to sauce; heat through. Serve in tortillas with lettuce and tomato if desired. **Yield:** 2 servings.

Ham 'n' Florets in a Basket

(Pictured at right)

I developed this recipe to sneak more vegetables into my husband's diet. It worked!
—Linden Staciokas, Fairbanks, Alaska

2 frozen puff pastry shells
1 cup small cauliflowerets
1 small onion, finely chopped
1/4 cup sliced fresh mushrooms
2 tablespoons butter *or* margarine
1 tablespoon all-purpose flour
3/4 teaspoon chicken bouillon granules
Dash pepper
1/2 cup milk
1/2 cup diced fully cooked ham (about 4 ounces)
1/4 cup shredded cheddar cheese

Prepare the pastry shells according to package directions; set aside. Place the cauliflower in steamer basket. Place in a saucepan over 1 in. of water; bring to a boil. Cover and steam for 5-8 minutes or until cauliflower is crisp-tender.

In a skillet, saute onion and mushrooms in butter until tender. Stir in the flour, bouillon and pepper until blended. Gradually add milk. Bring to a boil; cook and stir for 2 minutes or until thickened. Stir in ham and cauliflower. Remove from the heat. Stir in cheese until melted. Spoon into pastry shells. **Yield:** 2 servings.

Parmesan Sage Pork Chops

This recipe is simple and it goes together nicely. Tender chops are encased with a crunchy coating.
—Martha Barnes, Sheridan, Arkansas

2 tablespoons all-purpose flour
1/4 teaspoon salt
Dash pepper
3/4 cup soft bread crumbs
1/2 cup grated Parmesan cheese
1-1/2 teaspoons rubbed sage
1/2 teaspoon grated lemon peel
1 egg, lightly beaten
2 bone-in pork loin chops (about 6 ounces *each*)
1 tablespoon olive *or* vegetable oil
1 tablespoon butter *or* margarine

In a shallow dish, combine the flour, salt and pepper. In another shallow dish, combine the bread crumbs, Parmesan cheese, sage and lemon peel. Place egg in shallow bowl. Coat pork chops with flour mixture, dip in egg, then coat with bread crumb mixture. Let stand for 5 minutes.

In a skillet, brown chops in oil and butter for 2 minutes on each side. Transfer to a greased 11-in. x 7-in. x 2-in. baking dish. Bake, uncovered, at 425° for 10-15 minutes or until juices run clear and a meat thermometer reads 160°. **Yield:** 2 servings.

Sausage and Vegetable Skillet

(Pictured below)

This is an old recipe that has been handed down in our family through my sister-in-law. When I was a child, she did most of the cooking in our house, and this was my favorite meal.
—Ruby Williams, Bogalusa, Louisiana

1/2 pound fresh Italian sausage,
cut into 1/2-inch slices
1 tablespoon canola *or* vegetable oil
1 cup cubed yellow summer squash
(3/4-inch pieces)
1/2 cup chopped green onions
2 garlic cloves, minced
1-1/2 cups chopped fresh tomatoes
2 teaspoons Worcestershire sauce
1/8 teaspoon cayenne pepper

In a medium skillet, cook sausage in oil over medium heat until no longer pink; drain. Add the squash, onions and garlic; cook for 2 minutes. Stir in the tomatoes, Worcestershire sauce and cayenne pepper; heat through. **Yield:** 2 servings.

Nutritional Analysis: One serving (prepared with turkey Italian sausage) equals 309 calories, 18 g fat (4 g saturated fat), 61 mg cholesterol, 776 mg sodium, 16 g carbohydrate, 3 g fiber, 21 g protein. **Diabetic Exchanges:** 2-1/2 fat, 2 lean meat, 1 starch.

Lemon-Garlic Pork Tenderloin

I enjoy grilling, so I work hard to develop marinades and sauces to accompany the meats. This blend of tangy lemon and savory garlic mixes perfectly with pork.
—Nancy Schmitt, Hamilton, Ohio

2 tablespoons canola *or* vegetable oil
1-1/2 teaspoons lemon juice
1-1/2 teaspoons grated lemon peel
3 garlic cloves, minced
1-1/2 teaspoons dried oregano
1/4 teaspoon salt
1/4 teaspoon pepper
1 pork tenderloin (3/4 pound)

In a resealable plastic bag, combine the oil, lemon juice, peel, garlic, oregano, salt and pepper; add pork. Seal bag and turn to coat;

refrigerate for 8 hours or overnight.

Drain and discard marinade. Grill, covered, over medium coals for about 13-14 minutes on each side or until juices run clear and a meat thermometer reads 160°. Let stand for 5 minutes before slicing. **Yield:** 2 servings.

Nutritional Analysis: One serving equals 239 calories, 9 g fat (2 g saturated fat), 111 mg cholesterol, 159 mg sodium, 1 g carbohydrate, trace fiber, 36 g protein. **Diabetic Exchange:** 4-1/2 lean meat.

PORK AND CABBAGE SUPPER

This all-in-one dish makes a meal with great flavor. My mother-in-law shared this quick and easy recipe with me years ago.
—Tina Brown, Chico, California

2 pork loin chops (1/2 inch thick)
1 tablespoon vegetable oil
1 can (10-3/4 ounces) condensed cream of mushroom soup, undiluted
1/2 teaspoon garlic powder
1/4 teaspoon salt
1/4 teaspoon pepper
3 cups shredded cabbage

In an ovenproof skillet, brown chops in oil on both sides; remove and set aside. To drippings, add soup and seasonings; bring to a boil. Return chops to skillet; add cabbage. Cover and bake at 350° for 50-60 minutes or until meat is tender. **Yield:** 2 servings.

SMOKED SAUSAGE-STUFFED PEPPERS

(Pictured below)

This recipe evolved over time. It draws heavily on a stuffed pepper recipe passed on to me by my mother years ago.
—Helen Cornet, Carmel, Indiana

1/4 pound fully cooked smoked sausage, chopped
1 small onion, chopped
1 garlic clove, minced
2 teaspoons vegetable oil
1 cup chicken broth
3/4 cup canned kidney beans, rinsed and drained
1/2 cup uncooked instant rice
1/4 teaspoon Cajun seasoning
1 cup canned stewed tomatoes
2 medium sweet red *or* green peppers, cut in half lengthwise and seeded
2 tablespoons butter-flavored cracker crumbs
2 bacon strips, halved
1/2 cup shredded sharp cheddar cheese

In a skillet, cook the sausage, onion and garlic in oil until meat is browned. Add the broth, kidney beans, rice and Cajun seasoning. Bring to a boil. Reduce heat; cover and simmer for 5 minutes or until rice is tender. Add tomatoes. Simmer, uncovered, for 15 minutes or until thickened. Place pepper halves in a greased shallow 1-1/2-qt. baking dish. Place 1-1/2 teaspoons cracker crumbs in each pepper half. Fill with sausage mixture.

In a skillet, cook bacon over medium heat until lightly browned. Top each pepper with half of cheese and 1 bacon half. Bake, uncovered, at 375° for 25-30 minutes or until bacon is crisp. **Yield:** 2 servings.

THAI PORK BURRITOS

(Pictured at right)

*This is a unique version of sandwich wraps, which are so popular now.
The best thing about this tasty recipe is how fast it goes together.*
—Jennifer Gardner, Castle Rock, Colorado

1/4 pound ground pork
  2 thin onion slices
  2 tablespoons stir-fry sauce
  1 teaspoon minced fresh cilantro *or* parsley
1/8 teaspoon crushed red pepper flakes
3/4 cup coleslaw mix
  1 to 2 flour tortillas (7 inches)

In a skillet, cook pork over medium heat until no longer pink; drain. Add onion; saute for 1 minute. Add the stir-fry sauce, cilantro and red pepper flakes; cook for 1 minute. Add coleslaw mix; cook 2 minutes longer or until crisp-tender. Spoon filling down the center of tortilla. Fold end and sides over filling. **Yield:** 1 serving.

SWEET 'N' SPICY PORK CHOPS

(Pictured at right)

I found this recipe in a Kentucky newspaper some time ago. My husband asks for it often, saying it really hits the spot when he's hungry.
—Kim Hardin, Clarksville, Indiana

3 tablespoons brown sugar
3 tablespoons apple juice
2 teaspoons chili powder
1 teaspoon Dijon mustard
1/2 teaspoon salt
1/2 teaspoon pepper
  1 bone-in pork loin chop (3/4 inch thick)

In a bowl, combine the first six ingredients; mix well. Transfer 3 tablespoons to a resealable plastic bag; cover and refrigerate remaining marinade. Add pork to bag. Seal bag and turn to coat; refrigerate for at least 3 hours.

Drain and discard marinade. Broil pork chop 5-6 in. from the heat for 4-5 minutes on each side or until a meat thermometer reads 160°, basting several times with reserved marinade. **Yield:** 1 serving.

SERVING SUGGESTION

Apple, pineapple and tomato juice and apricot nectar are available in six-packs of individual cans. The small cans are handy when recipes call for a little juice. You won't need to worry about wasting a large can or bottle of juice.

THAI PORK BURRITOS
SWEET 'N' SPICY PORK CHOPS

ITALIAN SAUSAGE CHILI

I could barely boil water when I got out of the Navy, but I'm quite comfortable
in the kitchen now. This recipe is one I created.
—Paul Scott, New London, Connecticut

1 celery rib, chopped
1 small onion, chopped
1/4 cup chopped green pepper
1/4 cup chopped sweet red pepper
1 tablespoon vegetable oil
1 Italian sausage link (about 1/4 pound), casing removed
1 can (14-1/2 ounces) stewed tomatoes, undrained
1 cup canned kidney beans, rinsed and drained
1 cup water
5 tablespoons tomato paste
2 tablespoons chopped green chilies
3/4 teaspoon chili powder
1/4 teaspoon salt
1/4 teaspoon pepper
1/4 cup shredded cheddar cheese

In a small saucepan, saute the celery, onion and sweet peppers in oil until crisp-tender. Crumble the sausage into the skillet; cook over medium heat until meat is no longer pink; drain. Stir in the tomatoes, kidney beans, water, tomato paste, chilies and seasonings; bring to a boil. Reduce heat; simmer, uncovered, for 20-30 minutes or until thickened. Sprinkle with cheese. **Yield:** 2 servings.

SPICY SOUTHERN-STYLE TOMATO CUPS

I'm retired and enjoy collecting recipes. I only wish I had time to try every one of them!
I found this recipe in a local newspaper. My family loves the combination of flavors.
—Gwilia Lightle, Kansas City, Kansas

2 medium tomatoes, cored
4 tablespoons sliced green onions, *divided*
1 garlic clove, minced
2 tablespoons olive *or* vegetable oil, *divided*
1 tablespoon red wine vinegar *or* cider vinegar
1/8 teaspoon sugar
1/8 teaspoon salt
Pinch pepper
1/2 cup diced fully cooked ham *or* Canadian bacon
1/3 cup canned whole kernel corn, drained
2 cups shredded salad greens

Cut a thin slice off tops of tomatoes. Scoop out pulp, leaving a 1/4-in. shell; invert shells on paper towel to drain. Chop tops, pulp, and seeds; set aside. In a small skillet, saute 2 tablespoons onions and garlic in 1 teaspoon oil for about 2 minutes or until slightly softened. Remove from the heat. Add 1 tablespoon oil, vinegar, sugar, salt, pepper and 3 tablespoons chopped pulp; mix well. Pour into a small bowl; set aside.

In the same skillet, cook the ham, corn, remaining onions and remaining pulp in remaining oil for 4 minutes or until most of the liquid has evaporated, stirring occasionally. Spoon into tomato shells. Serve on a bed of lettuce; drizzle with the reserved tomato-vinegar mixture. **Yield:** 2 servings.

HAM LOAF

(Pictured at right)

This variation on meat loaf is quite tasty.
Creamy horseradish sauce adds the right spark.
—Sarah McClanahan, Mansfield, Ohio

    1 egg
1/4 cup milk
    3 tablespoons crushed saltines
1/4 pound ground fully cooked ham
1/4 pound ground pork
GLAZE:
    2 tablespoons brown sugar
    2 tablespoons water
    1 tablespoon white vinegar
    3/4 teaspoon prepared mustard
HORSERADISH SAUCE:
    1/4 cup mayonnaise
    3/4 teaspoon prepared horseradish
    3 tablespoons whipped topping

In a bowl, combine the egg, milk and cracker crumbs. Crumble meat over mixture and mix well. Pat into a greased 5-3/4-in. x 3-in. x 2-in. loaf pan or shape into loaf and place in a shallow baking pan.

In a small saucepan, bring glaze ingredients to a boil; pour over loaf. Bake at 350° for 35-40 minutes or until a meat thermometer reads 160°, basting occasionally. Meanwhile, for sauce, place mayonnaise and horseradish in a bowl. Fold in whipped topping. Serve with ham loaf. **Yield:** 2 servings.

SPICED HAM STEAK

This recipe came from my family's love of grilling and our inability to follow a recipe completely! We're always changing things to suit our tastes. We don't usually measure, but I did here so I could share this family favorite.
—Kimberly Craig, Menomonie, Wisconsin

1-1/3 cups pineapple juice
    1 teaspoon butter *or* margarine, melted
    1 teaspoon ground cloves
    1 teaspoon paprika
    2 garlic cloves, minced
1/2 teaspoon brown sugar
1/4 teaspoon ground mustard
    1 ham steak (about 1/2 pound and 1 inch thick)

In a 2-cup measuring cup, combine the juice, butter, cloves, paprika, garlic, sugar and mustard; mix well. Pour 2/3 cup marinade into a large resealable plastic bag; cover and refrigerate remaining marinade. Add ham to the bag. Seal bag and turn to coat; refrigerate for at least 3 hours or overnight.

Drain and discard marinade. Grill ham, uncovered, over medium heat for 4-6 minutes on each side or until meat is glazed and heated through, basting occasionally with reserved marinade. **Yield:** 2 servings.

SOUTHWESTERN GRILLED LAMB

(Pictured at right)

People seem to be eating food that's a little hotter nowadays, so I think this recipe has mass appeal.
—Margaret Pache, Mesa, Arizona

    1 cup salsa
 1/2 cup chopped onion
 1/4 cup molasses
 1/4 cup fresh lime juice (about 2 limes)
 1/4 cup chicken broth
    2 garlic cloves, minced
    1 to 3 tablespoons chopped seeded
      jalapeno peppers*
    2 teaspoons sugar
    4 lamb chops (1 inch thick)
Sour cream

In a saucepan, combine the first eight ingredients. Bring to a boil. Reduce heat; simmer, uncovered, for 15-20 minutes.

Meanwhile, grill lamb chops over medium heat on each side for 5-7 minutes for rare, 7-8 minutes for medium or 8-10 minutes for well-done. Brush with sauce during the last few minutes of grilling. Serve with sour cream. **Yield:** 2 servings.

    *Editor's Note: When cutting or seeding hot peppers, use rubber or plastic gloves to protect your hands. Avoid touching your face.

OVEN-BARBECUED SPARERIBS

I am fortunate to have both a mother and a mother-in-law who are wonderful cooks. My husband's mother shared this recipe with me at least 30 years ago, and it's still my favorite way to fix ribs.
—Sharon Moeller, Ceresco, Nebraska

 3/4 pound country-style pork ribs
 1/4 cup chopped onion
    2 teaspoons butter *or* margarine
 1/4 cup ketchup
    2 tablespoons chopped celery
    1 tablespoon lemon juice
    2 teaspoons brown sugar
    2 teaspoons cider vinegar
 3/4 teaspoon Worcestershire sauce
 1/4 teaspoon salt
 1/4 teaspoon prepared mustard
 1/8 teaspoon pepper
 1/8 teaspoon chili powder

Place ribs in a shallow baking pan. Bake, uncovered, at 350° for 1-1/2 hours. In a saucepan, saute onion in butter until tender. Add remaining ingredients; bring to a boil. Reduce heat; simmer, uncovered, for 10 minutes.

Pour sauce over ribs. Bake, uncovered, 30-45 minutes longer or until meat is tender. **Yield:** 1 servings.

ZITI CASSEROLE

Sometime I have to double this recipe because my husband has been known to have third or fourth helpings!
—Jennifer Anderson, Bloomington, Illinois

1-1/2 cups uncooked ziti *or* small tube pasta
   1 Italian sausage link (about 1/4 pound), casing removed
   1 small onion, chopped
   1 garlic clove, minced
1-1/2 cups spaghetti sauce
   2 tablespoons red wine *or* beef broth, optional
 1/2 teaspoon Italian seasoning
Salt and pepper to taste
 1/2 cup shredded mozzarella cheese

Cook pasta according to package directions; drain. Crumble sausage into a skillet; add onion and garlic. Cook over medium heat until meat is no longer pink; drain. Combine the sausage mixture, pasta, spaghetti sauce, wine or broth if desired and seasonings.

Transfer to a greased 1-qt. baking dish; top with cheese. Bake, uncovered, at 350° for 10-15 minutes or until heated through and cheese is melted. **Yield:** 2 servings.

SMOTHERED PORK CHOPS

(Pictured below)

I like to saute extra mushrooms and caramelize some onions for the side of this dish.
—Danielle Binkley, New Carlisle, Ohio

 1/2 cup olive *or* vegetable oil
   1 tablespoon lemon juice
   3 garlic cloves, minced
   2 teaspoons grated lemon peel
 1/2 teaspoon salt
 1/2 teaspoon pepper
 1/2 teaspoon *each* dried basil, parsley flakes and rosemary, crushed
   2 boneless butterflied pork loin chops (1/2 inch thick)
TOPPING:
   1 cup sliced fresh mushrooms
   2 tablespoons butter *or* margarine
 1/4 teaspoon salt
 1/8 teaspoon pepper
   2 slices pepper Jack cheese

In a large resealable plastic bag, combine the oil, lemon juice, garlic, lemon peel, salt, pepper, basil, parsley and rosemary; add the pork. Seal bag and turn to coat; refrigerate for 2 hours or overnight.

Drain and discard marinade. Broil pork chops 3-4 in. from the heat for 5-6 minutes on each side or until meat juices run clear.

Meanwhile, in a small skillet, saute mushrooms in butter until tender; sprinkle with salt and pepper. Using a slotted spoon, place mushrooms on pork chops. Cover each with a cheese slice. Broil for 1-2 minutes or until cheese is melted. **Yield:** 2 servings.

POLYNESIAN RIBS

(Pictured at right)

A friend shared this recipe more than 30 years ago, and I've been using it ever since. I make the ribs a day ahead to let the flavors meld, then I reheat and serve them the next day.
—Joyce Faust, Guelph, Ontario

1-1/2 to 2 pounds pork spareribs
1/2 cup packed brown sugar
4-1/2 teaspoons cornstarch
1/2 teaspoon celery salt
1/2 teaspoon ground ginger
1/2 cup undrained canned crushed
  pineapple
1/4 cup water
1/4 cup chopped onion
2 to 3 tablespoons cider vinegar
2 tablespoons soy sauce
1 tablespoon Worcestershire sauce
1-1/2 teaspoons grated orange peel
1/8 teaspoon hot pepper sauce

Cut ribs into serving size pieces. Place ribs bone side down on a rack in shallow roasting pan. Bake, uncovered, at 350° for 1 hour; drain.

In a saucepan, combine the brown sugar, cornstarch, celery salt and ginger. Combine the pineapple, water, onion, vinegar, soy sauce, Worcestershire sauce, orange peel and hot pepper sauce. Gradually stir into brown sugar mixture. Bring to a boil; cook for 2 minutes or until thickened. Brush ribs with sauce. Bake 25-35 minutes longer or until meat is tender, basting with sauce several times. **Yield:** 2 servings.

PORK SCHNITZEL

(Pictured at right)

German-style schnitzel is usually made with veal. I substituted pork to save money without sacrificing flavor. Whenever I serve it, I'm asked for the recipe.
—Diane Katzmark, Metamora, Michigan

2 pork cutlets (about 5 ounces *each*)
2 tablespoons all-purpose flour
1/4 teaspoon seasoned salt
1/8 teaspoon pepper
1 egg
2 tablespoons milk
1/4 cup dry bread crumbs
1/4 teaspoon paprika
1 to 2 tablespoons vegetable oil
SAUCE:
2/3 cup chicken broth, *divided*
1-1/2 teaspoons all-purpose flour
3 tablespoons sour cream
1/8 teaspoon dill weed
Salt and pepper to taste

Flatten meat to 1/2-in. thickness. In a shallow dish, combine the flour, seasoned salt and pepper. In another shallow bowl, combine egg and milk. Place bread crumbs and paprika in a third shallow dish. Coat meat with flour; dip in egg mixture, then coat with crumb mixture. Let stand for 5 minutes.

In a large skillet, cook pork in oil for 2 minutes on each side or until browned. Remove and keep warm. Stir 1/3 cup broth into skillet, scraping browned bits. In a bowl, combine flour and remaining broth until smooth. Stir into skillet. Bring to a boil; cook and stir for 1-2 minutes or until thickened. Reduce heat; stir in the sour cream, dill, salt and pepper; heat through. Serve with cutlets. **Yield:** 2 servings.

POLYNESIAN RIBS
PORK SCHNITZEL

HAM CORN AU GRATIN

*I found this recipe in one of my mother's cookbooks from back during the Depression.
It's still as satisfying today as it was back then.*
—Carren Chamberlin, New Waterford, Ohio

2 tablespoons butter *or* margarine
5 teaspoons all-purpose flour
1/4 teaspoon ground mustard
1/8 teaspoon pepper
1 cup milk
1 cup diced fully cooked ham
1-1/4 cups frozen corn, thawed
2 tablespoons finely chopped green
  pepper
1 tablespoon finely chopped onion
TOPPING:
1/4 cup shredded cheddar cheese
1/4 cup crushed butter-flavored
  crackers (about 7 crackers)
2 teaspoons butter *or* margarine,
  melted
Paprika

In a saucepan, melt butter. Stir in the flour, mustard and pepper until smooth; gradually add the milk. Bring to a boil; cook and stir for 2 minutes or until thickened.

In a greased 1-qt. baking dish, layer the ham, corn, green pepper and onion. Pour sauce over top. In a bowl, combine the cheese, crumbs and butter; sprinkle over top. Sprinkle with paprika. Bake, uncovered, at 375° for 10-15 minutes or until heated through and top is golden brown. **Yield:** 2 servings.

TERIYAKI BUTTERFLY PORK CHOPS

*My grandmother taught me how to cook years ago. All of my
friends rave over this dish and its hot sweet flavor.*
—Rick Keister, Houston, Texas

1/4 cup teriyaki sauce
1/4 cup white wine *or* chicken broth
3 tablespoons vegetable oil
2 to 3 tablespoons minced fresh
  cilantro *or* parsley
3 to 4 garlic cloves, minced
1/8 teaspoon crushed red pepper flakes
2 boneless butterfly pork chops (1/2
  inch thick)
1 teaspoon cornstarch

In a bowl, combine the teriyaki sauce, wine or broth, oil, cilantro, garlic and red pepper flakes. Pour 1/3 cup into a resealable plastic bag; cover and refrigerate remaining marinade for sauce. Add chops to the bag. Seal and turn to coat; refrigerate for at least 4 hours.

Drain and discard marinade. Grill chops, covered, over medium heat or broil 4 in. from heat for 9 minutes on each side or until juices run clear and a meat thermometer reads 160°.

In a saucepan, combine cornstarch and reserved marinade until smooth. Bring to a boil, cook and stir for 1-2 minutes or until thickened. Serve with chops. **Yield:** 2 servings.

LAMB SHEPHERD'S PIE

(Pictured at right and on page 180)

This is what I call "comfort food". My grandmother used to make it.
—Michele Hancox, Muskego, Wisconsin

   1 teaspoon all-purpose flour
Dash pepper
  1/2 pound lamb stew meat, cut into 1-inch cubes
   1 tablespoon vegetable oil
   1 can (8 ounces) tomato sauce
1-1/2 cups beef broth *or* water
   1 bay leaf
   4 to 8 frozen pearl onions
   1 cup frozen cut green beans
   1 medium carrot, sliced
   1 cup mashed potatoes (with added milk and butter)

In a large resealable plastic bag, combine the flour and pepper. Add lamb, a few pieces at a time, and shake to coat. In a nonstick skillet, brown lamb in batches in oil over medium heat until no longer pink; drain. Add the tomato sauce, broth and bay leaf. Bring to a boil. Reduce heat; cover and simmer for 1 hour. Add the onions, beans and carrot; cover and cook 20-30 minutes longer or until meat and vegetables are tender. Discard bay leaf.

Transfer stew to a greased 5-cup baking dish. Pipe or spoon mash potatoes around edges. Bake, uncovered, at 375° for 13-15 minutes or until potatoes are golden brown. **Yield:** 2 servings.

HAM FRIED RICE

This is a recipe that even my children love. When I make it for the whole family, I triple the ingredients and let the kids use chopsticks. It gets a little messy, but it's fun.
—Joyce Scholten, Dell Rapids, South Dakota

   2 eggs, lightly beaten
1-1/2 teaspoons canola *or* vegetable oil
   3/4 cup cold cooked rice
   2/3 cup diced fully cooked ham
   3/4 teaspoon garlic powder
   1/4 teaspoon ground ginger
Dash pepper
Dash chili powder, optional
1-1/2 teaspoons soy sauce

In a small skillet, cook and stir eggs in oil over medium heat until eggs are completely set. Remove and set aside. In same skillet, cook the rice, ham, garlic powder, ginger, pepper and chili powder if desired until heated through. Stir in soy sauce and reserved eggs. Serve immediately. **Yield:** 2 servings.

Nutritional Analysis: One 1-cup serving (prepared with egg substitute and reduced-sodium soy sauce) equals 193 calories, 6 g fat (1 g saturated fat), 14 mg cholesterol, 810 mg sodium, 16 g carbohydrate, 1 g fiber, 18 g protein. **Diabetic Exchanges:** 2 lean meat, 1 starch.

SWEET 'N' TANGY MEATBALLS

(Pictured at right)

A friend from church gave me this recipe. It's one of my all-time favorites.
—Robbie Hunt, Loyal, Wisconsin

  1 egg, lightly beaten
  1/3 cup soft bread crumbs
  1 tablespoon chopped onion
  1/4 teaspoon salt
Dash pepper
  1/4 pound bulk pork sausage
  1/4 pound ground beef
SAUCE:
  3/4 cup ketchup
  2 to 3 tablespoons brown sugar
  2 tablespoons cider vinegar
  2 tablespoons soy sauce
Hot cooked noodles *or* rice

In a bowl, combine the first five ingredients. Crumble meat over mixture and mix well. Shape into 1-1/2-in. balls. Place on a greased baking sheet. Bake, uncovered, at 350° for 13-15 minutes or until meatballs are no longer pink; drain.

In a large skillet, combine the ketchup, brown sugar, vinegar and soy sauce; add the meatballs. Bring to a boil. Reduce heat; simmer, uncovered, for 8-10 minutes or until heated through and sauce is thickened. Serve over noodles. **Yield:** 2 servings.

HAM AND POTATOES AU GRATIN

This is one of the dishes Grandma served during the holidays, so it brings back fond memories. I usually double the recipe, because the leftovers are fabulous.
—Novella Cook, Hinton, West Virginia

  2 cups sliced peeled potatoes, cooked
  1 cup diced fully cooked ham
  1 tablespoon minced onion
  1/3 cup butter *or* margarine
  3 tablespoons all-purpose flour
  3/4 teaspoon salt
Dash white pepper
1-1/2 cups milk
  1 cup (4 ounces) shredded cheddar cheese
Chopped fresh parsley

In a greased 1-qt. baking dish, combine the potatoes, ham and onion; set aside. In a saucepan, melt butter. Stir in the flour, salt and pepper until smooth. Gradually add milk. Bring to a boil; cook and stir for 2 minutes or until thickened. Reduce heat; stir in the cheese until melted. Pour over potato mixture and gently stir to coat. Bake, uncovered, at 350° for 35-40 minutes or until bubbly. Garnish with parsley. **Yield:** 2 servings.

EASY VEGETABLE LINGUINE

I like recipes that are simple yet tasty, and this one definitely fits the bill.
—Marie Herr, Berea, Ohio

6 slices bacon, cut into 1-inch pieces
1 cup broccoli florets *or* cauliflowerets
1/4 cup chopped onion
1 cup sliced fresh mushrooms
3 ounces linguine, cooked and drained
1/2 cup cherry tomato halves
1/2 cup grated Parmesan cheese

In a skillet, cook bacon over medium heat until crisp. Remove to paper towels. Drain, reserving 2 tablespoons drippings. In same skillet, saute the broccoli, onion and mushrooms in reserved drippings for 3-4 minutes or until crisp-tender. Add the linguine, tomato and cooked bacon; mix lightly. Sprinkle with cheese. Serve immediately. **Yield:** 2 servings.

MINI SAUSAGE LASAGNA

(Pictured below)

The home economists in our Test Kitchen created this tasty mini lasagna.
It strikes a perfect balance between cheese and tomato flavors.

4 lasagna noodles, cooked and drained
2 Italian sausage links (about 1/2 pound), casings removed
1-1/2 cups spaghetti sauce
1 cup ricotta cheese
1 egg, lightly beaten
2 tablespoons Parmesan cheese
1 tablespoon *each* dried thyme, parsley flakes, basil and rosemary, crushed
1/2 teaspoon garlic powder
1 cup shredded mozzarella cheese, *divided*

Cut 3 noodles widthwise in half. Cut remaining noodle widthwise into thirds. Crumble sausage into a skillet; cook over medium heat until no longer pink. Drain. Stir in spaghetti sauce; set aside. In a bowl, combine the ricotta, egg, Parmesan and seasonings; set aside.

Spread 3 tablespoons meat sauce in a shallow 1-qt. baking dish. Top with two large noodle pieces and one small piece. Layer with half of the ricotta cheese mixture and 1/3 cup mozzarella cheese. Repeat layers once, starting with sauce. Top with remaining noodles, meat sauce and mozzarella cheese.

Cover and bake at 375° for 30 minutes. Uncover; bake 10 minutes longer or until heated through. Let stand for 5 minutes before cutting. **Yield:** 2-3 servings.

INDIVIDUAL MEAT LOAVES

Pork gives this meat loaf a moist, tasty, old-fashioned flavor. It's one of our favorite dishes.
—Kim McMurl, Fargo, North Dakota

　1 egg
　3 tablespoons milk
1/2 teaspoon Worcestershire sauce
1/2 teaspoon onion salt
1/4 teaspoon pepper
1/4 cup cracker crumbs
1/2 pound ground pork
1/3 cup packed brown sugar
1/4 cup ketchup
　3 tablespoons cider vinegar
1/2 teaspoon prepared mustard

In a medium bowl, combine the first six ingredient. Crumble pork over mixture and mix well. Shape into two 5-in. x 2-1/2-in. loaves; place in a small baking dish. Combine remaining ingredients; pour over loaves. Bake, uncovered, at 325° for 1 hour or until a meat thermometer reaches 160°. **Yield:** 2 servings.

CLASSIC PIZZA

(Pictured below)

This Italian sausage pizza tastes just as good as its bigger counterparts.
The one-serving recipe comes from our Test Kitchen.

　1 Italian sausage link (about 1/4 pound), casing removed
　2 frozen bread dough rolls, thawed
1/4 cup pizza sauce
1/2 cup shredded mozzarella cheese, *divided*
1/4 cup chopped fresh mushrooms
　3 tablespoons chopped red onion
1/2 teaspoon Italian seasoning

Crumble sausage into a skillet. Cook over medium heat until no longer pink; drain. On a lightly floured surface, knead the two rolls together. Roll dough into a 7-1/2-in. circle. Transfer to a greased 7-1/2-in. pizza pan or baking sheet. Spread pizza sauce over dough; sprinkle with 1/4 cup mozzarella cheese, sausage, mushrooms, onion and remaining cheese. Top with Italian seasoning. Bake at 375° for 20-22 minutes or until crust is golden brown. **Yield:** 1 serving.

STUFFED PORK CHOPS

(Pictured at right)

I've had this recipe for almost 50 years, and it always brings me compliments. Any time I want the meal to be extra special—for dinner parties with friends, birthdays, anniversaries or holiday meals—I prepare these chops.
—Bessie Hulett, Shively, Kentucky

2 tablespoons chopped celery leaves
1 tablespoon chopped onion
2 tablespoons butter *or* margarine, *divided*
3/4 cup dry bread crumbs
2/3 cup chicken broth, *divided*
1 tablespoon minced fresh parsley *or* 1 teaspoon dried parsley flakes
1/2 teaspoon salt
1/2 teaspoon paprika
1/2 teaspoon rubbed sage
1/4 teaspoon dried thyme
1/4 teaspoon pepper
2 pork loin chops (1-1/4 inches thick)

In a skillet, saute celery leaves and onion in 1 tablespoon butter until soft. Remove from the heat; stir in bread crumbs, 1/3 cup broth and seasonings; mix well. Cut a pocket in each pork chop by slicing from the fat side almost to the bone. Spoon about 1/2 cup stuffing into each pocket. Secure with kitchen string or toothpicks. In a skillet, brown the chops on both sides in remaining butter.

Place in a greased 11-in. x 7-in. x 2-in. baking dish; pour remaining broth over the chops. Cover and bake at 350° for 40-50 minutes or until juices run clear. Remove string or toothpicks before serving. Thicken pan juices if desired. **Yield:** 2 servings.

LEMON HERB LAMB CHOPS

This recipe comes from my aunt, who thought we'd enjoy it because we like lamb. She was right.
—Mildred Sherrer, Bay City, Texas

1/4 cup olive *or* vegetable oil
1 tablespoon lemon juice
1 garlic clove, minced
1 teaspoon grated lemon peel
1/4 teaspoon salt
1/4 teaspoon dried basil
1/4 teaspoon dried rosemary, crushed
1/4 teaspoon pepper
2 bone-in lamb loin chops (6 ounces each)

In a large resealable plastic bag, combine the first eight ingredients; add the chops. Seal bag and turn to coat; refrigerate for at least 2 hours or overnight.

Drain and discard marinade. Broil lamb 3-4 in. from the heat for 4-6 minutes on each side or until meat reaches desired doneness (for rare, a meat thermometer should read 140°; medium, 160°; well-done, 170°). **Yield:** 1-2 servings.

SAUSAGE PASTA BAKE

(Pictured below)

This hearty dish is a favorite for weekday dinners. The combination of flavors makes it special.
—Patricia Anderson, Beavercreek, Ohio

1-1/4 cups uncooked wagon wheel pasta
1/4 pound bulk pork sausage
3 tablespoons chopped green pepper
2 tablespoons chopped green onion
1 garlic clove, minced
1 can (8 ounces) tomato sauce
1/4 cup spaghetti sauce with mushrooms
2/3 cup shredded mozzarella cheese, *divided*
5 slices pepperoni, cut into quarters, optional
1/2 teaspoon Italian seasoning
1/8 teaspoon pepper

Cook pasta according to package directions; drain. In a skillet, cook the sausage, green pepper, onion and garlic over medium heat until meat is no longer pink; drain. In a bowl, combine the pasta, sausage mixture, tomato sauce, spaghetti sauce, 1/3 cup mozzarella cheese, pepperoni, Italian seasoning and pepper.

Transfer to a greased shallow 3-cup baking dish. Cover and bake at 375° for 15 minutes. Uncover; sprinkle with remaining cheese. Bake, uncovered, 5-8 minutes longer or until bubbly and cheese is melted. **Yield:** 2 servings.

SAUSAGE RED BEANS 'N' RICE

This easy-to-make recipe has been a staple in my recipe file for about 10 years.
My husband and I both enjoy cooking it.
—Thelma Dye, Weatherford, Oklahoma

1/4 cup chopped green pepper
2 tablespoons onion, chopped
1 garlic clove, minced
1-1/2 teaspoons butter *or* margarine
1/4 pound fully cooked smoked sausage, cut into 1/2-inch slices
1 can (14-1/2 ounces) diced tomatoes, undrained
1 cup canned ranch-style *or* chili beans
1/8 teaspoon dried oregano

1/8 teaspoon pepper
Hot cooked rice

In a skillet, saute green pepper, onion and garlic in butter until crisp-tender. Add sausage; cook and stir until browned. Add the tomatoes, beans, oregano and pepper. Bring to a boil. Reduce heat; simmer, uncovered, for 20-25 minutes or until thickened. Serve over rice. **Yield:** 2 servings.

CHINESE RIBS

Folks who sample these are surprised to hear honey isn't one of the ingredients! These ribs are crisp on the outside and tender inside. I've also used the marinade for chicken wings.
—Rosemarie Balowas, New Port Richey, Florida

1-1/2 pounds pork spareribs
  3/4 **cup sugar**
  1/2 **cup cider vinegar**
  1/3 **cup soy sauce**
    3 **tablespoons apple juice**
Vegetable oil for deep-fat frying

Cut the ribs between the bones into single pieces; place in an 8-in. square baking dish. Bring the sugar, vinegar, soy sauce and apple juice to a boil. Pour over the ribs. Cover and refrigerate at least 1 hour.

Heat at least 1 in. of oil in an electric skillet or deep-fat fryer to 350°. Drain and pat ribs dry with paper towel. Fry, turning frequently, for 7-8 minutes or until meat is tender and no longer pink when cut with a knife and shrinks slightly from the bone. Drain on paper towels. **Yield:** 2 servings.

SWEET-AND-SOUR HAM

(Pictured below)

This recipe has become my standby for when I have leftover ham.
It's easy to prepare, and served over rice, it's delicious!
—Diane Widmer, Blue Island, Illinois

    1 **can (8 ounces) pineapple chunks**
  1/4 **cup ketchup**
    2 **teaspoons soy sauce**
    2 **teaspoons sugar**
    2 **cups cubed fully cooked ham**
  2/3 **cup cubed green** *or* **sweet red pepper**
    1 **tablespoon cornstarch**
    2 **tablespoons cold water**
Hot cooked rice, optional

Drain pineapple, reserving 1/3 cup of juice; set pineapple aside. In a bowl, combine the ketchup, soy sauce, sugar and reserved juice. Add ham and green pepper. If desired, cover and refrigerate for 30 minutes to marinate.

In a skillet, cook and stir ham mixture over medium heat for 5-7 minutes or until pepper is tender. Combine cornstarch and water until smooth; stir into skillet. Bring to a boil; cook and stir for 2 minutes or until thickened. Reduce heat. Stir in pineapple; heat through. Serve over rice if desired. **Yield:** 2 servings.

ITALIAN SAUSAGE CACCIATORE

This is one of my husband's favorite meals. I came up with this recipe after sampling a similar dish in a restaurant. This one is just as good.
—Mary Grace DiStasio, Kenmore, New York

1/4 medium green *or* sweet yellow pepper, julienned
3 tablespoons chopped onion
1 garlic clove, minced
1-1/2 teaspoons olive *or* vegetable oil
1 Italian sausage link (about 1/4 pound), casing removed
1 cup canned diced tomatoes with juice
2/3 cup tomato juice
15 slices pepperoni, halved
1/4 teaspoon dried oregano
1/8 teaspoon dried basil
Pepper to taste
1/3 cup sliced fresh mushrooms
1 tablespoon sliced ripe olives
2 tablespoons Romano *or* Parmesan cheese
Hot cooked linguine *or* fettuccine

In a skillet, saute the green pepper, onion and garlic in oil until crisp-tender. Crumble sausage into skillet; cook over medium heat until meat is no longer pink. Drain. Add the tomatoes, tomato juice, pepperoni, oregano, basil and pepper. Reduce heat; cover and simmer for 10 minutes. Add mushrooms and olives. Simmer, uncovered, for 10-15 minutes or until slightly thickened. Stir in cheese. Serve over pasta. **Yield:** 2 servings.

BAYOU SHRIMP RICE SKILLET

After I found this recipe in a cookbook, I fiddled with it to better suit my family. Now my husband and son love the ham and shrimp combination.
—Jessie Hale, Winn, Maine

1 small onion, chopped
1/4 cup chopped green pepper
1 garlic clove, minced
1 tablespoon butter *or* margarine
1 cup water
1/2 cup cubed fully cooked ham
1/2 cup tomato sauce
1-1/2 teaspoons white wine vinegar *or* cider vinegar
1/8 teaspoon pepper
3/4 cup uncooked instant rice
1/4 pound uncooked medium shrimp, peeled and deveined

In a skillet, saute the onion, green pepper and garlic in butter until crisp-tender. Stir in the water, ham, tomato sauce, vinegar and pepper. Bring to a boil. Reduce heat; cover and simmer for 3 minutes. Add the rice; cover and cook for 5 minutes. Add the shrimp; cook 3-5 minutes longer or until shrimp turn pink and rice is cooked. **Yield:** 2 servings.

Nutritional Analysis: One 1-cup serving equals 320 calories, 9 g fat (4 g saturated fat), 112 mg cholesterol, 916 mg sodium, 36 g carbohydrate, 2 g fiber, 23 g protein. **Diabetic Exchanges:** 2-1/2 lean meat, 2 starch, 1 vegetable.

HAM STEW FOR TWO

(Pictured at right)

My husband and I enjoy this stew any time of the year. If I don't have leftover ham, I buy a thick slice and use that.
—Judy Hall, Lockport, Illinois

2 medium potatoes, peeled and cut into 3/4-inch cubes
2 medium carrots, sliced
1-1/2 cups cubed fully cooked ham
1 cup water
1 small onion, chopped
1 bay leaf
1/2 teaspoon salt
1/4 teaspoon dried savory
1/8 teaspoon pepper
3 tablespoons all-purpose flour
1 cup milk

In a saucepan, combine the first nine ingredients. Bring to a boil. Reduce heat; cover and simmer until vegetables are tender. In a small bowl, combine the flour and milk until smooth. Stir into stew. Bring to a boil; cook and stir for 2 minutes or until thickened. Discard bay leaf before serving. **Yield:** 2 servings.

APPLE PORK CHOP CASSEROLE

I've loved this recipe since the first time I tried it. The apples and raisins give a nice homey flavor to the stuffing.
—Beverly Baxter, Kansas City, Kansas

2 boneless pork loin chops (3/4 inch thick)
2 teaspoons vegetable oil
3/4 cup water
1 tablespoon butter *or* margarine
1 small tart green apple, cored and chopped
2 tablespoons raisins
1-1/2 cups crushed chicken stuffing mix
2/3 cup condensed cream of mushroom soup, undiluted

In a skillet, brown meat in oil for about 5 minutes on each side. In a saucepan, combine the water, butter, apple and raisins; bring to a boil. Stir in stuffing mix. Remove from the heat; cover and let stand for 5 minutes. Fluff with fork.

Transfer to a greased shallow 1-qt. baking dish. Top with meat. Spoon soup over meat and stuffing. Cover and bake at 350° for 30-35 minutes or until a meat thermometer inserted into pork chops reads 160°. **Yield:** 2 servings.

FISH & SEAFOOD

If you're a fan of fish and seafood, this chapter will reel you in real fast. You'll find 32 tempting dishes featuring scallops, shrimp, catfish, crab, salmon and all your other favorites.

SALMON LOAF (P. 228)

MACADAMIA-CRUSTED SALMON (P. 212)
GARLIC SHRIMP PASTA (P.212)

MACADAMIA-CRUSTED SALMON

(Pictured on page 211)

One evening when my husband and I went out to dinner, he ordered a salmon dish that sounded interesting. It was wonderful. When I tried duplicating it at home, he said mine was as good as, if not better than, the original. That made my day!
—Dee Dee Rici, San Simeon, California

2 salmon steaks (about 1-1/8 inches thick)
1/4 teaspoon salt
1/4 teaspoon coarsely ground pepper
1 egg white
1/2 cup chopped macadamia nuts
2 tablespoons vegetable oil
2 tablespoons butter *or* margarine
2 tablespoons minced fresh parsley
1 teaspoon lemon juice
Hot cooked rice

Sprinkle fish with salt and pepper. In a shallow bowl, whisk egg white until frothy. Dip fish in egg white, then coat with nuts. Gently pat nut mixture onto fish.

In a skillet, cook fish in oil over medium heat for about 6-8 minutes on each side or until fish flakes easily with a fork. Meanwhile, melt butter. Stir in parsley and lemon juice. Drizzle over fish. Serve with rice. **Yield:** 2 servings.

GARLIC SHRIMP PASTA

(Pictured on page 211)

This recipe is elegant, yet it doesn't require hours of working in the kitchen. Everyone agrees it's quite a treat.
—Amy Varner, Rio Rancho, New Mexico

4 garlic cloves, minced
1/3 cup butter *or* margarine
3/4 cup whipping cream
1/4 cup minced fresh parsley
1 teaspoon minced fresh dill *or* 1/4 teaspoon dill weed
1/4 teaspoon salt
Dash pepper
1/2 pound uncooked medium shrimp, peeled and deveined
3 ounces thin spaghetti *or* angel hair pasta, cooked and drained

In a small skillet, cook garlic in butter for 1 minute. Whisk in cream, parsley, dill, salt and pepper. Bring to a boil. Reduce heat; simmer, uncovered, for about 13 minutes or until sauce is thickened, stirring occasionally. Add shrimp to pan. Cook and stir for about 2 minutes or until shrimp turn pink. Pour over pasta; toss to coat. Serve immediately. **Yield:** 2 servings.

SERVING SUGGESTION

Buy frozen vegetables in the bag instead of a box. It's easier to measure out the amount you need for one or two servings.

SOUTHWESTERN FISH TACOS

(Pictured at right)

These tacos, native to Southern California, are a real taste treat. This recipe has been on my family's most requested list for years.
—Joan Hallford, North Richland Hills, Texas

1/4 cup sour cream
1/4 cup mayonnaise
2 tablespoons minced fresh cilantro *or* parsley
4 teaspoons taco seasoning, *divided*
1 tablespoon lemon juice
1/2 pound cod, haddock *or* orange roughy fillets, cut into 1-inch pieces
1 tablespoon canola *or* vegetable oil
4 taco shells
Optional toppings: shredded lettuce *or* cabbage, chopped tomatoes, lime juice and salsa

In a small bowl, combine the sour cream, mayonnaise, cilantro and 2 teaspoons taco seasoning; set aside. In another bowl, combine the lemon juice and remaining taco seasoning. Add fish; toss to coat. In a small skillet, cook fish over medium-high heat in oil about 6 minutes. (Fish will break apart as it cooks.) Fill taco shells with fish mixture. Serve with toppings of your choice. Serve with sour cream mixture. **Yield:** 2 servings.

Nutritional Analysis: One serving (prepared with reduced-fat sour cream, fat-free mayonnaise and without additional toppings) equals 340 calories, 16 g fat (3 g saturated fat), 62 mg cholesterol, 963 mg sodium, 24 g carbohydrate, 2 g fiber, 24 g protein. **Diabetic Exchanges:** 3 lean meat, 1-1/2 starch, 1 fat.

SIMPLE HERBED SCALLOPS

Living in Kansas, fresh seafood can be hard to come by. Luckily, frozen scallops aren't. This dish offers an "East Coast" taste to those of us in the Midwest.
—Sarah Befort, Hays, Kansas

3 tablespoons butter *or* margarine, *divided*
3/4 teaspoon lemon juice
1/2 teaspoon minced chives
1/4 teaspoon dried parsley flakes
1/8 teaspoon garlic salt
1/8 teaspoon dried tarragon
Dash pepper
1/2 to 3/4 pound fresh *or* frozen sea scallops, thawed
2 tablespoons dry bread crumbs

In a small saucepan, melt 2 tablespoons butter. Add the lemon juice, chives, parsley, garlic salt, tarragon and pepper; stir well. Place scallops in a greased 1-qt. baking dish. Pour butter mixture over scallops. Melt remaining butter and toss with bread crumbs; sprinkle over scallops. Bake, uncovered, at 350° for 20-25 minutes or until scallops are opaque and topping is lightly browned. **Yield:** 2 servings.

SEAFOOD PASTA

(Pictured at right)

*This light dish is always welcome
on a warm spring night.*
—Becky Kudron, West Springfield, Massachusetts

2 garlic cloves, *divided*
2 tablespoons butter *or* margarine,
  divided
3 plum tomatoes, chopped
2 teaspoons minced fresh parsley
2 teaspoons minced fresh basil *or* 1/2
  teaspoon dried basil
1/8 to 1/4 teaspoon dried tarragon
3/4 cup chicken broth
4 ounces thin spaghetti
1/4 pound uncooked medium shrimp,
  peeled and deveined
1/4 pound bay scallops
Shredded Parmesan cheese, optional

In a medium skillet, saute 1 garlic clove in 1 tablespoon butter for 1 minute. Add the tomatoes, parsley, basil and tarragon; saute 2 minutes longer. Add the broth; bring to a boil. Reduce heat; simmer, uncovered, for 8-10 minutes or until mixture reaches desired thickness.

Meanwhile, cook pasta according to package directions. In another skillet, saute remaining garlic in remaining butter for 1 minute. Add shrimp; cook and stir for 1 minute. Add scallops and cook 3 minutes longer or until shrimp turn pink and scallops are firm and opaque. Add to tomato mixture. Drain pasta; transfer to a bowl. Pour seafood mixture over pasta; toss to coat. Sprinkle with Parmesan if desired. **Yield:** 2 servings.

TUNA AND RICE CASSEROLE

This recipe contains one of my favorite combinations, broccoli and rice, so I make it often.
—Margaret McNeil, Memphis, Tennessee

1 small onion, chopped
1-1/2 teaspoons vegetable oil
2/3 cup water
3 tablespoons Homemade Cream-
  Style Soup Mix (page 75)
3/4 cup frozen chopped broccoli,
  thawed
1 can (6 ounces) tuna, drained and
  flaked
1/2 cup milk
1/4 teaspoon salt
1/8 teaspoon lemon-pepper seasoning
1-1/2 cups cooked rice
2 tablespoons slivered almonds,
  toasted

In a small skillet, saute onion in oil until tender. In a microwave-safe dish, whisk together water and soup mix. Microwave, uncovered, on high for 2 to 2-1/2 minutes, whisking occasionally. Add soup to sauteed onions. Stir in the broccoli, tuna, milk, salt and lemon-pepper; bring to a boil. Reduce heat; simmer for 5 minutes or until broccoli is tender. Stir in rice. Cook and stir 2-3 minutes longer or until heated through. Sprinkle with almonds. **Yield:** 2 servings.

ORANGE ROUGHY PARMESAN

This simple fillet really hits the spot, and it's quick to make, too.
—Carole Davis, Kansas City, Missouri

1 orange roughy, red snapper, cod *or* haddock fillet (about 6 ounces)
1 tablespoon butter *or* margarine, melted
1/8 teaspoon salt, optional
Dash garlic powder
1 tablespoon seasoned bread crumbs
1 tablespoon grated Parmesan cheese

Place fish in a greased 11-in. x 7-in. x 2-in. baking dish. Brush fillet with butter. Sprinkle with salt if desired and garlic powder. In a shallow bowl, combine bread crumbs and Parmesan. Coat fish with bread crumb mixture and transfer to prepared pan. Bake at 425° for 12-15 minutes or until fish flakes easily with a fork. **Yield:** 1 serving.

Nutritional Analysis: One serving (calculated without salt) equals 269 calories, 14 g fat (8 g saturated fat), 69 mg cholesterol, 516 mg sodium, 5 g carbohydrate, trace fiber, 28 g protein. **Diabetic Exchanges:** 4 very lean meat, 2 fat, 1/2 starch.

MINTY HALIBUT PASTA

(Pictured below)

I love recipes like this that combine numerous colors, tastes and textures.
—Pam Rubenstein, Pacifica, California

1 large tomato, diced
2 tablespoons minced fresh mint *or* 2 teaspoons dried mint flakes
1 garlic clove, minced
1-1/2 teaspoons red wine vinegar *or* cider vinegar
5 teaspoons olive *or* vegetable oil, *divided*
1/2 teaspoon salt, *divided*
1/4 teaspoon pepper, *divided*
4 ounces uncooked penne *or* other medium tube pasta
1/2 teaspoon grated orange peel
1 halibut *or* swordfish steak (1/2 pound, 1 inch thick)

In a bowl, combine the first four ingredients. Add 3 teaspoons oil, 1/4 teaspoon salt and 1/8 teaspoon pepper; mix well. Let stand for 30 minutes.

Cook pasta according to package directions. Combine orange peel with the remaining oil, salt and pepper; rub over both sides of fish. Grill fish, uncovered, over medium heat or broil 3-4 in. from the heat for 5 to 6 minutes on each side or until fish flakes easily with a fork. Cut into 1-in. cubes. Drain pasta; transfer to a bowl. Add swordfish and mint vinaigrette; toss to coat. **Yield:** 2 servings.

TOMATO-TOPPED SOLE

(Pictured at right)

This dish is so simple to prepare, you won't believe it. My family adores it.
You can substitute flounder if you wish, but we prefer the delicate taste of sole.
—Esther Orgad, Staten Island, New York

1 small onion, thinly sliced
1 tablespoon olive *or* vegetable oil
1 sole *or* catfish fillet (about 5 ounces)
1/8 teaspoon salt
Dash pepper
1 plum tomato, sliced
2 tablespoons butter *or* margarine, melted
1/8 teaspoon garlic powder
2 tablespoons minced fresh parsley

In a small skillet, saute onion in oil until tender. Transfer to a greased 1-qt. baking dish. Place fillet over onions. Sprinkle with salt and pepper. Top with tomato slices. Combine butter and garlic powder; pour over tomato. Sprinkle with parsley.

Bake, uncovered, at 350° for 14-18 minutes or until fish flakes easily with a fork. **Yield:** 1 serving.

SALMON CAKES WITH LEMON-HERB SAUCE

(Pictured at right)

This recipe originally called for bread crumbs but I changed those to
cornmeal so my family would like it better. Now they love it!
—Susan Webster, Spokane, Washington

1/3 cup mayonnaise
1-1/2 teaspoons prepared horseradish
1 teaspoon lemon juice
2-1/4 teaspoons minced fresh thyme *or* 3/4 teaspoon dried thyme
1/8 teaspoon salt
Dash lemon-pepper seasoning
SALMON CAKES:
1 can (6 ounces) boneless skinless salmon, drained
1/4 cup mayonnaise*
2 tablespoons finely chopped green onion
2 tablespoons finely chopped sweet red pepper
3 to 4 teaspoons dry bread crumbs
1-1/2 teaspoons lemon juice
1/8 to 1/4 teaspoon seasoned salt
Dash cayenne pepper
3 tablespoons cornmeal
2 tablespoons butter *or* margarine

In a small bowl, combine the mayonnaise, horseradish, lemon juice, thyme, salt and lemon-pepper. Cover and refrigerate. For salmon cakes, in a bowl, combine the salmon, mayonnaise, green onion, red pepper, bread crumbs, lemon juice, seasoned salt and cayenne. Shape into four balls; roll in cornmeal. Flatten balls into 3-in. patties.

In a skillet, cook patties for 4 minutes on each side or until golden brown and heated through. Serve with lemon-herb sauce mixture. **Yield:** 2 servings.

*Editor's Note: Reduced-fat or fat-free mayonnaise is not recommended for this recipe.

TOMATO-TOPPED SOLE
SALMON CAKES WITH LEMON-HERB SAUCE

PECAN FISH

Even people who think they don't like fish gobble up this dish. It's wonderful.
—Elaine Nash, San Antonio, Texas

2 tablespoons plus 2 teaspoons
   seasoned bread crumbs
2 tablespoons finely chopped pecans,
   toasted
1-1/2 teaspoons toasted wheat germ
1/4 teaspoon dried thyme
1/8 teaspoon garlic powder
1/8 teaspoon onion powder
1/8 teaspoon salt
1/8 teaspoon pepper
1 to 2 tablespoons butter *or*
   margarine, melted, *divided*
1/2 pound cod, haddock *or* orange
   roughy fillets

In a shallow bowl, combine bread crumbs, pecans, wheat germ, thyme, garlic powder, onion powder, salt and pepper. Place half of the butter in another shallow dish. Dip fillet in butter, then coat with bread crumb mixture. Place in a greased 8-in. square baking dish. Bake at 425° for 13-15 minutes or until fish flakes easily with a fork. Drizzle with remaining butter. **Yield:** 2 servings.

Nutritional Analysis: One serving (prepared with 1 tablespoon butter) equals 189 calories, 7 g fat (4 g saturated fat), 64 mg cholesterol, 532 mg sodium, 8 g carbohydrate, 1 g fiber, 22 g protein. **Diabetic Exchanges:** 3 very lean meat, 1 fat, 1/2 starch.

CHEESE-TOPPED SWORDFISH

(Pictured below)

My husband, Alan, got this fantastic recipe from a college friend after his Alaskan fishing trip.
—Beth Campbell, Charlotte, North Carolina

1 swordfish *or* halibut steak (about 1
   inch thick)
1 tablespoon butter *or* margarine,
   melted
1/4 cup mayonnaise*
1/4 cup shredded Parmesan cheese

Place fish in a greased 1-qt. baking dish. Drizzle with butter. Combine mayonnaise and Parmesan cheese; spread over fish. Bake, uncovered, at 425° for 16-20 minutes or until fish flakes easily with a fork. **Yield:** 1 serving.

*Editor's Note: Reduced-fat or fat-free mayonnaise is not recommended for this recipe.

SEAFOOD A LA KING

(Pictured at right)

I like this recipe because it looks fancy yet it's very easy to make. It can be made with almost any mild cooked fish. We've enjoyed salmon, sole and leftover whitefish.
—Louise Graybiel, Toronto, Ontario

2 frozen puff pastry shells
2/3 cup water
3 tablespoons Homemade Cream-Style Soup Mix (page 75)
1/8 teaspoon celery salt
1 can (3 ounces) tuna, drained and flaked
1/3 cup shredded imitation crabmeat
1-1/2 teaspoons mayonnaise *or* salad dressing
1/4 cup sour cream

Bake pastry shells according to package directions. In a small saucepan, whisk together the water, soup mix and celery salt; bring to a boil, whisking frequently. Add the tuna, crab and mayonnaise; return to a boil. Reduce heat to low. Stir in sour cream; cook for 1-2 minutes or until heated through. Spoon tuna mixture into shells before serving. **Yield:** 2 servings.

Editor's Note: Reduced-fat or fat-free mayonnaise or sour cream may not be substituted for regular mayonnaise or sour cream in this recipe.

SPICY CATFISH WITH TOMATOES

I came up with this recipe after trying something similar at a catfish house in the mountains of northern Georgia. My husband and I both appreciate this healthful, flavor-packed dish.
—Marla Anthony, Loganville, Georgia

1 catfish fillet (about 1/2 pound)
1/4 teaspoon salt
1/8 teaspoon pepper
Dash to 1/8 teaspoon cayenne pepper
1 cup canned Mexican diced tomatoes with juice
1 to 2 green onions, thinly sliced
Hot cooked white *or* brown rice, optional

Sprinkle fish with salt, pepper and cayenne. In a nonstick skillet, cook fish over medium for about 3 minutes on each side or until lightly browned. Top with tomatoes and sprinkle with green onions. Bring to a boil. Reduce heat; simmer, uncovered, for about 2 minutes. Cover skillet and simmer 2-3 minutes longer or until liquid is reduced and fish flakes easily with a fork. Serve with rice if desired. **Yield:** 2 servings.

Nutritional Analysis: One serving (calculated without rice) equals 139 calories, 3 g fat (trace saturated fat), 52 mg cholesterol, 552 mg sodium, 7 g carbohydrate, 2 g fiber, 21 g protein. **Diabetic Exchanges:** 3 very lean meat, 1/2 starch.

TANGY LEMON CATFISH

(Pictured at right)

My husband turns up his nose at any fish dish I prepare except this one.
In fact, this one makes his eyes light up!
—Carol Mingia, Greensboro, North Carolina

2 tablespoons lemon juice
1 garlic clove, minced
1/4 teaspoon salt
Dash dried oregano
1/2 pound catfish *or* whitefish fillets
1/4 cup cornmeal
2 tablespoons all-purpose flour
1-1/2 teaspoons canola *or* vegetable oil
1-1/2 teaspoons butter *or* margarine
TARTAR SAUCE:
1/4 cup mayonnaise
1 tablespoon finely chopped dill pickle
2 teaspoons finely chopped onion
2 teaspoons minced fresh dill *or* 3/4 teaspoon dill weed

In a resealable plastic bag, combine the lemon juice, garlic, salt and oregano; add fillets. Seal bag and turn to coat; refrigerate for 30-60 minutes, turning several times.

Drain and discard marinade. In a shallow bowl, combine cornmeal and flour. Coat fillets with cornmeal mixture. In a skillet, cook fillets in oil and butter for 5 minutes on each side or until golden brown and fish flakes easily with a fork. Meanwhile, for tartar sauce, in a bowl, combine the mayonnaise, pickle, onion and dill. Serve with fish. **Yield:** 2 servings.

Nutritional Analysis: One serving (prepared with fat-free mayonnaise) equals 287 calories, 10 g fat (3 g saturated fat), 63 mg cholesterol, 717 mg sodium, 26 g carbohydrate, 2 g fiber, 22 g protein. **Diabetic Exchanges:** 3 lean meat, 1-1/2 starch.

SPICY CAJUN SHRIMP

(Pictured at right)

This dish is great for a meal or as an appetizer. It's so quick and easy.
—Scott Richardson, Bozeman, Montana

4-1/2 teaspoons salt
1-1/2 teaspoons onion powder
1-1/2 teaspoons garlic powder
1-1/2 teaspoons paprika
1-1/2 teaspoons cayenne pepper
3/4 teaspoon dried thyme
1/2 teaspoon pepper
1/4 teaspoon dried oregano
1/4 teaspoon white pepper
2 tablespoons olive *or* vegetable oil
1/2 pound uncooked large shrimp, peeled and deveined

In a bowl, combine the seasonings. In another bowl, combine oil and 1-1/2 teaspoons of seasoning mixture (save remaining mixture for another use). Add shrimp; toss until well coated. Thread shrimp onto two metal or soaked wooden skewers. Broil shrimp 4-6 in. from the heat for 2 minutes. Turn shrimp; baste with remaining oil mixture. Broil 1-2 minutes longer or until shrimp turn pink. **Yield:** 2 servings (about 1/4 cup seasoning mix).

Editor's Note: Store remaining Cajun seasoning mix in an airtight container at room temperature for up to 6 months.

TANGY LEMON CATFISH
SPICY CAJUN SHRIMP

FILLETS WITH GINGER SAUCE

This is a modification of a recipe I found in an old cookbook. It's quick, easy and delicious.
—C.W. Steve Stevenson, Newfoundland, Pennsylvania

1 tablespoon olive *or* vegetable oil
1 tablespoon butter *or* margarine
1 flounder *or* sole fillet (about 8 ounces)
2 garlic cloves, minced
1/4 teaspoon ground ginger *or* 1-1/2 teaspoons minced fresh gingerroot
4 teaspoons sugar
1 tablespoon cider vinegar
1 tablespoon soy sauce
1 tablespoon cornstarch
2/3 cup water
2 tablespoons thinly sliced chives
Thinly sliced green onion, optional

In a skillet, heat olive oil and butter until butter is melted. Fry fish over medium heat for 4 minutes on each side or until fish flakes easily with a fork. Remove to a plate and keep warm.

Add garlic and ginger to skillet; cook and stir for 1-2 minutes. Stir in the sugar, vinegar and soy sauce. Combine cornstarch and water until smooth. Stir into skillet. Bring to a boil; cook and stir for 1-2 minutes or until thickened. Pour over fish. Sprinkle with chives and onion if desired. **Yield:** 2 servings.

FRIED FISH NUGGETS

These cheesy bites are requested often on our annual fishing trip to Canada.
—Lynn Negaard, Litchfield, Minnesota

1 egg, lightly beaten
3 tablespoons dry bread crumbs
3 tablespoons shredded cheddar cheese
4-1/2 teaspoons finely chopped onion
1 garlic clove, minced
1/2 teaspoon minced fresh parsley
1/8 teaspoon dill weed
1/8 teaspoon pepper
2/3 cup flaked cooked fish

Oil for deep-fat frying
Tartar sauce, optional

In a bowl, combine the first eight ingredients; mix well. Stir in the fish. Roll mixture into 1-in. balls. Heat oil in a deep-fat fryer to 375°. Fry fish nuggets for 1-2 minutes or until golden brown; drain on paper towels. Serve with tartar sauce if desired. **Yield:** 2 servings.

SESAME SHRIMP

My husband tells me this quick recipe looks elegant and tastes awesome!
—Jennifer Breeden, Mobile, Alabama

2 tablespoons soy sauce
2 tablespoons sesame oil, *divided*
2 teaspoons lemon juice
1/4 teaspoon garlic powder
Dash lemon-pepper seasoning
1/2 pound medium shrimp, peeled and deveined
Hot cooked rice, optional
1 tablespoon sesame seeds, toasted

In a resealable plastic bag, combine the soy sauce, 1 tablespoon sesame oil, lemon juice, garlic powder and lemon-pepper; add shrimp. Seal bag and turn to coat; refrigerate for 30 minutes.

Drain and discard marinade. In a skillet, saute shrimp in remaining sesame oil until shrimp turn pink, about 3 minutes. Serve with rice if desired. Sprinkle with sesame seeds. **Yield:** 2 servings.

GRILLED ORANGE SALMON

I love nothing better than to cook for company. Folks say anything coming out of my kitchen made with a marinade or sauce is a winner.
—Cathy Comstock, Concord, Michigan

1/4 cup orange juice
1 tablespoon minced fresh tarragon
   or 1 teaspoon dried tarragon
1 tablespoon olive *or* vegetable oil
1-1/2 teaspoons minced chives
1/2 teaspoon grated orange peel
1/2 garlic clove, minced
1/4 teaspoon salt
1/8 teaspoon pepper
2 salmon fillets (8 ounces *each*)

In a bowl, combine the first eight ingredients; mix well. Set aside 2 tablespoons marinade for basting. Pour remaining marinade into a resealable plastic bag; add salmon. Seal bag and turn to coat; refrigerate for 2-3 hours.

Drain and discard marinade. Grill, uncovered, over medium heat or broil 6 in. from the heat for 12-15 minutes or until fish flakes easily with a fork. Baste occasionally with reserved marinade. **Yield:** 2 servings.

SWEET 'N' SOUR HALIBUT

(Pictured below)

My mother shared this recipe with me several years ago. I've found that even my friends who aren't fond of fish enjoy this particular dish and find themselves taking seconds.
—Kimberlie Sylvester, Litchfield Park, Arizona

4 to 6 tablespoons sugar
1 tablespoon cornstarch
1/3 cup white vinegar
1/4 cup water
1 to 2 teaspoons soy sauce
1/4 teaspoon hot pepper sauce
1 tablespoon all-purpose flour
1/4 teaspoon salt
1/8 to 1/4 teaspoon pepper
1/2 pound halibut *or* swordfish fillet,
   cut into 2-inch strips
2 tablespoons vegetable oil
1/2 cup green pepper chunks (1 inch)
1/2 cup sweet onion chunks (1 inch)
1/2 cup pineapple chunks, drained
Hot cooked rice

In a bowl, combine sugar and cornstarch. Stir in the vinegar, water, soy sauce and hot pepper sauce until smooth; set aside.

In a small resealable plastic bag, combine the flour, salt and pepper. Add fish and shake to coat. In a small skillet, saute fish in oil for 4-6 minutes or until fish flakes easily with a fork; remove and keep warm. In same skillet, saute green pepper and onion for 3 minutes or until crisp-tender. Add pineapple. Stir sauce and add to skillet. Bring to a boil; cook and stir for 2 minutes or until thickened. Return fish to skillet; heat through. Serve with rice. **Yield:** 2 servings.

CRAB SUPREME

(Pictured at right)

*I came across this recipe years ago in an old church cookbook. It's so good,
I've even served it for Christmas Eve dinner.*
—Cheryl Ryan, Timberville, Virginia

1 small onion, finely chopped
1/4 cup diced green pepper
3 tablespoons butter *or* margarine,
    divided
1 tablespoon all-purpose flour
3/4 cup milk
1/2 teaspoon chili powder
1/4 teaspoon salt
1/2 pound fresh *or* canned crabmeat,
    drained, flaked and cartilage
    removed *or* 1 cup imitation crab
    meat, flaked
1/3 cup mayonnaise*
Dash hot pepper sauce
2 tablespoons dry bread crumbs
Dash paprika

In a small saucepan, saute onion and green pepper in 2 tablespoons butter. Stir in flour until blended; gradually stir in the milk. Add chili powder and salt. Bring to a boil; cook and stir for 1 minute or until thickened. Remove from the heat; stir in the crab, mayonnaise and hot pepper sauce.

Transfer to a greased shallow 1-qt. baking dish. Melt the remaining butter and toss with bread crumbs. Sprinkle over crab mixture. Bake, uncovered, at 350° for 25-30 minutes or until heated through. Sprinkle with paprika. **Yield:** 2-3 servings.

*Editor's Note: Reduced-fat or fat-free mayonnaise is not recommended for this recipe.

SCALLOPS WITH RED PEPPER SAUCE

(Pictured at right)

*When scallop season is open here in Nova Scotia, I use scallops fresh from the ocean.
This dish is quick and easy yet tastes delicious.*
—Christine Hatt, Martins River, Nova Scotia

4 ounces uncooked linguine
1/4 pound fresh *or* frozen sea scallops,
    sliced into thin rounds
1/2 cup diced sweet red pepper
1 garlic clove, minced
1/8 to 1/4 teaspoon crushed red pepper
    flakes
1/8 teaspoon salt
1 tablespoon olive *or* canola oil
2 tablespoons grated Parmesan
    cheese

Cook linguine according to package directions. Meanwhile, in a skillet, saute the scallops, sweet red pepper, garlic, pepper flakes and salt in oil until scallops become firm and opaque. Remove from the heat. Drain pasta. Serve scallop mixture over linguini. Sprinkle with Parmesan. **Yield:** 2 servings.

Nutritional Analysis: One serving equals 348 calories, 10 g fat (2 g saturated fat), 23 mg cholesterol, 335 mg sodium, 46 g carbohydrate, 3 g fiber, 20 g protein. **Diabetic Exchanges:** 3 starch, 2 lean meat.

CRAB SUPREME
SCALLOPS WITH RED PEPPER SAUCE

Fish Italiano

(Pictured below)

I needed a new way to serve fish, so I came up with this recipe. My family thinks it's superb.
—Bonnie Martin, Wind Gap, Pennsylvania

2 tablespoons chopped onion
1 garlic clove, minced
1 tablespoon olive *or* canola oil
1 cup canned Italian diced tomatoes, drained
1/4 cup white wine *or* chicken broth
1/4 cup sliced ripe olives
1-1/2 teaspoons minced fresh parsley
1/4 teaspoon salt
1/2 pound cod, haddock *or* orange roughy fillets
Hot cooked rice

In a skillet, saute onion and garlic in oil until tender. Stir in the tomatoes, wine or broth, olives, parsley and salt. Bring to a boil. Cook, uncovered, for 5 minutes. Add fillets. Reduce heat; cover and simmer for 12-15 minutes or until fish flakes easily with a fork. Remove fish to serving plates; keep warm. Simmer sauce, uncovered, for about 4 minutes or until it reaches desired thickness. Serve fish and sauce with rice. **Yield:** 2 servings.

Bubbling Fish Bake

My mother-in-law gave me this great recipe soon after I got married.
—Soon-boon Lee, Agatha, Ontario

1/2 cup sliced fresh mushrooms
2 tablespoons chopped onion
1 tablespoon plus 1 teaspoon butter *or* margarine, *divided*
2/3 cup water
3 tablespoons Homemade Cream-Style Soup Mix (page 75)
1 cup cooked elbow macaroni
1 can (7-1/2 ounces) salmon, drained, bones and skin removed
1/2 cup shredded cheddar cheese, *divided*
1/4 cup milk
1 tablespoon dry bread crumbs

In a small saucepan, saute mushrooms and onion in 1 tablespoon butter until tender. Whisk in water and homemade cream-style soup mix; bring to a boil, whisking frequently. Add the macaroni, salmon, 6 tablespoons cheese and milk.

Pour into a greased 1-qt. baking dish. Melt remaining butter; stir in bread crumbs. Sprinkle over casserole. Top with remaining cheese. Bake, uncovered, at 350° for 24-28 minutes or until golden brown and bubbly. **Yield:** 2 servings.

BAKED SCALLOPS

This is a delicious alternative to traditional deep-fried scallops.
My family calls it their all-time favorite seafood dish.
—Amanda Sullivan, Fredericton, New Brunswick

1/4 cup all-purpose flour
1/4 teaspoon salt
Dash pepper
  1/2 pound fresh *or* frozen bay scallops,
     thawed
    2 tablespoons half-and-half cream
    2 teaspoons butter *or* margarine,
     melted
    1 tablespoon dry bread crumbs

In a small bowl, combine the flour, salt and pepper. Toss scallops in flour mixture, a few at a time, and place into two greased 6- to 8-oz. baking dishes. Top each with half the cream, butter and bread crumbs. Bake, uncovered, at 450° for 18-20 minutes or until scallops are opaque and topping is golden brown. **Yield:** 2 servings.

CREAMY SHRIMP TORTELLINI

(Pictured below)

My husband and I love entertaining. This recipe is easy yet elegant, allowing us to visit with company while serving a dish that's sure to impress. Here, it's sized for two.
—Susan Spigarelli, Cave Creek, Arizona

1/2 cup chopped green pepper
1/2 cup chopped sweet red pepper
1/2 cup sliced fresh mushrooms
1/4 cup chopped onion
  1 garlic clove, minced
1/4 cup butter *or* margarine
  1 tablespoon all-purpose flour
1/4 teaspoon garlic salt
Dash dried basil
Dash dried oregano
  1 cup half-and-half cream
1/4 cup white wine *or* chicken broth
  1 bay leaf
1-1/2 to 2 cups refrigerated three-cheese
    tortellini *or* tortellini of your choice
1/2 pound uncooked medium shrimp,
    peeled and deveined

In a skillet, saute the green pepper, red pepper, mushrooms, onion and garlic in butter until almost tender. Stir in the flour, garlic salt, basil and oregano until blended. Combine cream and wine; gradually stir into pepper mixture. Add bay leaf. Cook and stir until mixture comes to a boil. Reduce heat; simmer, uncovered, for about 8 minutes or until thickened, stirring several times.

Meanwhile, cook tortellini in boiling water for about 5 minutes or until tender; drain. Cook shrimp in boiling water for 3 minutes or until they turn pink; drain. Discard bay leaf. Stir tortellini and shrimp into sauce. **Yield:** 2 servings.

LEMON-BATTER FISH

A lot of fishing takes place here, and this is a delicious way to put this "catch" to good use.
—Jackie Hannahs, Muskegon, Michigan

1/2 cup all-purpose flour, *divided*
1/4 teaspoon baking powder
1/4 teaspoon salt
1/8 teaspoon sugar
  1 egg yolk
  3 tablespoons water
  5 tablespoons lemon juice, *divided*
3/4 pound perch, pike *or* walleye fillets,
    cut into serving-size pieces
Vegetable oil
Lemon wedges, optional

In a bowl, combine 6 tablespoons flour, baking powder, salt and sugar; set aside. In a small bowl, combine the egg yolk, water and 2 tablespoons lemon juice; add to the dry ingredients and mix until smooth. Dip fillets in remaining lemon juice and coat with remaining flour, then coat with the batter.

Heat 1 in. of oil in a skillet. Fry fish over medium-high heat for 2-3 minutes on each side or until fish flakes easily with a fork. Drain on paper towels. Serve with lemon if desired. **Yield:** 2 servings.

SALMON LOAF

(Pictured on page 210)

My children are a bit finicky when it comes to eating fish, but when I disguise it in this loaf, they think it's great. My husband, who isn't fussy, loves it, too.
—Heather Keens, Narvon, Pennsylvania

1 egg, lightly beaten
1 cup cubed day-old bread (1/2-inch
  cubes), crusts removed
1 can (7-1/2 ounces) salmon, drained,
  bones and skin removed
2 tablespoons milk
1 tablespoon butter *or* margarine,
  melted

2-1/4 teaspoons min ced fresh parsley
  1/2 teaspoon lemon juice

In a large bowl, combine all the ingredients. Press into a greased 5-3/4 in. x 3-in. x 2-in. loaf pan. Bake, uncovered, at 375° for 25-30 minutes or until lightly browned and set. **Yield:** 2 servings.

PEPPER AND SALSA COD

My husband created this recipe after sampling something similar at a local grocery store.
—Robyn Gallagher, Yorktown, Virginia

  1 teaspoon olive *or* canola oil
1/2 pound cod, haddock *or* orange
    roughy fillet
1/4 teaspoon salt
Dash pepper
  1/3 cup orange juice
  1/4 cup salsa
  1/3 cup julienned green pepper

1/3 cup julienned sweet red pepper
Hot cooked rice

Coat a 1-qt. baking dish with oil. Place fish in dish; sprinkle with salt and pepper. Pour orange juice over fish. Top with salsa and peppers. Cover and bake at 350° for 18-22 minutes or until peppers are tender and fish flakes easily with a fork. Serve with rice. **Yield:** 2 servings.

Linguine with Clam Sauce

(Pictured at right)

Green pepper gives a nice bite to this pasta dish. Add a loaf of crusty bread and a green salad, and dinner is served.
—Nicole Youngblood, Norcross, Georgia

4 ounces uncooked linguine
3/4 cup chopped green pepper
1 small onion, chopped
2 garlic cloves, minced
1 tablespoon olive *or* vegetable oil
1 tablespoon butter *or* margarine
1/4 to 1/3 cup clam juice
1/4 to 1/2 teaspoon dried basil
1/4 teaspoon salt
Dash pepper
Dash crushed red pepper flakes
1 can (6-1/2 ounces) minced clams, drained

Cook pasta according to package directions. In a small skillet, saute the green pepper, onion and garlic in oil and butter until almost tender. Stir in the clam juice, basil, salt, pepper and red pepper flakes. Bring to a boil. Reduce heat; simmer, uncovered, for 5-7 minutes. Stir in clams; heat through. Drain pasta; transfer to a bowl. Pour sauce over pasta; toss to coat. **Yield:** 2 servings.

Skillet Fish Dinner

This healthy recipe takes very little time. We enjoy it with a spinach salad and whole wheat rolls.
—Janet Cooper Claggett, Olney, Maryland

1 celery rib, chopped
1/2 cup chopped green pepper
1/2 cup chopped onion
1 teaspoon olive *or* canola oil
2 to 3 plum tomatoes, chopped
1/4 teaspoon salt
Dash pepper
1/2 pound cod, haddock *or* orange roughy fillets
1/4 to 1/2 teaspoon seafood seasoning
Hot cooked rice
Hot pepper sauce, optional

In a skillet, saute the celery, green pepper and onion in oil until almost tender. Add tomatoes; cook and stir for 1-2 minutes. Sprinkle with salt and pepper. Top with fish fillets and sprinkle with seafood seasoning. Reduce heat; cover and simmer for 6 minutes. Break fish into chunks. Cook about 3 minutes longer or until fish flakes easily with a fork. Serve over rice. Serve with hot pepper sauce if desired. **Yield:** 2 servings.

Nutritional Analysis: One serving (calculated without rice and hot pepper sauce) equals 156 calories, 3 g fat (1 g saturated fat), 49 mg cholesterol, 465 mg sodium, 10 g carbohydrate, 2 g fiber, 22 g protein. **Diabetic Exchanges:** 3 very lean meat, 1/2 starch.

SIDE DISHES

Rounding out your meals will be
a cinch when you turn
to this bountiful chapter.
You'll find more than 50 choices
for side dishes featuring
wholesome vegetables,
rice and pasta.

LEMONY BEETS (P. 254)

FRUITY ACORN SQUASH (P. 232)
LEMONY NEW POTATOES (P. 232)
GREEN BEAN BUNDLES (P. 233)

FRUITY ACORN SQUASH

(Pictured on page 231)

Here's an out-of-the-ordinary side dish that really perks up a fall menu.
—Barbara Meyers, Oregon, Ohio

1 small acorn squash (about 1-1/4 pounds)
1 medium tart apple, peeled and chopped
1/4 cup chopped celery
2 tablespoons raisins
1 tablespoon brown sugar
1/4 teaspoon pumpkin pie spice

Cut acorn squash in half lengthwise; remove and discard seeds and membranes. Place squash cut side down in a greased 11-in. x 7-in. x 2-in. microwave-safe dish. Microwave, uncovered, on high for 6-8 minutes or until almost tender.

Meanwhile, in a bowl, combine the apple, celery, raisins, brown sugar and pumpkin pie spice. Turn squash over; fill centers with apple mixture. Cover and microwave 4-5 minutes longer or until squash and apple filling are tender. Let stand for 3 minutes before serving. **Yield:** 2 servings.

Editor's Note: This recipe was tested in an 850-watt microwave.

LEMONY NEW POTATOES

(Pictured on page 231)

I can't recall where this recipe came from, but I know my family has enjoyed it for years.
—Cheryl Tichenor, Elgin, Illinois

4 to 6 small red potatoes
1 teaspoon butter *or* margarine
1-1/2 teaspoons lemon juice
1/4 teaspoon salt
1/4 teaspoon grated lemon peel
1 tablespoon sliced green onion (green part only)

Peel a strip from around each potato. Place potatoes in a small saucepan; cover with water. Bring to a boil. Reduce heat; cover and simmer for 15-20 minutes or until tender. Drain. Add the butter, lemon juice, salt and lemon peel; toss to coat. Sprinkle with green onion. **Yield:** 2 servings.

CHEESY POTATO BAKE

This dish not only tastes good, it looks good, too. I serve it with sliced beef or pork.
—Margie Spute, Pittsburgh, Pennsylvania

1 cup (4 ounces) shredded Swiss cheese
4-1/2 teaspoons butter *or* margarine, cubed
1/2 teaspoon salt
1/4 teaspoon pepper
1/8 teaspoon dried marjoram
3 medium potatoes, peeled and thinly sliced

In a bowl, combine the first five ingredients. In a greased 1-qt. baking dish, layer a fourth of the potatoes and a fourth of the cheese mixture. Repeat layers three times. Cover and bake at 400° for 60-75 minutes or until potatoes are tender. **Yield:** 2-3 servings.

COLORFUL BRAISED VEGETABLES

(Pictured at right)

The parsley, carrots and onion grown in my garden star in this succulent side dish. It's a perfect partner for pork.
—Lynn Fripps, Aldergrove, British Columbia

   1/3 **cup chopped onion**
      1 **tablespoon butter** *or* **stick margarine**
      2 **cups coleslaw mix**
      1 **medium carrot, shredded**
      2 **tablespoons minced fresh parsley**
   1/4 **teaspoon salt**
   1/8 **teaspoon pepper**
   1/3 **cup water**

In a saucepan, saute onion in butter until tender. Stir in the coleslaw mix, carrot, parsley, salt and pepper. Add water. Bring to a boil. Reduce heat; cover and simmer for 3 minutes. Uncover; simmer 3 minutes longer or until tender. **Yield:** 2 servings.

   Nutritional Analysis: One serving (2/3 cup) equals 99 calories, 6 g fat (4 g saturated fat), 16 mg cholesterol, 391 mg sodium, 11 g carbohydrate, 3 g fiber, 2 g protein. **Diabetic Exchanges:** 2 vegetable, 1 fat.

GREEN BEAN BUNDLES

(Pictured on page 231)

I carry this dish to all the potluck dinners I attend because it's always a hit. I take extra recipe cards because everyone wants a copy.
—Gretchen Copeland, Marble Falls, Texas

     20 **fresh green beans**
      2 **maple-flavored bacon strips, halved**
   1/4 **cup butter** *or* **margarine**
      1 **tablespoon brown sugar**
      2 **teaspoons orange juice concentrate**

Place beans in a saucepan and cover with water. Bring to a boil. Cook, uncovered, for 3 minutes; drain. Place bacon on a microwave-safe plate. Microwave on high for 1 to 1-1/2 minutes or until edges curl. Wrap 5 green beans with a half bacon strip; secure with a wooden toothpick. Repeat.

Place bundles in a greased 1-qt. baking dish. In a small saucepan, combine the butter, brown sugar and orange juice concentrate. Cook and stir over medium heat until butter is melted and sugar is dissolved. Pour over bundles. Bake, uncovered, at 350° for 10 minutes or until beans are crisp-tender, basting once. **Yield:** 2 servings.

   Editor's Note: This recipe was tested in an 850-watt microwave.

SKILLET RED POTATOES

(Pictured at right)

When I'm in a hurry to prepare potatoes, I reach for this recipe, which I created myself. The mix of seasonings is just right and makes a delicious, attractive side dish that never fails to satisfy.
—Lois Collier, Vineland, New Jersey

2 medium red potatoes, cooked and cut into 1/2-inch chunks
2 tablespoons vegetable oil
1/2 teaspoon dried parsley flakes
1/4 to 1/2 teaspoon garlic powder
1/4 to 1/2 teaspoon onion powder
1/4 to 1/2 teaspoon paprika

In a skillet, cook potatoes in oil over medium heat for 10 minutes, stirring occasionally. Stir in the remaining ingredients; cook and stir 5 minutes longer or until potatoes are browned and tender. **Yield:** 2 servings.

CREAM CHEESE CORN BAKE

This recipe gives corn a whole new look. Don't be surprised if your pickiest eater loves it!
—Tamma Foster, Blanchard, Oklahoma

1-3/4 cups frozen corn
4 ounces cream cheese, cubed
2 tablespoons butter *or* margarine, cubed
2 tablespoons canned chopped green chilies
1 small garlic clove, minced

1/8 teaspoon salt
Dash pepper

In a bowl, combine all the ingredients. Place in a greased 3-cup baking dish. Bake, uncovered, at 350° for 25-30 minutes or until bubbly around the edges. Stir before serving. **Yield:** 2 servings.

FETTUCCINE ALFREDO

My 9-year-old son earned his cooking merit badge in Cub Scouts by making this tasty dish.
—Moriah Earl, Trementon, Utah

4 ounces uncooked fettuccine
1/4 cup milk
1/4 cup butter *or* margarine
1 package (3 ounces) cream cheese, softened and cubed
1/3 cup grated Parmesan cheese
White pepper, optional

Cook pasta according to package directions. In a saucepan, heat milk and butter until butter is melted. Stir in cream cheese and heat until melted. Add Parmesan cheese and pepper if desired; cook and stir until blended and heated through. Drain pasta and transfer to a serving bowl. Pour sauce over fettuccine; toss to coat. **Yield:** 2 servings.

HERBED NOODLES

This simple dish is a complement to just about any kind of meat or fish.
We enjoy it often, no matter what the season.
—Edie Farm, Farmington, New Mexico

1-1/2 cups uncooked noodles
1 tablespoon butter *or* stick margarine
1/4 teaspoon dried thyme
1/4 teaspoon dried basil
1/4 teaspoon minced fresh parsley
1/4 teaspoon minced chives
Salt and pepper to taste, optional

In a saucepan, cook noodles according to package directions; drain and return to saucepan. Add the remaining ingredients; toss well to coat. **Yield:** 2 servings.

Nutritional Analysis: One 3/4-cup serving (prepared with yolk-free noodles and calculated without salt) equals 170 calories, 6 g fat (4 g saturated fat), 16 mg cholesterol, 76 mg sodium, 23 g carbohydrate, 2 g fiber, 5 g protein. **Diabetic Exchanges:** 1-1/2 starch, 1 fat.

IMPOSSIBLE GARDEN PIE

(Pictured below)

This pie featuring a popular biscuit/baking mix makes a nice lunch or dinner.
I serve it with a tossed or fruit salad and dessert.
—Rita Ann Preuss, Portage, Wisconsin

2/3 cup chopped fresh broccoli
3 tablespoons chopped onion
3 tablespoons chopped sweet red pepper
1/3 cup shredded cheddar cheese
1 egg
1/2 cup milk
1/4 cup biscuit/baking mix
1/4 teaspoon salt
1/8 teaspoon pepper

ed fat), 14 mg cholesterol, 728 mg sodium, 18 g carbohydrate, 1 g fiber, 12 g protein. **Diabetic Exchanges:** 1 starch, 1 lean meat, 1/2 fat.

Place 1 in. of water and broccoli in a small saucepan; bring to a boil. Reduce heat; cover and simmer for 3-4 minutes or until crisp-tender. Drain.

In a well greased 5-1/2-in. pie plate, combine the broccoli, onion and red pepper. Sprinkle with cheese. In a bowl, combine the egg, milk, biscuit mix, salt and pepper just until combined; pour over cheese. Bake at 400° for 18-22 minutes or until golden brown. **Yield:** 2 servings.

Nutritional Analysis: One serving (prepared with reduced-fat cheese, egg substitute, fat-free milk and reduced-fat biscuit/baking mix) equals 162 calories, 5 g fat (3 g saturat-

GLAZED CARROTS AND SNOW PEAS

(Pictured at right)

This simple but colorful side dish goes with just about any kind of meat or fish.
—Lisa Denham, South Bend, Indiana

    1 cup sliced carrots
    2 tablespoons water
    1 cup fresh *or* frozen snow peas,
      thawed
    1 green onion, sliced
1-1/2 teaspoons brown sugar
    1/4 teaspoon cornstarch
    1 tablespoon butter, melted
    1/8 teaspoon salt
Dash pepper

Place carrots and water in a microwave-safe dish. Cover and microwave on high for 4 minutes or until crisp-tender. Add snow peas and onion. Cover and microwave for 1 minute or until tender; drain. In a bowl, combine the brown sugar, cornstarch, butter, salt and pepper until smooth. Stir into vegetables. Microwave, uncovered, for 1 to 1-1/2 minutes or until bubbly around the edges, stirring once. **Yield:** 2 servings.

    Nutritional Analysis: One serving (2/3 cup) equals 124 calories, 6 g fat (4 g saturated fat), 16 mg cholesterol, 232 mg sodium, 16 g carbohydrate, 4 g fiber, 3 g protein. **Diabetic Exchanges:** 1 starch, 1 fat.

    Editor's Note: This recipe was tested in an 850-watt microwave.

COMPANY CAULIFLOWER

(Pictured at right)

This recipe came from a women's group benefit. We think it tastes great with beef.
—Mary Lou Holtgeerts, Brinnon, Washington

1-1/2 cups fresh cauliflowerets
    1/2 cup sliced celery
    1/4 cup chopped onion
    1 tablespoon butter *or* margarine
    1/2 teaspoon chicken bouillon granules
    1/4 cup white wine *or* chicken broth
    1/8 teaspoon pepper
Grated Parmesan cheese

Place 1 in. water in a small saucepan; add cauliflower. Bring to a boil. Reduce heat; cover and simmer for 5-8 minutes or until crisp-tender. Drain and set aside.

    In a small skillet, saute celery and onion in butter until tender. Add the cauliflower, bouillon, wine or broth and pepper. Bring to a boil. Reduce heat; simmer, uncovered, for 1 minute or until heated through. Sprinkle with Parmesan cheese. **Yield:** 2 servings.

BAKED APPLESAUCE

Once you try this applesauce, you won't want the store-bought variety anymore.
—Mary Mootz, Cincinnati, Ohio

    2 large tart apples, peeled and sliced
    3 tablespoons sugar
1/4 to 1/2 teaspoon ground cinnamon
    1/4 teaspoon vanilla extract

Place apples in a greased 1-qt. baking dish. In a small bowl, combine sugar, cinnamon and vanilla; mix well. Sprinkle over apples. Cover and bake at 350° for 40-45 minutes or until apples are tender. Uncover and mash with a fork. Serve warm. **Yield:** 2 servings.

GLAZED CARROTS AND SNOW PEAS
COMPANY CAULIFLOWER

HONEY-TOPPED SWEET POTATO

*I came up with this recipe after tasting something similar in a restaurant.
I decided I couldn't afford to go out every time I wanted one!*
—Kathy Fleming, Lisle, Illinois

1 small sweet potato
2 tablespoons butter *or* margarine, softened
4 teaspoons brown sugar
2 teaspoons honey
1/8 teaspoon ground cinnamon

Wrap potato in foil; bake at 400° for 45-50 minutes or until soft when gently squeezed. In a bowl, combine the butter, brown sugar, honey and cinnamon until smooth. Cut an "X" on top of potato. Using a fork, fluff the pulp. Add the butter mixture; fluff with potato until melted. **Yield:** 1 serving.

SPINACH AND RICE ALFREDO

*Even folks who don't like spinach enjoy this rich, cheesy rice and spinach combination.
We prefer it with pork chops, but it goes well with chicken or steak as well.*
—Diana Knight, Reno, Nevada

1 garlic clove, minced
2 tablespoons butter *or* margarine
1/2 cup whipping cream
1/4 cup grated Parmesan cheese
2 cups packed torn fresh spinach
1/8 teaspoon salt
1/8 teaspoon white pepper
1-1/2 cups hot cooked rice

In a small saucepan, saute garlic in butter. Stir in cream and Parmesan cheese; cook for 1 minute or until the cheese is melted. Add spinach, salt and white pepper. Cook for 1 minute or until spinach is wilted. Stir in rice. **Yield:** 2 servings.

SAUCY LIMA BEANS

*This side dish was always a staple at my grandmother's delicious dinners
when I was a child. It has continued to be a favorite for my entire family.*
—Jeanne Easterly, Easton, Pennsylvania

1 package (10 ounces) frozen lima beans
1/4 cup chopped onion
1 tablespoon butter *or* margarine
2/3 cup half-and-half cream
1-1/2 teaspoons minced fresh parsley
1/2 teaspoon dill weed
1/4 teaspoon salt
1/8 teaspoon pepper

In a small saucepan, cook lima beans according to package directions; drain, reserving 1 tablespoon cooking liquid. In a small skillet, saute onion in butter. Stir in the cream, parsley, dill, salt, pepper and reserved cooking liquid. Cook 1-2 minutes longer or until butter is melted. **Yield:** 2 servings.

CRUMB-COATED TOMATOES

(Pictured at right)

This recipe brings back memories of my grandmother. It was her favorite dish for family get-togethers. It's easy to make, takes little time to prepare and is especially tasty with garden-fresh tomatoes.
—Connie Simon, Cleveland, Ohio

1/2 cup crushed butter-flavored crackers (about 13)
1/2 teaspoon salt
1/4 teaspoon pepper
1 medium fresh tomato, cut into 1/4-inch slices
1 egg, beaten
2 tablespoons butter *or* margarine

In a shallow bowl, combine the cracker crumbs, salt and pepper. Dip tomato slices into egg, then into crumbs. In a skillet, cook tomatoes in butter for 2 minutes on each side or until golden brown. Serve immediately. **Yield:** 2 servings.

VEGETABLE LASAGNA

Our Test Kitchen created the recipe for this creamy herbed vegetable lasagna. It's also a great option for a vegetarian main dish.

4 lasagna noodles, cooked and drained
2 medium carrots, grated
1 small zucchini, grated
1 small sweet red pepper, diced
1/2 cup chopped fresh mushrooms
1 garlic clove, minced
2 tablespoons olive *or* vegetable oil
1/4 cup butter *or* margarine
1/4 cup all-purpose flour
2 cups milk
1/4 cup grated Parmesan cheese
2 tablespoons minced fresh basil *or* 2 teaspoons dried basil
1/4 teaspoon onion salt
1/4 teaspoon garlic powder
3/4 cup ricotta cheese
1 egg, lightly beaten
1 teaspoon Italian seasoning
2/3 cup shredded mozzarella cheese

Cut 3 noodles widthwise in half. Cut remaining noodle widthwise into thirds. In a skillet, saute the carrots, zucchini, red pepper, mushrooms and garlic in oil until tender; set aside. In a saucepan, melt butter. Stir in flour until smooth; gradually add the milk. Bring to a boil; cook and stir for 1-2 minutes or until thickened. Add the Parmesan cheese, basil, onion salt and garlic powder. In a bowl, combine the ricotta, egg, cheese and seasoning.

Spread 1/4 cup white sauce in an ungreased 7-in. x 5-in. x 1-1/2-in. (3 cup) baking dish. Cover bottom of dish with 2 large noodle pieces and one small piece. Layer with 1/3 cup mozzarella cheese, 1/2 cup white sauce, half of the vegetables and half of the ricotta cheese mixture. Repeat layers once, starting with the noodles. Top with remaining noodles and sauce.

Cover and bake at 350° for 30 minutes. Uncover; bake 10 minutes longer or until heated through. Let stand for 5 minutes before cutting. **Yield:** 2-3 servings.

TACO-TOPPED POTATO

(Pictured at right)

This quick-and-easy recipe fits in well with a busy schedule. Along with a garden salad, it makes a nice light meal for two. When we want something more filling, I serve it with a broiled steak.
—Linda Brausen, Janesville, Wisconsin

    1 large baking potato
1/4 pound ground beef
    1 tablespoon chopped onion
1/4 cup salsa
1/4 teaspoon Worcestershire sauce
    2 tablespoons shredded cheddar cheese
Sour cream

Scrub and pierce potato; place on a microwave-safe plate. Microwave, uncovered, on high for 4-5 minutes or until tender, turning once. Let stand while preparing topping. Crumble meat into a shallow microwave-safe bowl; add onion. Cover and microwave on high for 2 to 2-1/2 minutes or until meat is no longer pink, stirring once; drain. Stir in salsa and Worcestershire sauce. Cut potato in half lengthwise; fluff pulp with fork. Top each half with meat mixture, cheese and sour cream. **Yield:** 2 servings.

Editor's Note: This recipe was tested in an 850-watt microwave. To prepare in a conventional oven, bake potato at 400° for 40 minutes or until tender. Cook beef and onion in a skillet until meat is no longer pink; drain. Stir in salsa and Worcestershire sauce. Assemble as directed.

SAVORY STRING BEANS

I love making this dish when I can pick the beans right out of the garden and put them into the pot. The fresh taste is unbeatable.
—Ina Reed, Kingman, Arizona

    4 bacon strips
    2 cups fresh *or* frozen cut green beans (1-1/2-inch pieces)
    1 cup water
1/2 cup chopped onion
    2 tablespoons minced fresh basil *or* 2 teaspoons dried basil
    1 bay leaf
1/4 teaspoon dill seed
1/4 teaspoon garlic powder

1/8 to 1/4 teaspoon salt
1/8 teaspoon pepper

In a skillet, cook bacon over medium heat until crisp. Remove bacon to paper towels; crumble and set aside. Drain, reserving 1 tablespoon drippings. Add the beans, water, onion and seasonings to drippings; bring to a boil. Cook, uncovered, for 15-20 minutes or until beans are tender. Discard bay leaf. Stir in bacon. **Yield:** 2 servings.

CREAMED BROCCOLI AND CAULIFLOWER

You can change the cheese in this recipe to suit your tastes. I use whatever I have on hand. Cheddar adds a nice flavor.
—Cynthia Byars, Morocco, Indiana

3/4 cup fresh broccoli florets
3/4 cup fresh cauliflowerets
1/2 cup water
1 tablespoon butter *or* margarine
1-1/2 teaspoons all-purpose flour
1/2 cup milk
1 slice American cheese
1 tablespoon grated Parmesan cheese
Additional Parmesan cheese, optional

Place the first three ingredients in a small saucepan. Bring to a boil. Reduce heat; cover and simmer for 4-5 minutes or until vegetables are crisp-tender. Drain and keep warm. In another small saucepan, melt butter. Stir in flour. Gradually stir in milk. Bring to a boil; cook and stir for 1 minute or until thickened. Reduce heat. Add American and Parmesan cheeses; cook and stir until cheeses are melted. Pour over vegetables and serve with additional Parmesan cheese if desired. **Yield:** 2 servings.

BAKED APPLE-RAISIN STUFFING

(Pictured below)

After sampling a friend's turkey dressing one Thanksgiving, I was inspired to add apples, raisins and sage to my own stuffing recipe.
—Cindy Wirtanen, Hibbing, Minnesota

1/4 cup chopped onion
1 celery rib, chopped
2 tablespoons butter *or* margarine
1/2 cup cubed peeled tart apple
1/4 cup golden raisins
1/2 teaspoon chicken bouillon granules
1/4 teaspoon salt
1/4 teaspoon rubbed sage
1/4 teaspoon poultry seasoning
Dash to 1/8 teaspoon pepper
1/3 to 1/2 cup chicken broth
2 cups cubed day-old bread, crusts removed

In a skillet, saute onion and celery in butter until tender. Add the apple, raisins, bouillon, salt, sage, poultry seasoning and pepper. Cook and stir 1-2 minutes longer. Stir in broth. Pour over bread cubes; toss to coat.

Transfer to a greased 1-qt. baking dish. Cover and bake at 350° for 25 minutes. Uncover; bake 20-25 minutes longer or until top is golden brown. **Yield:** 2 servings.

ZUCCHINI PROVENCAL

(Pictured at right)

Here's a delicious side dish I turn to often. Vegetarians can make it into a main dish by simply adding vegetables to the pasta.
—Liane Davenport, Greensboro, North Carolina

1 small onion, thinly sliced
1 tablespoon olive *or* vegetable oil
1 medium zucchini, cubed
2 plum tomatoes, peeled, quartered and chopped
2 tablespoons chopped green pepper
1 garlic clove, minced
1/4 teaspoon salt
1/8 teaspoon pepper
1 tablespoon grated Parmesan cheese
2 teaspoons minced fresh parsley

In a small skillet, saute onion in oil until tender. Add the zucchini, tomatoes, green pepper, garlic, salt and pepper. Reduce heat; simmer, uncovered, for 8-10 minutes or until vegetables are tender. Sprinkle with Parmesan cheese and parsley. **Yield:** 2 servings.

TOMATO PASTA TOSS

(Pictured at right)

I came up with this end-of-summer pasta toss while trying to figure out how to use up tomatoes from my grandmother's garden. It's quick, easy and tasty.
—Rebecca Poole, Cortland, New York

1-1/2 cups uncooked bow tie pasta
1 medium tomato, chopped
1 garlic clove, minced
1 teaspoon olive *or* vegetable oil
Salt and pepper to taste
2 tablespoons shredded Parmesan cheese

Cook pasta according to package directions. In a bowl, combine the tomato, garlic, oil, salt and pepper. Drain pasta and add to tomato mixture. Sprinkle with Parmesan cheese; toss to coat. Serve immediately. **Yield:** 2 servings.

POPPY SEED NOODLES

This side dish is great because it goes with just about any meat main dish.
—Joan Smith, Ellensburg, Washington

1-1/2 cups uncooked egg noodles
1 teaspoon butter *or* stick margarine
1 green onion, chopped
1/2 teaspoon poppy seeds
1/8 teaspoon garlic salt
1/8 teaspoon pepper
1/3 cup sour cream

Cook noodles according to package directions; drain and return to pan. Add the butter, green onion, poppy seeds, garlic salt and pepper; stir until butter is melted. Stir in sour cream; serve immediately. **Yield:** 2 servings.

Nutritional Analysis: One 1-cup serving (prepared with yolk-free noodles and reduced-fat sour cream) equals 194 calories, 6 g fat (4 g saturated fat), 18 mg cholesterol, 124 mg sodium, 26 g carbohydrate, 2 g fiber, 7 g protein. **Diabetic Exchanges:** 1-1/2 starch, 1 lean meat, 1/2 fat.

ZUCCHINI PROVENCAL
TOMATO PASTA TOSS

GARLIC BROCCOLI

There's nothing like good down-home cooking, and this recipe proves the point.
—Domenick Palmer, Rohrersville, Maryland

1-1/2 cups fresh broccoli florets
1-1/2 teaspoons sesame oil
   1 teaspoon canola *or* vegetable oil
  1/8 teaspoon crushed red pepper flakes
   1 tablespoon soy sauce
   2 garlic cloves, minced
  3/4 teaspoon sugar
  3/4 teaspoon lemon juice

Place 1 in. of water in a saucepan; add broccoli. Bring to a boil. Reduce heat; cover and simmer for 5-8 minutes or until crisp-tender.

Meanwhile, in a small saucepan, heat the sesame oil, canola oil and red pepper flakes over medium heat for 2 minutes or until hot. Stir in the soy sauce, garlic, sugar and lemon juice. Cook and stir for 1-2 minutes or until sugar is dissolved. Remove from the heat.

Drain broccoli and transfer to a serving bowl. Pour garlic sauce over; toss to coat. Serve warm or chilled with a slotted spoon. **Yield:** 2 servings.

Nutritional Analysis: One 2/3-cup serving (prepared with reduced-sodium soy sauce) equals 92 calories, 6 g fat (1 g saturated fat), 0 cholesterol, 318 mg sodium, 8 g carbohydrate, 2 g fiber, 3 g protein. **Diabetic Exchanges:** 1 vegetable, 1 fat.

CHINESE-STYLE CABBAGE

This speedy cabbage dish picks up nice flavor from the onion and soy sauce.
—Edie Farm, Farmington, New Mexico

1-1/2 cups shredded Chinese *or* Napa
     cabbage
  1/2 cup sliced celery
  1/3 cup chopped onion
   1 tablespoon vegetable oil
  1/8 teaspoon salt

Dash pepper
1-1/2 teaspoons soy sauce

In a small skillet, saute the cabbage, celery and onion in oil for 4-5 minutes or until crisp-tender. Sprinkle with salt, pepper and soy sauce. **Yield:** 1-2 servings.

CHEDDAR SOUFFLE

My sweet mother-in-law gave me this recipe many years ago. It's a keeper.
—Dollypearle Martin, Douglastown, New Brunswick

1/2 cup milk
  5 teaspoons quick-cooking tapioca
1/4 teaspoon salt
1/3 cup shredded cheddar cheese
  2 eggs, *separated*

In a saucepan, combine the milk, tapioca and salt. Let stand for 5 minutes. Bring to a boil over medium heat, stirring constantly. Remove from the heat; stir in cheese until melted. In a small bowl, beat egg yolks; add to tapioca mixture. In a small mixing bowl, beat egg whites on high speed until stiff peaks form; fold into tapioca mixture.

Pour into a greased 1-qt. baking dish. Place the dish in a larger pan. Fill large pan with hot water halfway up the sides. Bake, uncovered, at 350° for 25-30 minutes or until a knife inserted near the center comes out clean. **Yield:** 2 servings.

Spicy Brussels Sprouts and Carrots

(Pictured at right)

A teacher friend, who knew I liked to try different dishes, shared this recipe with me. Guests always rave about the unique flavor of this casserole.
—Barbara Ferster, Richfield, Pennsylvania

3/4 cup fresh *or* frozen brussels sprouts, thawed and halved
3/4 cup sliced carrot
1/2 cup water
1/4 cup mayonnaise
2 teaspoons prepared horseradish
1 tablespoon finely chopped onion
1/8 teaspoon salt
Dash pepper
1/4 cup soft bread crumbs
1-1/2 teaspoons butter *or* margarine, melted
Minced fresh parsley

In a small saucepan, combine the first three ingredients. Bring to a boil. Cover and cook for 6-7 minutes or until crisp-tender; drain, reserving 1 tablespoon cooking liquid. In a bowl, combine the mayonnaise, horseradish, onion, salt, pepper and reserved

cooking liquid; mix well. Add the sprouts and carrot; toss to coat.

Transfer to a greased 2-cup baking dish. Combine bread crumbs and butter; sprinkle on top. Bake, uncovered, at 350° for 11-13 minutes or until lightly browned. Sprinkle with parsley. **Yield:** 2 servings.

Nutritional Analysis: One 3/4-cup serving (prepared with fat-free mayonnaise) equals 100 calories, 4 g fat (2 g saturated fat), 11 mg cholesterol, 486 mg sodium, 15 g carbohydrate, 4 g fiber, 2 g protein. **Diabetic Exchanges:** 1 starch, 1/2 fat.

Vegetable Cheese Bake

You can't go wrong with creamed veggies in a cheese sauce. What a delight!
—Barbara Lantz, Roseville, Ohio

2 cups frozen mixed vegetables
1/4 cup chopped onion
2 tablespoons butter *or* margarine
2 tablespoons all-purpose flour
1/4 teaspoon salt
1/8 teaspoon pepper
3/4 cup milk
1/3 cup shredded cheddar cheese

Place 1 in. of water in a saucepan; add vegetables. Bring to a boil. Reduce heat; cover and simmer for 5 minutes or until vegetables

are crisp-tender. Drain. In a saucepan, saute onion in butter until tender. Stir in the flour, salt and pepper until blended. Gradually whisk in milk. Bring to a boil; cook and stir for 1-2 minutes or until thickened. Remove from the heat; stir in cheese until cheese is melted. Stir in vegetables.

Transfer to a greased 2-1/2-cup baking dish. Bake, uncovered, at 350° for 20-25 minutes or until bubbly and vegetables are tender. Let stand for 3-5 minutes before serving. **Yield:** 2 servings.

OVEN-CRISPED POTATOES

(Pictured at left)

I often make this easy potato dish when I invite someone over for lunch. It goes well with salads or sandwiches.
—Precious Owens, Elizabethtown, Kentucky

2 medium potatoes, peeled and thinly sliced
3 tablespoons butter *or* margarine, melted
1 tablespoon finely chopped onion
1/8 teaspoon pepper

Arrange potatoes in an ungreased 1-1/2-qt. baking dish. Combine the butter, onion and pepper; pour over potatoes. Bake, uncovered, at 425° for 1 hour or until potatoes are tender. **Yield:** 2 servings.

GREEK RICE

My husband is of Greek descent, so I'm always interested in Greek recipes. This dish goes together easily and cooks quickly, plus it costs less than packaged rice mixes.
—Katie Parker, Salt Lake City, Utah

1/2 cup uncooked long grain rice
1 cup plus 2 tablespoons water
1-1/2 teaspoons butter *or* margarine
1 teaspoon chicken bouillon granules
1 teaspoon minced fresh mint *or* 1/4 teaspoon dried mint
1 teaspoon lemon juice
1/8 teaspoon garlic powder

In a small saucepan, combine all of the ingredients. Bring to a boil. Reduce heat; cover and simmer for 12-15 minutes or until rice is tender and liquid is absorbed. **Yield:** 2 servings.

CANDIED PARSNIPS

I clipped this recipe 20 years ago. It's a great substitute for candied sweet potatoes.
—Helen Barrett, Bend, Oregon

2 tablespoons butter *or* margarine
2 tablespoons brown sugar
3 tablespoons orange juice
2 teaspoons honey
1/8 teaspoon salt
2 medium parsnips, peeled and sliced
1/2 teaspoon grated orange peel

In a skillet, melt butter over medium heat. Stir in the brown sugar, orange juice, honey and salt until smooth. Add parsnips. Bring to a boil. Reduce heat; simmer, uncovered, for 12-15 minutes or until parsnips are tender. Add orange peel. **Yield:** 2 servings.

STIR-FRY SNAP BEANS

The recipe for this delicious dish came from a Chinese student who lived with us.
—Carol Hicks, Pensacola, Florida

1/4 **pound fresh green beans, trimmed**
  1 **teaspoon canola *or* vegetable oil**
1-1/2 **teaspoons soy sauce**
  3/4 **teaspoon sesame seeds**
  1/4 **teaspoon sesame oil, optional**
  1/8 **teaspoon garlic powder**
  1/8 **teaspoon onion powder**
Dash pepper

In a small skillet, saute beans in canola oil for 5 minutes. Add the soy sauce, sesame seeds, sesame oil if desired, garlic powder, onion powder and pepper. Cook and stir 1-2 minutes longer or until beans are tender and evenly coated with soy sauce mixture. Serve immediately. **Yield: 2 servings.**

MAPLE-GLAZED CARROTS

I like to make this side dish when I want to add some color to my meal.
—Sharon Bickett, Chester, South Carolina

1-1/2 **cups baby carrots *or* sliced carrots**
  1/2 **cup water**
   1 **tablespoon butter *or* margarine**
   2 **tablespoons maple syrup**
  1/4 **cup chopped pecans**

In a small saucepan, bring carrots and water to a boil. Reduce heat; cover and cook for 10 minutes or until tender. Drain. Stir in the butter, syrup and pecans until the butter is melted. **Yield: 2 servings.**

SPRING CORN

(Pictured at right)

Although this is known as Spring Corn, the taste reminds me of summer's sweet varieties of those golden kernels. My aunt shared the recipe in a family cookbook.
—Elizabeth Crowder, Germantown, Tennessee

1-1/2 **cups frozen yellow and white corn**
  2 **tablespoons chopped onion**
  1 **tablespoon butter *or* margarine**
  1/4 **teaspoon sugar**
  1/8 **teaspoon ground mustard**
  2 **teaspoons minced fresh parsley**

Cook corn according to package directions; drain and set aside. In a small skillet, saute onion in butter. Add the sugar, mustard, parsley and reserved corn. Cook 2-3 minutes longer or until heated through. **Yield: 1-2 servings.**

PINEAPPLE-STUFFED SWEET POTATOES

(Pictured at right)

This is an unusual way to served baked sweet potatoes, but if your family is like mine, they'll love it. It's a regular on our menu at Thanksgiving and Christmas.
—Joy McMillan, The Woodlands, Texas

2 small sweet potatoes
1/2 cup crushed pineapple
4-1/2 teaspoons brown sugar
1 tablespoon butter *or* margarine
1/8 teaspoon salt
1 tablespoon dried cranberries
2 tablespoons chopped pecans, *divided*

Wrap potatoes in foil and bake at 400° for 45-50 minutes or until soft when gently squeezed. Let stand until cool enough to handle. Cut a thin slice off the top of each potato and discard. Scoop out the pulp, leaving a thin shell.

In a bowl, mash the pulp; add the pineapple, brown sugar, butter and salt. Stir in cranberries and 1 tablespoon pecans. Spoon into potato shells. Top with the remaining pecans. Place on a baking sheet. Bake at 400° for 8-12 minutes or until heated through. **Yield:** 2 servings.

OREGANO CUBED POTATOES

(Pictured at right)

This tastes just like the roasted potatoes served at a neighborhood Greek restaurant.
—Carole Lantheir, Courtice, Ontario

2 medium uncooked potatoes, peeled and cubed
2 tablespoons lemon juice
5-1/2 teaspoons olive *or* vegetable oil
1 garlic clove, minced
1-1/2 teaspoons minced fresh oregano *or* 1/2 teaspoon dried oregano
1/2 teaspoon salt
1/8 teaspoon pepper

In a bowl, combine all of the ingredients. Transfer to a greased 1-qt. baking dish. Bake, uncovered, at 425° for 45-50 minutes or until tender, stirring twice. **Yield:** 2 servings.

GREEN RICE

Chopped fresh spinach produces pretty color in this simple but substantial side dish.
—Edie Farm, Farmington, New Mexico

3/4 cup boiling water
1/3 cup uncooked long grain rice
1/4 cup chopped fresh spinach
1-1/2 teaspoons butter *or* stick margarine, melted
1 teaspoon dried minced onion
1/4 teaspoon salt, optional

In a bowl, combine the water, rice, spinach, butter, onion and salt if desired; mix well. Transfer to a greased 2-cup baking dish. Cover and bake at 350° for 30-35 minutes or until liquid is absorbed and rice is tender. Stir before serving. **Yield:** 2 servings.

Nutritional Analysis: One 2/3-cup serving (calculated without salt) equals 149 calories, 3 g fat (2 g saturated fat), 8 mg cholesterol, 33 mg sodium, 27 g carbohydrate, trace fiber, 3 g protein. **Diabetic Exchanges:** 1-1/2 starch, 1 vegetable.

PINEAPPLE-STUFFED SWEET POTATOES
OREGANO CUBED POTATOES

VEGETABLE COUSCOUS

We love couscous, especially when we tire of potatoes, rice or pasta.
—Helen Holmes, Austin, Manitoba

1/4 cup chopped onion
1-1/2 teaspoons canola *or* vegetable oil
1/4 cup sliced fresh mushrooms
1/4 cup shredded carrot
1 garlic clove, minced
Dash ground ginger *or* 1/4 teaspoon
    minced fresh gingerroot
1/2 cup chicken broth
3/4 teaspoon soy sauce
3/4 teaspoon lemon juice
1/3 cup uncooked couscous

In a saucepan, saute onion in oil for 1 minute. Stir in the mushrooms, carrot, garlic and ginger. Cook and stir until vegetables are almost tender. Stir in the broth, soy sauce and lemon juice. Bring to a boil. Stir in couscous. Remove from the heat; cover and let stand for 5 minutes. Fluff with a fork. **Yield:** 2 servings.

Nutritional Analysis: One 3/4-cup serving (prepared with reduced-sodium chicken broth and reduced-sodium soy sauce) equals 160 calories, 4 g fat (trace saturated fat), 0 cholesterol, 240 mg sodium, 26 g carbohydrate, 2 g fiber, 5 g protein. **Diabetic Exchanges:** 2 vegetable, 1 starch, 1/2 fat.

OVEN-BAKED BEANS

This recipe starts with a can of beans, then I dress them up for a special homemade taste.
—Edie Farm, Farmington, New Mexico

2 bacon strips, diced
1 small onion, diced
2 tablespoons brown sugar
2 tablespoons ketchup
1 teaspoon Worcestershire sauce
1/2 teaspoon prepared mustard
1 can (15 ounces) pork and beans

In a skillet, cook bacon over medium heat until crisp. Using a slotted spoon, remove to paper towels to drain. Saute onion in drippings until tender; drain. Stir in the brown sugar, ketchup, Worcestershire sauce and mustard until blended. Stir in pork and beans; heat through.

Transfer to a greased 3-cup baking dish. Bake, uncovered, at 350° for 40-45 minutes or until bubbly and mixture reaches desired thickness. **Yield:** 2-3 servings.

HASH BROWN CASSEROLE

This is a scaled-down version of a wonderful casserole I traditionally serve at family get-togethers and holidays.
—Nancy Blankenship, Franklin, West Virginia

1 cup frozen southern-style hash
    brown potatoes, thawed
1/4 cup shredded cheddar cheese
2 tablespoons Homemade Cream-
    Style Soup Mix (page 75)
1 tablespoon water
1/4 cup sour cream
1 tablespoon finely chopped onion
2 teaspoons grated Parmesan cheese

In a bowl, combine the first two ingredients. In another bowl, whisk together the soup mix and water; mix well. Add the sour cream, butter and onion. Stir soup mixture into the potato mixture. Place in a greased 12-oz. baking dish; sprinkle with Parmesan cheese. Bake, uncovered, at 350° for 30-35 minutes or until bubbly around the edges. **Yield:** 1 serving.

SPANISH RICE

(Pictured at right)

This is my own recipe. It's easy, economical and good for you, but the best part is it tastes great and goes with everything from hamburgers to steaks.
—Amy Swenson, Champlin, Minnesota

2/3 cup uncooked instant rice
2/3 cup chicken broth
1/4 cup chopped green pepper
  2 tablespoons chopped celery
  2 tablespoons chopped onion
1/8 teaspoon minced garlic
  2 tablespoons water
1/2 cup chopped fresh tomato
1/4 teaspoon seasoned salt, optional
1/8 teaspoon chili powder
1/8 teaspoon pepper

Cook rice according to package directions, using broth instead of water; set aside. In a small skillet, saute the green pepper, celery, onion and garlic in water until tender. Add the tomato, seasoned salt if desired, chili powder, pepper and cooked rice. Cook 3-4 minutes or until heated through. **Yield:** 2 servings.

Nutritional Analysis: One 3/4-cup serving (prepared with reduced-sodium chicken broth and calculated without seasoned salt) equals 133 calories, trace fat (trace saturated fat), 0 cholesterol, 223 mg sodium, 28 g carbohydrate, 2 g fiber, 4 g protein. **Diabetic Exchange:** 2 starch.

SWISS SPINACH CASSEROLE

I'm a nurse who works 12-hour shifts, so I don't have much time to cook. This goes together quickly and can easily be shared with my husband.
—Mary Ellen Minter, North Ridgeville, Ohio

  1 egg
  3 tablespoons milk
  4 cups chopped fresh spinach
1/2 cup chopped water chestnuts
1/2 cup shredded Swiss cheese, *divided*
  1 tablespoon chopped pimientos
  1 tablespoon chopped green onion
1/4 to 1/2 teaspoon salt
1/8 teaspoon ground nutmeg, optional

In a bowl, whisk together the egg and milk. Stir in the spinach, water chestnuts, 1/4 cup Swiss cheese, pimientos, green onion, salt and nutmeg if desired; mix well. Transfer to a greased 1-qt. baking dish. Cover and bake at 350° for 25 minutes. Sprinkle with remaining cheese. Bake, uncovered, 5 minutes longer or until cheese is melted. **Yield:** 2 servings.

Nutritional Analysis: One 3/4-cup serving (prepared with fat-free milk, reduced-fat cheese and 1/4 teaspoon salt) equals 150 calories, 5 g fat (2 g saturated fat), 118 mg cholesterol, 478 mg sodium, 12 g carbohydrate, 5 g fiber, 16 g protein. **Diabetic Exchanges:** 1 lean meat, 1 vegetable, 1/2 reduced-fat milk.

PASTA PRIMAVERA

Since I eat very little meat, I'm always on the lookout for good vegetarian recipes.
I came up with this one after a lot of experimenting.
—Clara DelVitto, Venice, Florida

1/2 cup sliced onion
1/2 cup julienned green *or* sweet red pepper
 2 teaspoons olive *or* vegetable oil
1/2 cup sliced zucchini
1/2 cup sliced yellow summer squash
 2 medium fresh mushrooms, sliced
3/4 cup canned stewed tomatoes with liquid
1/4 to 1/2 teaspoon dried basil

 2 cups hot cooked pasta
Shredded Parmesan cheese, optional

In a skillet, saute onion and pepper in oil until crisp-tender. Add the zucchini, yellow squash and mushrooms; saute for 1 minute. Add tomatoes and basil. Bring to a boil; reduce heat. Cover and simmer for 8-10 minutes or until vegetables are tender. Toss with pasta; sprinkle with cheese if desired. **Yield:** 2 servings.

AU GRATIN POTATO CASSEROLE

I've been making this casserole for a few years now. It's rich, creamy and comforting.
—Laura Manning, Lilburn, Georgia

 2 cups sliced peeled potatoes (1/4-inch slices)
2/3 cup condensed cream of mushroom soup, undiluted

1/4 cup milk
1/4 cup shredded cheddar cheese
1/8 teaspoon pepper
 2 to 4 tablespoons French-fried onions

Place potatoes in a saucepan and cover with water. Bring to a boil. Reduce heat; cover and cook for 12 minutes or until potatoes are almost tender. Drain. In a bowl, combine soup and milk. Stir in cheese and pepper.

In a greased shallow 1-qt. baking dish, layer half of potatoes and half of soup mixture. Repeat layers. Bake, uncovered, at 350° for 20 minutes. Sprinkle with onions. Bake 5-10 minutes longer or until bubbly and onions are golden brown. **Yield:** 2 servings.

HONEY CASHEW GREEN BEANS

(Pictured on front cover)

Folks always comment how tasty this dish is with home-grown beans.
—Donna Gonda, North Canton, Ohio

1/2 pound fresh green beans, trimmed
 2 tablespoons coarsely chopped cashews
4-1/2 teaspoons butter *or* margarine
 1 tablespoon honey

Place beans in a steamer basket. Place in a saucepan over 1 in. of water; bring to a boil. Cover and steam for 8-10 minutes or until crisp-tender. Meanwhile, in a small skillet, saute cashews in butter for about 2 minutes or until golden brown. Stir in honey; heat through. Transfer beans to a serving bowl; toss to coat. Serve immediately. **Yield:** 2-3 servings.

VEGGIE PIZZA

(Pictured at right)

For a twist on the traditional vegetable side dish, our Test Kitchen home economists came up with this pizza for one. You can use vegetables to suit your tastes.

2 frozen bread dough rolls, thawed
3/4 cup Monterey Jack cheese, *divided*
1 small sweet red pepper, julienned
1 small carrot, grated
1 green onion, chopped

Let dough rise according to package directions. On a lightly floured surface, knead the 2 rolls together. Roll dough into a 7-1/2-inf. circle.

Place on a greased 7-1/2-in. pizza pan or baking sheet. Top with 1/2 cup Monterey Jack cheese and peppers. Sprinkle with carrot and green onion. Top with remaining cheese. Bake at 375° for 20 minutes or until crust is golden brown. **Yield:** 1 serving.

OLIVE-CHEESE ZUCCHINI BOATS

I was anxious the first time I tried this recipe, wondering if my family would like it. It was a big hit, though, and I was happy to find another idea for serving this prolific garden vegetable. I serve it most often with chicken. It adds so much color to the plate.
—Dorothy Pritchett, Wills Point, Texas

1 medium zucchini
1/4 cup water
1/8 teaspoon salt
1 tablespoon butter *or* margarine
1/4 cup soft bread crumbs
2 tablespoons chopped stuffed olives
2 tablespoons shredded cheddar cheese

Cut zucchini in half lengthwise; scoop out and reserve pulp, leaving 1/4-in. shells. Place zucchini shells, cut side down, in a skillet. Add water. Bring to a boil; reduce heat. Cover and simmer for 5-6 minutes or until tender; drain. Turn shells cut side up; sprinkle with salt. Chop zucchini pulp; saute in a small saucepan in butter for 5 minutes or until tender. Stir in bread crumbs and olives. Spoon into the zucchini shells; sprinkle with cheese. Cover and cook over medium heat (with no added water) for 5 minutes or until cheese is melted. **Yield:** 2 servings.

CARROTS AU GRATIN

(Pictured at right)

I'm an onion lover, so I sometimes double the amount called for in this recipe.
—Agnes Carone, East Windsor, Connecticut

3 medium carrots, sliced
2 tablespoons chopped onion
5 teaspoons butter *or* margarine,
   divided
1 tablespoon all-purpose flour
1/4 teaspoon salt
Dash pepper
1/2 cup milk
1/3 cup shredded cheddar cheese
1 tablespoon minced fresh parsley
2 tablespoons crushed cornflakes

Place 1 in. of water in a saucepan; add carrots. Bring to a boil. Reduce heat. Cover and simmer for 6-8 minutes or until carrots are almost tender. Meanwhile, in a small saucepan, saute onion in 3 teaspoons butter until tender. Stir in flour, salt and pepper until blended. Gradually whisk in milk. Bring to a boil; cook and stir 1-2 minutes or until thickened. Remove from heat; stir in cheese and parsley until cheese is melted. Drain carrots; add to sauce.

Transfer to a greased 2-cup baking dish. Melt remaining butter; stir in cornflakes. Sprinkle over carrots. Bake, uncovered, at 350° for 15-20 minutes or until bubbly and golden brown. **Yield:** 2 servings.

VEGETABLE RICE MEDLEY

(Pictured at right)

A relative brought this dish to a family get-together. I got the recipe on the spot.
—Shannon Wasielewski, Milwaukee, Wisconsin

3/4 cup chicken broth
1/4 cup water
1/3 cup chopped yellow summer
   squash
1/3 cup chopped zucchini
1/8 teaspoon salt
1/8 teaspoon dill weed
1 cup uncooked instant rice
1/4 cup chopped fresh tomato

3 tablespoons grated Parmesan
   cheese

In a saucepan, bring the broth, water, summer squash, zucchini, salt and dill weed to a boil. Stir in rice. Remove from the heat. Cover and let stand for 5 minutes. Stir in the tomato and Parmesan cheese. **Yield:** 2 servings.

LEMONY BEETS

(Pictured on page 230)

This is a sure-fire way to get people who say they don't like beets to enjoy them.
—Carol Hemker, Phenix City, Alabama

1 tablespoon chopped onion
1 teaspoon butter *or* margarine
1 can (15 ounces) whole beets,
   drained and quartered
1 tablespoon water
1 tablespoon lemon juice
1/8 teaspoon salt

1/8 teaspoon pepper
Dash sugar

In a small saucepan, saute onion in butter. Stir in the remaining ingredients. Cover and cook for 5 minutes or until heated through. **Yield:** 2 servings.

CARROTS AU GRATIN
VEGETABLE RICE MEDLEY

BREADS, ROLLS & MUFFINS

This chapter's appealing
assortment of breads, rolls
and muffins will rise to the
occasion and fill your kitchen
with wonderful aromas.
Choose from 15 delicious
tried-and-true favorites.

SOUR CREAM BANANA COFFEE CAKE (P. 265)

RAISIN MOLASSES YEAST BREAD (P. 258)
SWISS CHEESE MUSHROOM BREAD (P. 259)
CHERRY COFFEE CAKE (P. 258)

RAISIN MOLASSES YEAST BREAD

(Pictured on page 257)

My family loves this bread toasted and topped with butter or jam.
It's a different kind of raisin bread because it's not sweet.
—Mary West, Marstons Mills, Massachusetts

3/4 cup boiling water
1/2 cup quick-cooking oats
1/4 cup molasses
1/2 teaspoon butter *or* margarine, softened
3/4 teaspoon salt
1-1/8 teaspoons active dry yeast
1/4 cup warm water (110° to 115°)
2 to 2-1/2 cups all-purpose flour
1/2 cup raisins
1/4 cup chopped walnuts

In a large bowl, combine the water and oats; let stand for 30 minutes. Add the molasses, butter and salt. In a small bowl, dissolve yeast in warm water; add to oat mixture. Stir in enough flour to form a soft dough. Stir in raisins and nuts. Turn onto a lightly floured surface; knead until smooth and elastic, about 8 minutes. Place in a greased bowl, turning once to grease top. Cover and let rise in a warm place until doubled, about 45 minutes.

Punch dough down. Turn out onto a lightly floured surface; divide in half. Shape into two loaves. Place into two greased 5-3/4 x 3-in. x 2-in. loaf pans. Cover and let rise until doubled, about 30 minutes. Bake at 375° for 25-30 minutes or until golden brown. Remove from pans to a wire rack to cool. **Yield:** 2 loaves.

Editor's Note: The baked bread may be frozen for up to 3 months.

CHERRY COFFEE CAKE

(Pictured on page 257)

During the 21 years my husband was in the Navy, the wives got together
to exchange recipes. This one's from a California woman, and it's great.
All five of my daughters have added this to their recipe collections.
—Mary Zetterholm, Clinton, Mississippi

1/4 cup butter *or* margarine, softened
1/2 cup sugar
1 egg
1/2 teaspoon vanilla extract
1 cup all-purpose flour
1 teaspoon baking powder
1/4 cup milk
1/2 cup cherry 100% spreadable fruit
4 drops red food coloring, optional
TOPPING:
1/4 cup sugar
2 tablespoons all-purpose flour
1 tablespoon cold butter *or* margarine
1/4 cup chopped walnuts

In a small mixing bowl, cream butter and sugar until fluffy. Beat in egg and vanilla. Combine flour and baking powder; add to creamed mixture alternately with milk. Spread half of batter in a greased 8-in. square baking dish. Combine cherry spread and food coloring if desired; spread over batter. Top with remaining batter.

In a bowl, combine sugar and flour. Cut in butter until crumbly; add walnuts. Sprinkle over top. Bake at 350° for 40-45 minutes or until a toothpick inserted near the center comes out clean. Cool on a wire rack. **Yield:** 6-8 servings.

POPPY SEED LEMON LOAVES

(Pictured at right)

These light golden loaves have just a hint
of almond flavor mixed in with the lemon.
—Mrs. Richard Bridges, Absarokee, Montana

1-1/2 cups all-purpose flour
  2/3 cup sugar
    2 teaspoons poppy seeds
  1/2 teaspoon baking soda
  1/2 teaspoon lemon peel
  2/3 cup plain yogurt
  1/3 cup butter *or* margarine, melted
    1 egg, lightly beaten
    1 egg yolk, beaten
  3/4 teaspoon vanilla extract
  1/4 teaspoon almond extract

In a bowl, combine the flour, sugar, poppy seeds, baking soda and lemon peel. Combine the remaining ingredients; stir into dry ingredients just until moistened. Spoon into two greased 5-3/4-in. x 3-in. x 2-in. loaf pans. Bake at 350° for 35-40 minutes or until a toothpick inserted near the center comes out clean. Cool for 5 minutes before removing from pans to wire racks. **Yield:** 2 mini loaves.

Editor's Note: The baked bread may be frozen for up to 2 months.

SWISS CHEESE MUSHROOM BREAD

(Pictured on page 257)

This recipe doctors up store-bought bread into a wonderful, tasty mini loaf.
You can pull it apart into bite-size pieces.
—Bonnie Zentner, Falls City, Nebraska

  1 Vienna *or* Hoagie roll (6 to 8 inches)
  2 tablespoons butter *or* margarine, melted
3/4 teaspoon poppy seeds
3/4 teaspoon minced dried onion
1/2 teaspoon ground mustard
1/8 teaspoon seasoned salt
1/8 teaspoon lemon juice
1/2 cup sliced fresh mushrooms
  2 tablespoons finely shredded Swiss cheese

Cut bread diagonally into 1-in. slices to within 1/2 in. of bottom loaf. Repeat cuts in opposite direction. In a bowl, combine the butter, poppy seeds, onion, mustard, salt and lemon juice. Drizzle over cut bread and into cut slits. Place mushrooms and cheese in slits. Wrap bread in foil. Bake at 350° for 15-20 minutes or until warmed. **Yield:** 2 servings.

POPOVERS FOR TWO

(Pictured at right)

Simply served with butter and honey, these popovers are delicious anytime. They're also easy to make.
—Alpha Wilson, Roswell, New Mexico

1/2 cup milk
1 egg
1/2 cup all-purpose flour
1/4 teaspoon salt
1/4 teaspoon poultry seasoning, optional

Let milk and egg stand at room temperature for 30 minutes. Combine all ingredients in a mixing bowl; beat just until smooth. Pour into four greased 6-oz. custard cups; place on a baking sheet. Bake at 425° for 15 minutes. Reduce heat to 350° (do not open door). Bake 15-20 minutes longer or until popovers are deep golden brown (do not underbake). Serve warm. **Yield:** 4 popovers.

Nutritional Analysis: Two popovers (prepared with fat-free milk) equals 175 calories, 3 g fat (1 g saturated fat), 108 mg cholesterol, 358 mg sodium, 28 g carbohydrate, 1 g fiber, 9 g protein. **Diabetic Exchange:** 2 starch.

CARROT MUFFINS

When I need a great accompaniment for soup, stew or a casserole, I reach for this recipe. The carrot gives the muffins a nice texture.
—Judith Lippens, Escanaba, Michigan

1 cup all-purpose flour
1-1/4 teaspoons baking powder
1/2 teaspoon salt
1/3 cup milk
1 egg
2 tablespoons canola *or* vegetable oil
2 tablespoons sugar
1 medium carrot, sliced

In a bowl, combine the flour, baking powder and salt. In a blender or food processor, combine remaining ingredients; cover and process until carrots are finely chopped.

Pour carrot mixture over dry ingredients; stir just until combined.

Fill greased muffin cups three-fourths full. Bake at 425° for 15-18 minutes or until a toothpick comes out clean. Cool for 5 minutes before removing from pan to a wire rack. Serve warm. **Yield:** 6 muffins.

Nutritional Analysis: One muffin (prepared with fat-free milk) equals 157 calories, 6 g fat (1 g saturated fat), 36 mg cholesterol, 268 mg sodium, 22 g carbohydrate, 1 g fiber, 4 g protein. **Diabetic Exchanges:** 1-1/2 starch, 1 fat.

HAZELNUT CRUMB COFFEE CAKE

This was a plain brunch cake that I played around with until I came up with this recipe.
My husband says it tastes like a hot fudge sundae.
—Donna Cattanach, Redding, California

2 tablespoons all-purpose flour
1/4 cup packed brown sugar
2 tablespoons cold butter *or* margarine
1/4 cup finely chopped hazelnuts
BATTER:
1 square (1 ounce) semisweet chocolate
1 cup all-purpose flour
1/2 cup sugar
1/2 teaspoon baking soda
1/4 teaspoon salt
1/2 cup sour cream
1/4 cup butter *or* margarine, softened
1 egg, beaten

In a small bowl, combine the flour and sugar; cut in butter until crumbly. Stir in nuts; set aside. In a small saucepan, melt chocolate over low heat. Stir until smooth; cool. In a small mixing bowl, combine the flour, sugar, baking soda and salt. Add the sour cream, butter and egg; beat until well mixed. Remove 1 cup of batter; stir in chocolate.

Spread the remaining batter into a greased 8-in. square baking dish; spoon chocolate batter over the top. Cut through batters with a knife to swirl. Sprinkle with reserved nut topping. Bake at 350° for 35-40 minutes or until a toothpick inserted near the center comes out clean. Cool on a wire rack. **Yield:** 4 servings.

RED ONION FOCACCIA

(Pictured at right)

Our Test Kitchen suggests this delicious but quick way to make focaccia using frozen bread dough.

3 frozen bread dough rolls, thawed
1/2 teaspoon olive *or* canola oil
2 red onion slices, separated into rings
1/2 teaspoon Italian seasoning
2 tablespoons shredded Parmesan cheese
1 tablespoon butter *or* margarine, melted
1/8 teaspoon salt

On a lightly floured surface, knead dough together. Roll out into a 7-in. circle. Place on greased 7-1/2-in. pizza pan or baking sheet. Brush with oil. Top with onion slices. Sprinkle with Italian seasoning and Parmesan cheese. Bake at 350° for 28-32 minutes or until golden brown.

In a small bowl, combine the butter and garlic salt; brush over warm foccacia. Cool for 10 minutes on a wire rack before cutting. **Yield:** 2 servings.

Nutritional Analysis: One serving equals 244 calories, 11 g fat (5 g saturated fat), 19 mg cholesterol, 573 mg sodium, 31 g carbohydrate, 2 g fiber, 8 g protein. **Diabetic Exchanges:** 2 starch, 2 fat.

CHOCOLATE CHIP CINNAMON ROLLS

(Pictured at right)

I found this recipe in one of my mother's old cookbooks. My family doesn't like raisins, so they were thrilled to hear it contains chocolate chips instead.
—Cindy Padgett, Centralia, Washington

3/4 teaspoon active dry yeast
1 tablespoon warm water (110° to 115°)
1 cup plus 2 tablespoons all-purpose flour
2 tablespoons sugar, *divided*
1/4 teaspoon salt
3 tablespoons cold butter *or* margarine, *divided*
1/4 cup warm milk (110° to 115°)
1 egg yolk
2 tablespoons brown sugar
1/4 teaspoon ground cinnamon
1/3 cup miniature semisweet chocolate chips
GLAZE:
1/3 cup confectioners' sugar
1-1/2 teaspoons butter *or* margarine, softened
1/4 teaspoon vanilla extract
1-1/2 to 2 teaspoons hot water

In a small bowl, dissolve yeast in warm water. In a bowl, combine the flour, 1 tablespoon sugar and salt. Cut in 2 tablespoons of the butter until crumbly. Add the milk, egg yolk and yeast mixture; stir well. Cover with plastic wrap; refrigerate for at least 4 hours or overnight.

Turn dough onto a lightly floured surface. Roll out into a 10-in. x 6-in. rectangle. Melt remaining butter; brush butter to within 1/2 in. of edges. Combine the brown sugar, cinnamon and remaining sugar. Sprinkle over dough, then sprinkle with chocolate chips. Roll up jelly-roll style, starting with a short side; pinch seam to seal. Cut into 1-in. slices; place cut side down in a greased 8-in. square baking dish. Cover and let rise in a warm place until doubled, about 1-1/2 hours.

Bake at 375° for 15-18 minutes or until golden brown. In a bowl, combine the confectioners' sugar, butter, vanilla and enough milk to achieve drizzling consistency; drizzle over warm rolls. Serve warm. **Yield:** 6 rolls.

Editor's Note: Rolls may be frozen for up to 2 months. Reheat in the microwave before serving if desired.

STICKY BUNS

(Pictured at right)

This quick and easy way to make sticky buns starts with frozen bread dough. These are always a hit when I serve them for brunch.
—Becky Learmont, Waukegan, Illinois

6 frozen bread dough rolls
1/4 cup butter *or* margarine
1/3 cup sugar
1/3 cup chopped pecans
3 tablespoons brown sugar
3/4 teaspoon ground cinnamon

Thaw rolls for 10 minutes or until each roll can be cut into 3 pieces. In a large saucepan, melt butter. Add the sugar, pecans, brown sugar and cinnamon; simmer for 1 minute. Add rolls and stir to coat.

Transfer to a greased 6-cup fluted tube pan. Cover and refrigerate for at least 8 hours or overnight. Bake at 350° for 25-30 minutes or until golden brown. Immediately invert onto a serving plate. **Yield:** 2-4 servings.

ORANGE BREAKFAST ROLLS

A friend served these rolls at a gathering, and I just loved them. She shared the recipe
and I've been making them for family and friends ever since.
—Ann Burton, Rochester, Minnesota

6 frozen bread dough rolls, thawed
4 teaspoons butter *or* margarine,
    softened
2 tablespoons sugar
1 teaspoon orange juice
1/2 teaspoon grated orange peel
ORANGE GLAZE:
1/2 cup confectioners' sugar
1 tablespoon orange juice
1/8 teaspoon grated orange peel

On a lightly floured surface, roll each piece of dough into an 8-in. rope. Flatten to 1-1/2-in.-wide strip. Combine the butter, sugar, orange juice and peel; spread over dough. Roll up jelly-roll style, starting with a short side. Pinch ends to seal. Place in a greased 8-in. square baking dish. Cover and let stand in a warm place until doubled, about 45 minutes.

Bake at 350° for 18-22 minutes or until golden brown. Combine glaze ingredients and drizzle over warm rolls. **Yield:** 6 rolls.

Nutritional Analysis: One roll equals 178 calories, 4 g fat (2 g saturated fat), 7 mg cholesterol, 237 mg sodium, 32 g carbohydrate, 1 g fiber, 4 g protein. **Diabetic Exchanges:** 1 starch, 1 fruit, 1 fat.

Editor's Note: The baked rolls may be frozen for up to 3 months.

OLD-FASHIONED PLUM LOAVES

This moist quick bread has a sweet light glaze. The secret ingredient
that makes it so easy and convenient is baby food.
—Laura Andrew, Newaygo, Michigan

1 cup all-purpose flour
3/4 cup sugar
1/2 teaspoon baking soda
1/2 teaspoon ground cinnamon
1/4 teaspoon salt
1/8 teaspoon ground nutmeg
1 egg, lightly beaten
1 egg yolk, lightly beaten
1 jar (4 ounces) plum baby food
1/4 cup vegetable oil
1/2 cup chopped pecans *or* walnuts
1/4 cup sugar
2 tablespoons buttermilk
2 tablespoons butter *or* margarine
1/4 teaspoon vanilla extract

In a large bowl, combine the first six ingredients. Stir in the egg, egg yolk, baby food and oil just until moistened. Fold in nuts. Spoon into two greased 5-3/4-in. x 3-in. x 2-in. loaf pans. Bake at 325° for 35-40 minutes or until a toothpick inserted near the center comes out clean.

Meanwhile, in a saucepan, combine the sugar, buttermilk and butter; bring to a boil. Cook and stir for 3 minutes. Remove from the heat; stir in vanilla. Poke holes with a fork in top of loaves. Pour topping over loaves. Cool in pans for 10 minutes or until topping is absorbed. Remove from pans to wire racks to cool. **Yield:** 2 mini loaves.

Editor's Note: The baked bread may be frozen for up to 2 months.

SOUR CREAM BANANA COFFEE CAKE

(Pictured on page 256)

This is the best way I've found to use up ripe bananas.
—Julee Wallberg, Carson City, Nevada

1/4 cup butter *or* margarine, softened
8 tablespoons sugar, *divided*
1 egg
1/4 teaspoon vanilla extract
1/2 cup mashed ripe banana
1/4 cup sour cream
1 cup all-purpose flour
1/2 teaspoon baking powder
1/2 teaspoon baking soda
1/8 teaspoon salt
1/4 cup chopped walnuts
1/4 teaspoon ground cinnamon

In a small mixing bowl, cream butter and 6 tablespoons sugar. Beat in egg and vanilla. Stir in banana and sour cream. Combine the flour, baking powder, baking soda and salt; gradually add to creamed mixture. Combine the walnuts, cinnamon and remaining sugar.

Spoon half of batter into a greased 6-cup fluted tube pan. Sprinkle with nut mixture; top with remaining batter. Bake at 350° for 32-38 minutes or until a toothpick inserted near the center comes out clean. Cool for 10 minutes before removing from pan to a wire rack. **Yield:** 1 loaf.

GARLIC CHEESE BREAD

I serve this recipe often because my family likes it with just about anything!
—Susan Spence, Lawrenceville, Virginia

3 tablespoons mayonnaise
1 tablespoon grated Parmesan cheese
1 garlic clove, minced
Dash paprika
2 tablespoons finely shredded cheddar cheese
2 French bread rolls, halved lengthwise

In a small bowl, combine the mayonnaise, Parmesan cheese, garlic and paprika; stir in cheddar cheese. Place rolls cut side up on a baking sheet; broil 6 in. from the heat for 1 minute or until lightly browned. Spread with cheese mixture. Broil 1 minute longer or until bubbly and lightly browned. **Yield:** 2 servings.

CHOCOLATE CHIP SCONES

These scones are delicious warm, served with butter, when the chips are melted and gooey.
—Diane LaFurno, College Point, New York

1 cup all-purpose flour
3 tablespoons sugar
1-1/2 teaspoons baking powder
Dash salt
2 tablespoons cold butter *or* margarine
1 egg
3 tablespoons whipping cream
1/2 cup miniature semisweet chocolate chips

In a bowl, combine the flour, sugar, baking powder and salt. Cut in butter until the mixture resembles coarse crumbs. In a small bowl, combine egg and cream; stir into dry ingredients just until moistened. Fold in chocolate chips. Turn onto a floured surface; knead gently 6-8 times. Pat into a 6-in. circle. Cut dough into 6 wedges. Separate wedges and place on an ungreased baking sheet. Bake at 350° for 18-20 minutes or until golden brown. Serve warm. **Yield:** 6 scones.

COOKIES & BARS

The only thing better than
the wonderful aroma of
fresh-baked cookies is the taste.
This chapter features 15
recipes for delicious bars
and cookies flavored with fruit,
nuts, chocolate and more.

CRACKLE COOKIES (P. 272)

ORANGE COCONUT COOKIES (P. 268)
CAPPUCCINO TRUFFLE BROWNIES (P. 274)
HAWAIIAN WEDDING CAKE COOKIES (P. 268)

ORANGE COCONUT COOKIES

(Pictured on page 267)

The sunny taste of these crisp cookies always makes me smile—no matter what the weather.
—Evelyn Acheson, Nanaimo, British Columbia

1/2 cup butter (no substitutes),
    softened
1/2 cup confectioners' sugar
1/2 teaspoon grated orange peel
1/2 cup all-purpose flour
1/4 cup cornstarch
  1 cup flaked coconut

In a small mixing bowl, cream butter and sugar. Stir in orange peel. Combine flour and cornstarch; add to creamed mixture. Shape into 1-in. balls, then roll in coconut. Place 2 in. apart on ungreased baking sheets. Bake at 350° for 14-16 minutes or until coconut is lightly browned and cookies are set. Remove to wire racks to cool. **Yield:** 15 cookies.
    Editor's Note: This recipe uses no eggs.

HAWAIIAN WEDDING CAKE COOKIES

(Pictured on page 267)

Macadamia nuts and pineapple help give these sweet treats their tropical name.
—Darlene Markel, Sublimity, Oregon

1/2 cup butter (no substitutes),
    softened
1/4 cup confectioners' sugar
1/2 teaspoon vanilla extract
  1 cup all-purpose flour
1/2 cup finely chopped macadamia
    nuts, toasted
  2 tablespoons finely chopped candied
    pineapple
Additional confectioners' sugar

In a small mixing bowl, cream the butter, confectioners' sugar and vanilla. Beat in flour. Stir in nuts and pineapple. Shape into 1-in. balls. Place 2 in. apart on ungreased baking sheets. Bake at 350° for 14-16 minutes or until lightly browned. Remove to wire racks to cool completely. Roll cooled cookies in additional confectioners' sugar. **Yield:** about 1-1/2 dozen.
    Editor's Note: This recipe uses no eggs.

BLONDE BROWNIE NUT SQUARES

These moist, rich bars get a small but satisfying crunch from pecans.
—Edie Farm, Farmington, New Mexico

1/4 cup butter (no substitutes), melted
  1 cup packed brown sugar
  1 egg
  1 teaspoon vanilla extract
3/4 cup all-purpose flour
  1 teaspoon baking powder
1/4 teaspoon salt
1/2 cup finely chopped pecans

In a mixing bowl, beat the butter, sugar, egg and vanilla. Combine the flour, baking powder and salt; gradually add to sugar mixture and mix well. Fold in nuts. Spread in a greased 8-in. baking dish. Bake at 350° for 15-20 minutes or until toothpick comes out clean. Cool on a wire rack. Cut into squares. **Yield:** 16 squares.

ALMOND RASPBERRY DIAMONDS

(Pictured at right)

In case there was any doubt, here's proof that diamonds are a girl's best friend. Yum!
—Louise Brown, Warren, Michigan

1/2 cup butter (no substitutes)
1 package (10 to 12 ounces) vanilla *or* white chips, *divided*
2 eggs
1/2 cup sugar
1/2 to 1 teaspoon almond extract
1 cup all-purpose flour
1/2 teaspoon salt
1/2 cup seedless raspberry jam *or* preserves, warmed
1/2 cup sliced almonds, toasted

In a saucepan, melt butter over low heat. Remove from heat and add 1 cup chips. Let stand, without stirring, to soften chips. In a mixing bowl, beat eggs until foamy. Add sugar; beat until thickened and lemon-colored. Beat in chip mixture and extract. Combine flour and salt; gradually add to creamed mixture.

Spread half of the batter into a greased 9-in. square baking pan. Bake at 325° for 17-20 minutes or until golden brown. Spread raspberry jam over warm crust. Stir remaining vanilla chips into the remaining batter. Spoon over raspberry layer. Sprinkle with almonds. Bake for 20-23 minutes or until toothpick comes out clean. Cool on a wire rack before cutting. **Yield:** 16 bars.

DOUBLE CHOCOLATE BROWNIES

I've made these tempting brownies many times and also given them as gifts.
—Isolde Meadows, Santa Rosa, California

1 square (1 ounce) unsweetened chocolate
2 tablespoons butter (no substitutes)
1 egg
1/2 cup sugar
1/2 teaspoon vanilla extract
1/3 cup all-purpose flour
1/4 teaspoon baking powder
1/8 teaspoon salt
1/4 cup chopped pecans
1/4 cup semisweet chocolate chips

In a small heavy saucepan or microwave-safe dish, melt unsweetened chocolate and butter; stir until smooth. In a small mixing bowl, combine egg and sugar. Stir in the chocolate mixture and vanilla. Combine the flour, baking powder and salt; gradually add to chocolate mixture and mix well. Stir in nuts.

Spread into a greased 8-in. x 4-in. x 2-in. loaf pan. Sprinkle with chocolate chips. Bake at 350° for 15-18 minutes or until toothpick comes out clean. Cool on a wire rack. **Yield:** 8 brownies.

CHOCOLATE CHIP ICEBOX COOKIES

(Pictured at right)

Putting chocolate chips in these refrigerator cookies make them deliciously different. This treat is always welcome at my house.
—Betty Holzinger, West Olive, Michigan

3 tablespoons butter (no substitutes), softened
2 tablespoons shortening
1/4 cup sugar
1/4 cup packed brown sugar
1 egg yolk
1/2 teaspoon vanilla extract
2/3 cup all-purpose flour
1/4 teaspoon baking soda
1/4 teaspoon salt
1/4 cup miniature semisweet chocolate chips
1/4 cup finely chopped pecans

In a small mixing bowl, cream the butter, shortening and sugars. Beat in egg yolk and vanilla; mix well. Combine the flour, baking soda and salt; gradually add to creamed mixture and mix well. Stir in chips and pecans. Shape into a 9-in. roll; wrap in plastic wrap. Refrigerate overnight.

Unwrap and cut into 1/4-in. slices. Place 2 in. apart on ungreased baking sheets. Bake at 375° for 8-10 minutes or until edges are golden brown. Cool for 2 minutes before removing to wire racks to cool completely. **Yield:** 20 cookies.

FROSTED BROWN SUGAR COOKIES

(Pictured at right)

These old-fashioned, cake-like cookies are sweet and buttery. They pair equally well with a glass of cold milk or a cup of hot coffee.
—Loretta Patterson, Mentor, Ohio

1/2 cup butter (no substitutes), softened
1 cup packed brown sugar
1 egg
1/2 cup sour cream
1-3/4 cups all-purpose flour
1/2 teaspoon baking soda
1/4 teaspoon salt
BROWN SUGAR FROSTING:
1/4 cup butter
1/2 cup packed brown sugar
2 tablespoons milk
1 cup confectioners' sugar

In a small mixing bowl, cream butter and brown sugar. Beat in egg and sour cream; mix well. Combine the flour, baking soda and salt; gradually add to creamed mixture and mix well. Drop by tablespoonfuls 2 in. apart onto greased baking sheets. Bake at 375° for 9-11 minutes or until golden brown. Remove to wire racks to cool.

For frosting, in a small saucepan, melt butter over low heat; add brown sugar. Cook and stir for 2 minutes. Gradually add the milk. Bring to a boil, stirring constantly. Remove from the heat. Stir in confectioners' sugar. Cool for 20-30 minutes. Frost cooled cookies. **Yield:** about 2 dozen.

CHOCOLATE CHIP ICEBOX COOKIES
FROSTED BROWN SUGAR COOKIES

CRACKLE COOKIES

(Pictured on page 266)

My granddaughter thinks the crackles in these cookies are a mistake, but she loves to eat them.
—Ruth Cain, Hartselle, Alabama

1/2 cup sugar
1 egg
2 tablespoons vegetable oil
1 square (1 ounce) unsweetened chocolate, melted and cooled
1/2 teaspoon vanilla extract
1/2 cup all-purpose flour
1/2 to 3/4 teaspoon baking powder
1/8 teaspoon salt
Confectioners' sugar

In a mixing bowl, combine the sugar, egg, oil, chocolate and vanilla; mix well. Combine the flour, baking powder and salt; gradually add to creamed mixture and mix well. Refrigerate dough for at least 2 hours.

With sugared hands, shape dough into 1-in. balls. Roll in confectioners' sugar. Place 2 in. apart on greased baking sheets. Bake at 350° for 10-12 minutes or until set. Remove to a wire rack to cool. **Yield:** about 1-1/2 dozen.

APRICOT CHEESECAKE BARS

(Pictured at right)

With such an appealing blend of flavors, these bars never seem to last long!
—June Moffett, Santa Ana, California

1/3 cup butter (no substitutes), softened
1/3 cup packed brown sugar
1 cup all-purpose flour
1/2 cup chopped walnuts
1 package (8 ounces) cream cheese, softened
1/4 cup sugar
1 egg
2 tablespoons milk
1 tablespoon lemon juice
1 teaspoon vanilla extract
3/4 cup apricot jam, warmed

In a small mixing bowl, cream butter and brown sugar. Stir in flour and nuts; mix well. Set aside 1 cup for topping. Press remaining mixture into a greased 8-in. square baking dish. Bake at 350° for 15-20 minutes or until lightly browned. Cool on a wire rack.

In another small mixing bowl, beat cream cheese and sugar. Add the egg, milk, lemon juice and vanilla; mix well. Spread the jam over cooled crust. Pour cream cheese mixture over jam. Sprinkle with reserved topping mixture; press down lightly. Bake at 350° for 17-20 minutes or until center is almost set. Cool on a wire rack. Store in the refrigerator. **Yield:** 16 bars.

CHOCOLATE-DRIZZLED SHORTBREAD

(Pictured at right)

The home economists in our Test Kitchen came up with this recipe for cookies that are as pretty as they are tasty.

1/2 **cup butter (no substitutes), softened**
1/2 **cup confectioners' sugar**
  1 **teaspoon vanilla extract**
  1 **cup all-purpose flour**
1/4 **teaspoon salt**
1/4 **cup semisweet chocolate chips**
1/4 **teaspoon shortening**

In a small mixing bowl, cream butter and confectioners' sugar. Beat in vanilla; mix well. Combine flour and salt; gradually add to creamed mixture and mix well. Shape into 1-in. balls. Place 2 in. apart on ungreased baking sheets; flatten slightly with a glass dipped in sugar. Bake at 350° for 10-12 minutes or until edges are golden brown. Immediately remove to wire racks to cool.

For drizzle, in a heavy saucepan or microwave, melt the chips and shortening; stir until smooth. Remove from the heat. Drizzle over cookies. **Yield:** 18 cookies.

LEMON CRISSCROSS COOKIES

This is a favorite cookie that my sister used to bake when we were kids.
—Mrs. John Ottosen, Fairfield, Washington

1/2 **cup butter-flavored shortening**
1/2 **cup plus 3 tablespoons sugar,** *divided*
1/3 **cup packed brown sugar**
  1 **egg**
1/2 **teaspoon grated lemon peel**
1/2 **teaspoon lemon extract**
1/4 **teaspoon vanilla extract**
1-1/3 **cups all-purpose flour**
1/2 **teaspoon baking soda**
1/2 **teaspoon cream of tartar**
1/4 **teaspoon salt**

In a mixing bowl, cream the shortening, 1/2 cup sugar and brown sugar. Beat in the egg, lemon peel and extracts; mix well. Combine the flour, baking soda, cream of tartar and salt; gradually add to creamed mixture and mix well. Refrigerate dough for 1-2 hours or until firm.

Shape dough into 1-in. balls; roll in remaining sugar. Place 2 in. apart on greased baking sheets. Flatten with a fork, forming a crisscross pattern. Bake at 375° for 8-10 minutes or until lightly browned. Remove to wire racks to cool. **Yield:** about 2 dozen.

Editor's Note: To freeze cookie dough, shape cookies on a waxed paper-lined baking sheet. Freeze until firm. Remove from baking sheet; place in a resealable plastic freezer bag. Dough may be frozen for up to 2 months. To bake, place 2 in. apart on greased baking sheets. Bake at 375° for 7-10 minutes or until lightly browned.

CAPPUCCINO TRUFFLE BROWNIES

(Pictured on page 267)

I created these brownies by combining my favorite beverage and chocolate together for a cooking contest. I was so pleased with the results, I knew the recipe was a keeper.
—Karen Yetter, Oceanside, California

    2 squares (1 ounce *each*) semisweet
      chocolate
  1/2 cup butter (no substitutes)
    2 eggs
  3/4 cup packed brown sugar
    1 teaspoon vanilla extract
  3/4 cup all-purpose flour
  1/2 teaspoon baking powder
  1/2 teaspoon ground cinnamon
FILLING:
    1 package (8 ounces) cream cheese,
      softened
  1/4 cup confectioners' sugar
    1 teaspoon instant coffee granules
    1 tablespoon hot water
    1 cup (6 ounces) semisweet chocolate
      chips
  1/2 teaspoon butter
GLAZE:
  1/2 cup semisweet chocolate chips
    1 teaspoon shortening
Whole blanched almonds

In a heavy saucepan or microwave, melt chocolate and butter; stir until smooth. Cool slightly. In a small mixing bowl, beat eggs, brown sugar and vanilla. Beat in chocolate mixture. Combine the flour, baking powder and cinnamon; stir into chocolate mixture. Spread into a greased 9-in. square baking pan. Bake at 350° for 20-22 minutes or until toothpick comes out clean. Cool on a wire rack.

For filling, in a mixing bowl, beat the cream cheese and confectioners' sugar until light and fluffy. Dissolve coffee in water. Stir into cream cheese mixture. In a heavy saucepan or microwave, melt chips and butter; stir until smooth. Add to cream cheese mixture; beat well. Spread over brownies.

For glaze, in a heavy saucepan or microwave, melt chips and butter; stir until smooth. Dip each almond halfway into glaze and place on a waxed paper-lined baking sheet. Let stand until chocolate is set. Drizzle remaining glaze over bars. Place almond in the center of each bar. Refrigerate leftovers. **Yield:** 16 bars.

CHOCOLATE WAFFLE COOKIES

I've had this recipe for years. It's economical to make, yet results in a delicious cookie.
—Pat Oviatt, Zimmerman, Minnesota

  1/4 cup butter (no substitutes),
      softened
    6 tablespoons sugar
    1 egg
  1/2 teaspoon vanilla extract
    1 square (1 ounce) unsweetened
      chocolate, melted
  1/2 cup all-purpose flour
Confectioners' sugar

In a mixing bowl, cream butter and sugar; beat in egg and vanilla until light and fluffy. Blend in chocolate. Add flour; mix well. Drop by rounded teaspoonfuls 1 in. apart onto a preheated waffle iron. Bake for 1 minute. Remove to a wire rack to cool. Dust with confectioners' sugar. **Yield:** about 1-1/2 dozen.

BRICKLE COOKIES

The only problem with these cookies is that once you eat one, you want more.
—Robert Moon, Tampa, Florida

1 package (9 ounces) yellow cake mix
1/4 cup vegetable oil
1 egg, lightly beaten
1/2 teaspoon vanilla extract
1/2 cup chopped pecans
1/2 cup almond brickle chips *or* English toffee bits

In a mixing bowl, combine the dry cake mix, vegetable oil, egg and vanilla; mix well. Stir in pecans. Refrigerate for 1 hour or until firm enough to handle.

Roll into 1-in. balls; dip top of each ball into toffee bits and set 2 in. apart on greased baking sheets. Bake at 350° for 10-12 minutes or until golden brown. Cool for 3 minutes before removing to wire racks. **Yield:** about 1-1/2 dozen.

CRANBERRY VANILLA CHIP COOKIES

(Pictured below)

Every time I share these cookies, I'm asked for the recipe. I'm happy to oblige.
—Dana Tschannen, Brighton, Michigan

1/4 cup butter (no substitutes), softened
2/3 cup sugar
1 egg
1/2 teaspoon butter flavoring *or* vanilla extract
3/4 cup plus 2 tablespoons all-purpose flour
1/2 cup quick-cooking oats
1/2 teaspoon baking soda
1/4 teaspoon salt
1/2 cup dried cranberries
1/3 cup vanilla *or* white chips

In a small mixing bowl, cream butter and sugar. Add egg and butter flavoring; mix well. Combine the flour, oats, baking soda and salt. Add to creamed mixture; mix well. Stir in cranberries and chips.

Roll a rounded tablespoonful of dough into a ball. Place 2 in. apart onto lightly greased baking sheets. Bake at 350° for 9-11 minutes or until cookies are set and edges begin to brown. Cool for 2 minutes before removing to wire racks. **Yield:** 2 dozen.

JUST DESSERTS

Whether you want a
traditional dessert or something
a bit out of the ordinary,
you'll find it right here.
Choose from 55 cakes, pies,
tarts, puddings and more, all
of which taste extraordinary.

PUMPKIN STREUSEL CUSTARD
(P. 294)

HOT FUDGE ICE CREAM DESSERT (P. 278)
LUSCIOUS LEMON LAYER CAKE (P. 278)
CRUMB-TOPPED APPLE RASPBERRY TARTS (P. 281)

HOT FUDGE ICE CREAM DESSERT

(Pictured on page 277)

I have to make this dessert for all our family get-togethers because my children like it so much. It's very rich, so start with a small piece.
—Mary Smith, Bradenton, Florida

    1 cup miniature marshmallows
    3/4 cup evaporated milk
    1/2 cup semisweet chocolate chips
    1/4 cup butterscotch chips
    1/4 cup milk chocolate chips
     10 vanilla wafers
      1 quart butter pecan ice cream,
        softened
      9 pecan halves, toasted
      4 maraschino cherries

For fudge sauce, in a saucepan, combine the marshmallows, milk and chips. Cook and stir over low heat until mixture is melted and smooth. Remove from the heat and refrigerate until chilled.

Line the bottom of a 6-in. springform pan with vanilla wafers. Top with about 1 cup ice cream; press into a smooth layer. Top with a third of the fudge sauce. Freeze for 30 minutes or until set.

Repeat layers twice, freezing in between layers. Top with pecans and cherries. Cover and freeze until firm. Remove from freezer 10-15 minutes before serving. **Yield:** 6 servings.

LUSCIOUS LEMON LAYER CAKE

(Pictured on page 277)

This is my mom's variation of an old favorite. It's pleasantly tangy, but not too tart.
—Joan Parks, Boise, Idaho

      1 package (9 ounces) yellow cake
        mix*
FILLING:
      3 tablespoons sugar
      1 tablespoon cornstarch
Dash salt
      3 tablespoons water
    3/4 teaspoon butter *or* margarine,
        softened
    1/4 teaspoon grated lemon peel
      1 drop yellow food coloring, optional
4-1/2 teaspoons lemon juice
FROSTING:
      3 tablespoons butter *or* margarine,
        softened
1-1/2 cups confectioners' sugar
      1 teaspoon lemon juice
      1 teaspoon finely grated lemon peel
      1 to 2 tablespoons milk

Prepare cake mix according to package directions; pour into a greased 9-in. square baking pan. Bake at 350° for 18-20 minutes or until a toothpick inserted near the center comes out clean. Cool for 10 minutes before removing from pan to a wire rack to cool completely.

For filling, combine the sugar, cornstarch and salt in a saucepan. Gradually stir in water until smooth. Bring to a boil; cook and stir for 2 minutes or until thickened. Remove from heat; stir in the butter, lemon peel and food coloring if desired. Gradually stir in lemon juice. Cool completely.

For frosting, in a mixing bowl, beat butter until fluffy. Gradually add confectioners' sugar. Add lemon juice, peel and enough milk to achieve spreading consistency.

To assemble, cut cake in half. Trim outside edges. Place one half on a serving plate. Spread with the lemon filling. Top with remaining cake; spread with frosting. **Yield:** 6 servings.

*Editor's Note: This recipe was tested with Jiffy cake mix.

STRAWBERRY MERINGUE CAKE

(Pictured at right)

This beautiful strawberry cake is the best I've ever tasted. It's hard to believe it starts with a boxed cake mix.
—Mary Ann Higgins, Rushville, Indiana

- 1 **package (9 ounces) yellow cake mix***
- 1/2 **cup orange juice**
- 2 **eggs,** *separated*
- 3/4 **teaspoon grated orange peel**
- 1/8 **teaspoon cream of tartar**
- 1/2 **cup plus 2 tablespoons sugar,** *divided*
- 1 **cup sliced fresh strawberries,** *divided*
- 1 **cup heavy whipping cream**

Line a 9-in. springform pan with parchment paper. Grease paper and sides of pan; set aside. In a mixing bowl, combine the cake mix, orange juice, egg yolks and orange peel; beat for 3 minutes. Pour into prepared pan. In another mixing bowl, beat egg whites and cream of tartar on medium speed until soft peaks form. Gradually beat in 1/2 cup sugar, 1 tablespoon at a time, on high until stiff glossy peaks form and sugar is dissolved. Spread evenly over batter, sealing to edge of pan.

Bake at 350° for 40-45 minutes or until golden brown. Cool on a wire rack for 10 minutes (meringue will crack). Carefully run a knife around edge of pan to loosen.

Remove sides of pan. Cool completely. Cut in half widthwise.

In a small mixing bowl, mash 1/4 cup berries with remaining sugar. Add cream and beat on high until stiff peaks form. Place one cake layer half meringue side up on a serving plate. Spread half the whipped cream mixture over cake. Top with remaining cake and topping. Garnish with remaining berries. Store in the refrigerator. **Yield: 4-6 servings.**

*Editor's Note: This recipe was tested with Jiffy cake mix.

SUMMER'S HERE ICE CREAM

My mother worked up this recipe years ago. Because it's so delicious, we serve it year-round, not just during our hot Phoenix summers.
—Virginia Speaker, Phoenix, Arizona

- 1 **pint vanilla ice cream, softened**
- 1/3 **cup apricot preserves**
- 4-1/2 **teaspoons pink lemonade concentrate**

In a freezer container, combine ice cream, apricot preserves and lemonade concentrate. Cover and freeze. **Yield: about 1 pint.**

FROSTY FREEZE TARTS

(Pictured below)

*You can make these quick tarts with orange, lime or raspberry sherbet,
depending on your preference. All are tasty.*
—Karen Meehan, Roodhouse, Illinois

1/2 cup plus 2 tablespoons crushed
   chocolate wafers (about 9)
2 tablespoons sugar
2 tablespoons butter *or* margarine,
   melted
1 package (3 ounces) cream cheese,
   softened
1/2 cup marshmallow creme
1/2 cup orange sherbet *or* flavor of
   your choice, softened
1 cup whipped topping
Additional whipped topping and crushed
   chocolate wafers, optional

In a bowl, combine the wafer crumbs, sugar and butter. Press onto the bottom and up the sides of two ungreased 4-1/2-in. fluted tart pans with removable bottoms. Bake at 375° for 7-9 minutes or until crust is set. Cool.

In a mixing bowl, beat the cream cheese until smooth. Add marshmallow creme; beat until blended. Fold in sherbet. Fold in whipped topping. Fill tart shells. Cover and freeze. Remove from the freezer 15 minutes before serving. Garnish with additional whipped topping and wafer crumbs if desired. **Yield:** 2 servings.

TWO-BERRY PARFAITS

Sour cream and ice cream complement the raspberries and strawberries in these pretty parfaits.
—Nancy Maguire, Stony Plain, Altanta

1-1/4 cups fresh raspberries, *divided*
1 tablespoon sugar
1-1/2 teaspoons cornstarch
1/2 cup sliced fresh strawberries
1/2 teaspoon lemon juice
1 cup vanilla ice cream
1/4 cup sour cream

Mash 1 cup raspberries and press through a strainer. Reserve enough juice to measure 1/4 cup. Discard seeds and pulp. In a small saucepan, combine sugar and cornstarch; stir in reserved juice until smooth. Add strawberries and cook over low heat until mixture comes to a boil; cook and stir for 1 minute or until thickened. Remove from the heat; stir in remaining raspberries; cool.

In 2 parfait glasses, layer half the ice cream, a fourth of the berry sauce, half the sour cream and a fourth of the berry sauce. Repeat layers. **Yield:** 2 servings.

Nutritional Analysis: One serving (prepared with reduced-fat frozen yogurt and reduced-fat sour cream) equals 222 calories, 5 g fat (3 g saturated fat), 20 mg cholesterol, 91 mg sodium, 40 g carbohydrate, 6 g fiber, 7 g protein. **Diabetic Exchanges:** 2 fruit, 1 fat, 1/2 fat-free milk.

CRUMB-TOPPED
APPLE RASPBERRY TARTS

(Pictured on page 277)

*When I was a girl, my dad raised and sold red and black
raspberries for extra money. When berries were at their peak, the whole family
was out there picking. This pie was our favorite.*
—Margie Portenier, Orleans, Nebraska

> 1 cup fresh *or* frozen unsweetened
>   raspberries, thawed
> 3/4 cup halved thinly sliced peeled tart
>   apple
> 1/4 cup sugar
> 1 tablespoon quick-cooking tapioca
> Dash to 1/8 teaspoon ground cinnamon
> Dash ground nutmeg
> 1 sheet refrigerated pie pastry
> 2 teaspoons butter *or* margarine,
>   melted
> **TOPPING:**
> 1 tablespoon all-purpose flour
> 1-1/2 teaspoons brown sugar
> 1 teaspoon cold butter *or* margarine

In a bowl, combine raspberries and apple. In a small bowl, combine the sugar, tapioca, cinnamon and nutmeg. Sprinkle over apple mixture; gently toss to coat evenly. Let stand for 15 minutes.

Divide pie pastry in half and roll each half into a 7-in. circle. Transfer pastry to two ungreased 4-in. fluted tart pans with removal bottoms. Trim pastry even with edge. Spoon raspberry mixture into pastry shells. Drizzle with melted butter.

For topping, in a bowl, combine flour and brown sugar. Cut in butter until crumbly. Sprinkle over raspberry mixture. Bake at 375° for 35-40 minutes or until bubbly. **Yield:** 2 servings.

TOFFEE CRUNCH ICE CREAM

*I grew up on a farm where we had fresh eggs, milk and cream, so we often made
homemade ice cream. Many years later, I'm back on a small farm where
we have fresh eggs and I'm making ice cream again.*
—Barbara Proctor, Carthage, Missouri

> 1 egg, lightly beaten
> 2/3 cup sugar
> Dash salt
> 1 cup milk
> 3 ounces German sweet chocolate,
>   melted and cooled
> 2/3 cup heavy whipping cream
> 2 tablespoons strong brewed coffee
> 3/4 teaspoon vanilla extract
> 2 Heath candy bars (1.4 ounces *each*),
>   crushed
> 1/3 cup chopped pecans

In a saucepan, combine the egg, sugar and salt. Gradually add milk. Cook and stir over medium heat until mixture reaches 160° and coats the back of a metal spoon. Remove from the heat. Whisk in chocolate, then add the cream, coffee and vanilla. Refrigerate for at least 2 hours.

Fold in candy and nuts. Fill cylinder of ice cream freezer; freeze according to manufacturer's directions. Allow to ripen in ice cream freezer or firm up in the freezer for 2-4 hours before serving. **Yield:** 6 servings (3 cups).

GINGERSNAP BERRY DESSERT

(Pictured at right and on back cover)

This cheesecake-like dessert is loaded with fresh fruit, making it perfect for summer.
—Susan Petty-Bailer, West Hartford, Connecticut

1/2 cup finely crushed gingersnap cookies (about 9 cookies)
1/3 cup finely crushed vanilla wafers (about 8 wafers)
2 tablespoons finely chopped walnuts
2 tablespoons butter *or* margarine, melted

FILLING:
2 packages (3 ounces *each*) cream cheese, softened
1/4 cup sugar
1 teaspoon vanilla extract
1-1/2 cups fresh blueberries, *divided*
3/4 cup sliced fresh strawberries

In a bowl, combine the gingersnap crumbs, wafer crumbs, walnuts and butter. Press onto the bottom and 1-1/2 in. up the sides of a greased 6-in. springform pan. Bake at 375° for 5-7 minutes or until the crust is set. Cool on a wire rack.

In a small mixing bowl, beat cream cheese and sugar until smooth. Add vanilla. Carefully spread about 1/3 cup over crust. Top with half of blueberries. Spread with about 1/3 cup of cream cheese mixture. Top with strawberries. Spread with remaining cream cheese mixture. Arrange remaining blueberries on top. Cover and refrigerate for at least 4 hours. **Yield:** 4 servings.

STRAWBERRY TRUFFLE TARTS

(Pictured at right and on back cover)

In my quest for the perfect dessert a couple of years ago, I found this "berried treasure".
My husband and children love it, and that's saying a lot!
—Bobbi Carney, Aurora, Colorado

1/2 cup plus 2 tablespoons all-purpose flour
1/4 teaspoon salt
2 tablespoons plus 2 teaspoons shortening
2 tablespoons plus 1 to 2 teaspoons cold water
1/4 cup semisweet chocolate chips
1 teaspoon butter *or* margarine
1 package (3 ounces) cream cheese, cubed
1-1/2 teaspoons orange juice
1 tablespoon confectioners' sugar
14 to 16 large strawberries, stems removed
1/4 cup currant jelly, melted
Slivered orange peel, optional

In a bowl, combine flour and salt. Cut in shortening until crumbly. Gradually add cold water, tossing with a fork until a ball forms. Divide dough in half. On a lightly floured surface, roll each portion into a 6-in. circle. Press onto the bottom and up the sides of ungreased 4-in. fluted tart pans with removable bottom. Line unpricked shells with a double thickness of heavy-duty foil. Bake at 450° for 8 minutes. Remove foil; bake 5 minutes longer. Cool on a wire rack.

In a small heavy saucepan, melt chocolate chips and butter over low heat, stirring constantly. Stir in cream cheese and orange juice. Cook and stir until cream cheese is melted and mixture is smooth. Remove from the heat. Stir in confectioners' sugar until blended. Spread over bottoms of baked crust. Arrange berries over chocolate mixture. Brush jelly over berries. Refrigerate for at least 4 hours. Garnish with orange peel if desired. **Yield:** 2 servings.

GINGERSNAP BERRY DESSERT
STRAWBERRY TRUFFLE TARTS

HAZELNUT BUNDT CAKE

*My mother, a wonderful German lady, used to make this cake often, since she knew how much
I loved hazelnuts and chocolate together. Now I make it for my family.*
—Elizabeth Blondefield, San Jose, California

1/2 cup butter *or* margarine, softened
3/4 cup sugar
  2 eggs
1/4 teaspoon almond extract
  1 cup all-purpose flour
1-1/2 teaspoons baking powder
1/2 cup finely ground hazelnuts
1/4 cup miniature semisweet chocolate
    chips

In a mixing bowl, cream butter and sugar. Beat in eggs and extract. Combine flour and baking powder. Stir in nuts and chocolate chips; add to creamed mixture and stir until well mixed.

Pour into a greased 6-cup fluted tube pan. Bake at 350° for 30-35 minutes or until a toothpick inserted near the center comes out clean. Cool for 10 minutes before removing from pan to a wire rack to cool completely. **Yield:** 6-8 servings.

RUBY FRUIT COMPOTE

(Pictured below)

*This easy anytime dessert is beautiful and delicious all by itself, so imagine it
over ice cream or pound cake! It's a dream come true.*
—Gladys Abee, McKee, Kentucky

  1 can (14-1/2 ounces) tart cherries
1/3 cup sugar
  1 tablespoon cornstarch
Pinch salt
  1 teaspoon lemon juice
Liquid red food coloring, optional
  1 cup whole fresh strawberries,
    halved
  2 tablespoons sour cream
1/4 teaspoon confectioners' sugar

Drain cherries, reserving juice in a 2-cup measuring cup. Set cherries aside. Add enough water to the reserved juice to measure 1-1/4 cups. In a small saucepan, combine the sugar, cornstarch and salt. Stir in juice mixture until smooth. Bring to a boil; cook and stir for 2 minutes or until thickened. Remove from the heat; stir in lemon juice. Cool for 10 minutes; stir in food coloring if desired.

Fold in strawberries and reserved cherries. Refrigerate for 2-3 hours. Spoon into individual serving dishes. In a small bowl, combine sour cream and confectioners' sugar. Dollop over fruit. **Yield:** 2-3 servings.

BLUEBERRY BREAD PUDDING

(Pictured at right)

My husband cooks breakfast for a men's Bible study group every Sunday. When he makes this dish, there's never any left.
—Sue Camara, Greensburg, Pennsylvania

   2 slices day-old Italian bread
   1 egg yolk
1/4 cup heavy whipping cream
   3 tablespoons milk
   2 tablespoons sugar
   2 tablespoons butter *or* margarine, melted
3/4 teaspoon vanilla extract
1/8 teaspoon ground nutmeg
Dash ground cinnamon
1/2 cup fresh *or* frozen blueberries
Confectioners' sugar

Cut bread into 1/2-in. cubes; place into a greased 20-oz. baking dish. In a bowl, combine the egg yolk, cream, milk, sugar, butter, vanilla, nutmeg and cinnamon. Stir in blueberries. Pour over bread cubes. Cover and refrigerate for 30 minutes.

Bake, uncovered, at 350° for 30 minutes or until top is golden brown and a knife inserted near the center comes out clean. Sprinkle with confectioners' sugar and serve warm. **Yield:** 2 servings.

SOFT BAKED CUSTARD

The creamy texture of this soft-set custard is so inviting, you could call it comfort food. It has a pleasant vanilla flavor complemented by nutmeg.
—Mary Ann Pearce, Sparks, Nevada

   1 egg
   1 cup milk
   3 tablespoons sugar
3/4 teaspoon vanilla extract
1/8 teaspoon salt
Dash ground nutmeg

In a mixing bowl, beat egg. Add the milk, sugar, vanilla and salt; stir well. Pour into two ungreased 6-oz. custard cups. Sprinkle with nutmeg.

Place cups in a baking pan. Fill pan with hot water to a depth of 1 in. Bake, uncovered, at 350° for 35-40 minutes or until a knife inserted near the center comes out clean. **Yield:** 2 servings.

BROWN SUGAR CAKE

I can remember my mom making this cake more than 30 years ago.
It's still a great dessert for special occasions today.
—Rita Schwass, Kirkwood, Illinois

1/4 cup shortening
1/2 cup packed brown sugar
1/4 cup sugar
1 egg
1 egg yolk
3/4 teaspoon vanilla extract
1 cup all-purpose flour
1-1/2 teaspoons baking powder
1/2 teaspoon salt
1/4 teaspoon baking soda
2/3 cup milk
1/2 cup miniature semisweet chocolate
   chips
CREAMY NUT FILLING:
2 tablespoons brown sugar
1 tablespoon all-purpose flour
1/4 cup milk
1/4 cup chopped walnuts
1 tablespoon butter *or* margarine
1 teaspoon vanilla extract
GLAZE:
1/4 cup miniature semisweet chocolate
   chips
1 tablespoon butter *or* margarine
1-1/2 teaspoons light corn syrup

In a mixing bowl, cream shortening and sugars. Beat in the egg, egg yolk and vanilla. Combine the flour, baking powder, salt and baking soda. Add to creamed mixture alternately with milk. Beat well. Stir in chocolate chips. Pour into a greased and waxed paper-lined 9-in. round baking pan. Bake at 350° for 30-35 minutes or until a toothpick inserted near the center comes out clean. Cool for 5 minutes before removing from the pan to a wire rack to cool completely.

Meanwhile, for filling, combine brown sugar and flour in a small saucepan; stir in milk. Bring to a boil; cook and stir for 3 minutes or until thickened. Remove from the heat; stir in nuts, butter and vanilla; cool completely.

Cut cake widthwise in half. Place one layer on a serving plate. Spread with filling; top with other layer. In a microwave or small saucepan, melt chocolate chips and butter with corn syrup, stirring until smooth. Cool slightly and drizzle over top of cake. **Yield:** 4-6 servings.

MARSHMALLOW FUDGE TOPPING

My sister and I have both served this for family gatherings and we've always received
compliments. Not only is it great over ice cream, it's also tasty with fresh fruit or pound cake.
—Charlotte Jones, Huron, South Dakota

1/4 cup packed brown sugar
2 tablespoons milk
1 tablespoon baking cocoa
1 teaspoon butter *or* margarine
1/4 teaspoon vanilla extract
1/4 cup miniature marshmallows
Ice cream

In a small saucepan, combine the brown sugar, milk and cocoa. Bring to a boil, stirring constantly. Cook and stir for 5 minutes. Remove from the heat; stir in butter and vanilla. Cool for 5 minutes. Stir in marshmallows. Serve warm over ice cream. **Yield:** about 1/3 cup.

CHERRY ENCHILADAS

This easy dessert recipe reminds me of French crepes. It's the perfect meal-ending treat for those Tex-Mex brunches we have so often here.
—Mary Lou Chambers, Houston, Texas

2/3 cup cherry pie filling **or** pie filling of your choice
2 flour tortillas (6 inches)
3 tablespoons sugar
3 tablespoons butter **or** margarine
3 tablespoons water

Spoon pie filling off center on each tortilla; roll up. Place seam side down in a greased 8-in. square baking dish; set aside. In a small saucepan bring the sugar, butter and water to a boil over medium heat; pour over enchiladas. Bake, uncovered, at 350° for 20-25 minutes or until lightly browned. Serve immediately. **Yield:** 2 servings.

CRANBERRY PECAN TARTS

(Pictured below)

This recipe was passed on to me as an alternative to traditional pecan pie. The cranberries inspire me to make this tart at Thanksgiving, but it gets rave reviews all year long.
—Melanie Bredeson, Milwaukee, Wisconsin

1 sheet refrigerated pie pastry
1/4 cup fresh **or** frozen cranberries, thawed
1/4 cup vanilla **or** white chips
1/4 cup pecan halves
1 egg
3 tablespoons packed brown sugar
3 tablespoons light corn syrup
1-1/2 teaspoons all-purpose flour
1/4 teaspoon grated orange peel
Whipped cream, optional

Cut pastry sheet in half and roll each half into a 7-in. circle. Transfer pastry to two ungreased 4-in. fluted tart pans with removable bottoms. Trim pastry even with edge. Layer the cranberries, vanilla chips and pecans in pastry. In a small mixing bowl, beat the egg, brown sugar, corn syrup, flour and peel until smooth; pour over nuts. Place pans on a baking sheet.

Bake at 400° for 15 minutes. Cover with foil; bake 15-20 minutes longer or until crust is golden brown and filling near center is set. Cool on a wire rack. Serve with whipped cream if desired. **Yield:** 2 servings.

PLUM TART

(Pictured at right)

We have a plum tree in our yard, and some years it's so full of fruit that its branches have to be propped up. I always make one or two extra tarts to freeze for later.
—Liz Myers, Plymouth, Wisconsin

1 cup all-purpose flour
1/4 cup sugar
1/4 teaspoon salt
1/4 cup butter-flavored shortening
2 to 3 tablespoons cold water
FILLING:
2 cups sliced fresh plums (about 3 large)
3 tablespoons plus 1/4 teaspoon sugar, *divided*
1 tablespoon all-purpose flour
1 egg white, lightly beaten

In a bowl, combine the flour, sugar and salt; cut in the shortening until crumbly. Gradually add water, tossing with a fork until a ball forms. Cover and refrigerate for at least 1-1/2 hours. On a lightly floured surface, roll pastry into a 9-in. circle. Transfer to a foil-lined 15-in. x 10-in. x 1-in. baking pan.

In a bowl, combine the plums, 3 tablespoons sugar and flour. Place on the center of pastry. Bring edges of pastry over filling, leaving 3-1/2 in. of filling uncovered. Brush crust with egg white, then sprinkle with remaining sugar. Bake at 375° for 40-45 minutes or until bubbly and crust is golden brown. **Yield:** 2-4 servings.

FROZEN LEMON PIE

(Pictured at right and on front cover)

This refreshing dessert is simple to whip up and serve. I've also made it with pink lemonade concentrate using red food coloring and limeade concentrate with green coloring.
—Dai Smith, York, Nebraska

3/4 cup graham cracker crumbs (about 12 squares)
2 tablespoons plus 2 teaspoons butter *or* stick margarine, melted
2 tablespoons sugar
FILLING:
1/3 cup lemonade concentrate
2 drops yellow food coloring, optional
1 cup vanilla ice cream, softened
1-3/4 cups whipped topping
Grated lemon peel, optional

In a bowl, combine the cracker crumbs, butter and sugar; blend well. Press onto the bottom and 1 in. up the sides of a greased 6-in. springform pan. Bake at 375° for 6-8 minutes or until the crust is lightly browned.

Cool crust completely on a wire rack.

For filling, in a mixing bowl, beat lemonade concentrate and food coloring if desired for 30 seconds. Gradually spoon in ice cream and blend. Fold in whipped topping. Spoon into prepared crust. Freeze until solid, about 2 hours. Remove from the freezer 10-15 minutes before serving. Garnish with lemon peel if desired. **Yield:** 6 servings.

Nutritional Analysis: One piece (prepared with reduced-fat graham crackers, reduced-fat margarine, reduced-fat frozen yogurt and reduced-fat whipped topping) equals 190 calories, 6 g fat (3 g saturated fat), 3 mg cholesterol, 122 mg sodium, 32 g carbohydrate, trace fiber, 2 g protein. **Diabetic Exchanges:** 1 starch, 1 fruit, 1 fat.

PLUM TART
FROZEN LEMON PIE

HONEY-MAPLE PECAN TOPPING

It's tough to decide whether this sweet syrup is better over vanilla or chocolate ice cream.
It also can be served with pancakes or waffles.
—Mary McCollum, Haskell, Texas

1/2 cup maple syrup
2 tablespoons honey
1/8 teaspoon ground cinnamon
3 tablespoons chopped pecans
Ice cream

In a bowl, combine the maple syrup, honey and cinnamon. Stir in pecans. Serve over ice cream. **Yield:** about 2/3 cup.

SOUR CREAM WALNUT CAKE

Over the years, with much trial and error, I have developed into a good basic cook.
It's so nice to hear friends say, "If you're cooking, we'll be there."
—Lois Denardo, Camarillo, California

1/4 cup butter *or* margarine, softened
1/2 cup sugar
1 egg, *separated*
1 egg yolk
4-1/2 teaspoons grated lemon peel
1 cup all-purpose flour
1/2 teaspoon baking soda
1/2 teaspoon baking powder
1/8 teaspoon salt
1/2 cup sour cream
1/2 cup semisweet chocolate chips
1/2 cup chopped walnuts
GLAZE:
1/4 cup sugar
1 tablespoon orange juice
1 tablespoon lemon juice

In a mixing bowl, cream the butter and sugar; beat in egg yolks and lemon peel. Combine the flour, baking soda, baking powder and salt; add to creamed mixture alternately with sour cream. Stir in the chocolate chips and walnuts. In another mixing bowl, beat egg white until soft peaks form; fold into the batter.

Pour into a greased 6-cup fluted tube pan. Bake at 350° for 35-40 minutes or until a toothpick inserted near the center comes out clean. Cool for 10 minutes before removing from pan to a wire rack.

In a small saucepan, combine sugar and juices. Bring to a boil. Brush over warm cake. Cool completely. **Yield:** 6-8 servings.

STRAWBERRY BANANA FLUFF

Desserts don't come any easier than this recipe, which is quite good, too.
—Terri Egnater, Oak Park, Michigan

1 small firm banana, diced
1/2 cup sliced fresh strawberries
1/4 cup miniature marshmallows
1/4 cup salted peanuts
1/2 to 3/4 cup whipped topping
2 whole strawberries

In a bowl, combine the banana, sliced strawberries, marshmallows and peanuts. Fold in whipped topping. Place into two small serving dishes. Garnish with strawberries. Serve immediately. **Yield:** 2 servings.

PECAN PIE FOR TWO

(Pictured at right)

Pecan pie was always requested by my family for special occasions. When we became empty nesters, it was hard to give up some of our favorites. Smaller recipes were hard to come by, so I was delighted to find this one.
—Noreen Johnson, Leesburg, Florida

1/3 **cup all-purpose flour**
1/8 **teaspoon salt**
  1 **tablespoon shortening**
  1 **tablespoon cold butter** *or* **margarine**
  1 **teaspoon cold water**
FILLING:
1/4 **cup chopped pecans**
  2 **tablespoons brown sugar**
  1 **tablespoon all-purpose flour**
  1 **egg, beaten**
1/4 **cup corn syrup**
1/4 **teaspoon vanilla extract**

In a bowl, combine flour and salt. Cut in shortening and butter until crumbly. Add water, tossing with a fork until a ball forms. Roll out pastry to fit an 18-oz. baking dish. Press onto the bottom and up the sides of the dish. Combine filling ingredients; mix well. Pour into pastry shell. Bake at 375° for 35-40 minutes or until a knife inserted near the center comes out clean. **Yield:** 2 servings.

BERRY GOOD PIZZA

This cute dessert pizza tastes good anytime, but it's a natural for Memorial Day or the Fourth of July with its red, white and blue ingredients.
—Judy Morgan, Chattanooga, Tennessee

2/3 **cup refrigerated sugar cookie dough**
  2 **ounces cream cheese, softened**
  2 **tablespoons sugar**
1/4 **teaspoon vanilla extract**
1/2 **cup sliced fresh strawberries**
1/2 **cup fresh blueberries**
GLAZE:
2/3 **cup pineapple juice**
4-1/2 **teaspoons sugar**
1-1/2 **teaspoons quick-cooking tapioca**

With lightly floured hands, pat dough into two greased 7-1/2-in. pizza pans. Bake at 350° for 9-11 minutes or until crust is lightly browned. Cool.

In a small mixing bowl, cream the cream cheese, sugar and vanilla. Spread over crust. Refrigerate for 30 minutes. Arrange strawberries and blueberries over cream cheese mixture.

In a small saucepan, combine the pineapple juice, sugar and tapioca; let stand for 5 minutes. Cook and stir over medium heat until mixture comes to a boil and thickens. Cool; pour over top of fruit. Refrigerate for up to 1 hour before serving. **Yield:** 2 servings.

ICE CREAM LOAF

(Pictured at right)

A co-worker shared this recipe with me a few years back.
Anyone who likes ice cream and chocolate can't resist this one.
—Faye Parker, Bedford, Nova Scotia

1/4 cup chocolate wafer crumbs (about 5 wafers)
1 tablespoon butter *or* margarine, melted
1 pint vanilla ice cream, softened
1/4 cup chopped peanuts
1/4 cup semisweet chocolate chips
3 tablespoons evaporated milk
2 tablespoons confectioners' sugar
2 tablespoons butter *or* margarine

Cut a piece of foil into a 12-in. x 3-in. rectangle. Line the bottom of a 5-3/4-in. x 3-in. x 2-in. loaf pan with the foil, so that the foil comes up over the ends of the pan. Combine wafer crumbs and melted butter; press onto bottom of prepared pan. Spoon ice cream over crumbs; smooth with a spatula. Sprinkle with nuts. Freeze until firm.

In a small saucepan, combine the remaining ingredients; bring to a boil over medium heat. Reduce heat to simmer. Cook and stir for 4 minutes or until thickened. Refrigerate mixture until completely cool, stirring occasionally. Spread over ice cream. Cover and freeze until firm. Remove from refrigerator 10-15 minutes before serving. **Yield:** 4 servings.

MERINGUE-TOPPED RASPBERRY DESSERT

(Pictured at right)

This recipe was presented by a local gas company to a women's club in Ann Arbor, Michigan almost 30 years ago. The home economist's name, appropriately enough, was Mrs. Cook!
—Susan Hamilton, Pomona, California

1/2 cup plus 2 tablespoons all-purpose flour, *divided*
3 tablespoons confectioners' sugar
1/4 cup cold butter *or* margarine
2 cups frozen unsweetened raspberries, thawed and patted dry
1/3 cup chopped walnuts
1 egg
1/2 cup sugar
1/2 teaspoon baking powder
1/2 teaspoon vanilla extract
1/4 teaspoon salt
RASPBERRY SAUCE:
1/2 cup frozen sweetened raspberries, thawed
2 teaspoons cornstarch
1/4 cup currant jelly
1/2 cup heavy whipping cream, whipped
Additional chopped walnuts

In a bowl, combine 1/2 cup flour and confectioners' sugar. Cut in butter until crumbly. Press onto the bottom of an ungreased 8-in. square baking dish. Bake at 350° for 12-15 minutes or until edges are light brown. Sprinkle with raspberries and walnuts.

In a mixing bowl, combine egg and sugar. Beat on medium speed for about 1 minute or until lemon-colored. Stir in the baking powder, vanilla, salt and remaining flour. Pour over raspberries. Bake 20-25 minutes longer or until lightly browned. Cool on a wire rack.

For sauce, drain sweetened raspberries, reserving juice. In a small saucepan, combine cornstarch and reserved raspberry juice until smooth. Add jelly. Bring to a boil; cook and stir for 1-2 minutes or until thickened. Remove from the heat; stir in raspberries. Cut dessert into squares. Top with the raspberry sauce, whipped cream and chopped walnuts. **Yield:** 6 servings.

ICE CREAM LOAF
MERINGUE-TOPPED RASPBERRY DESSERT

LEMON CHEESECAKE

*I love cheesecake. This is a wonderful summertime recipe that seems to go well
with whatever main dish my husband happens to grill.*
—Terri Folz, Tarawa Terrace, North Carolina

2/3 cup vanilla wafer crumbs (about 17
   wafers)
1/3 cup slivered almonds
   3 tablespoons sugar
   2 tablespoons butter *or* margarine,
   melted
   2 packages (one 8 ounces, one 3
   ounces) cream cheese, softened
1/3 cup sugar
   3 tablespoons heavy whipping cream
   2 tablespoons lemon juice
   1 to 1-1/4 teaspoons grated lemon
   peel
1/2 teaspoon vanilla extract
   2 eggs, lightly beaten
TOPPING:
   1 cup sliced fresh strawberries
   1 tablespoon sugar

In a blender or food processor, combine the
wafer crumbs, almonds and sugar. Add butter; cover and process until blended. Press
on the bottom and 1-1/2 in. up the sides of
a greased 6-in. springform pan. Bake at
350° for 7-9 minutes, until crust is set and
just starting to brown. Cool on a wire rack.

In a mixing bowl, beat cream cheese until smooth. Gradually beat in sugar. Beat on
high speed for 2 minutes. Stir in the cream,
lemon juice, peel and vanilla. Add eggs;
beat just until blended. Pour into crust.

Bake at 350° for 35-40 minutes or until
center is almost set. Cool for 10 minutes.
Carefully run a knife around edge of pan to
loosen; cool 1 hour longer. (Cheesecake
may dip in center.) Refrigerate overnight.
Remove sides of pan.

For sauce, in a bowl, combine strawberries and sugar. Let stand for 15-30 minutes.
Serve over cheesecake. **Yield:** 4-6 servings.

PUMPKIN STREUSEL CUSTARD

(Pictured on page 276)

*This is a delectable dessert for chilly fall and winter days.
The streusel topping complements the smooth, spicy custard to perfection.*
—Maxine Smith, Owanka, South Dakota

   1 egg
1/4 cup packed brown sugar
1/4 teaspoon vanilla extract
1/4 teaspoon salt
1/4 teaspoon ground cinnamon
1/8 teaspoon *each* ground allspice,
   ginger and nutmeg
2/3 cup canned pumpkin
1/2 cup evaporated milk
TOPPING:
   1 tablespoon brown sugar
   2 teaspoons all-purpose flour
1/4 teaspoon ground cinnamon
   1 teaspoon cold butter *or* margarine
   tablespoons chopped pecans

In a mixing bowl, beat the egg. Add the
brown sugar, vanilla, salt and spices. Stir
in the pumpkin and milk. Pour into two
greased 8- or 10-oz. custard cups. Bake at
325° for 20 minutes.

For topping, combine the brown sugar,
flour and cinnamon in a small bowl. Cut in
the butter until crumbly; stir in pecans.
Sprinkle over custard. Bake 15 minutes
longer or until a knife inserted near the center comes out clean. **Yield:** 2 servings.

BUTTERSCOTCH BREAD PUDDING

This old-fashioned dessert has a nice custard flavor with just the right touch of cinnamon.
—Edie Farm, Farmington, New Mexico

1 cup soft bread cubes (1/2 inch)
1 egg
1 tablespoon butter *or* stick margarine, melted
2/3 cup milk
3 tablespoons brown sugar
1/2 teaspoon ground cinnamon
1/8 teaspoon ground nutmeg
Dash salt, optional
1/4 cup raisins

Place bread cubes in a greased 2-cup baking dish. In a bowl, whisk the egg. Whisk in the butter, milk, sugar, cinnamon, nutmeg and salt if desired. Stir in raisins. Pour over bread cubes.

Bake at 350° for 35-40 minutes or until a knife inserted near the center comes out clean. Serve warm or chilled. **Yield:** 2 servings.

Nutritional Analysis: One serving (prepared with reduced-fat margarine, fat-free milk and without salt) equals 273 calories, 6 g fat (2 g saturated fat), 108 mg cholesterol, 207 mg sodium, 48 g carbohydrate, 1 g fiber, 8 g protein. **Diabetic Exchanges:** 2 starch, 1 fruit, 1 fat.

CHEESE DANISH

(Pictured at right)

When company drops by, I simply double this recipe to accommodate my guests. They love the sweet treat, and so do I. It's delicious and preparation time is minimal.
—Mary Margaret Merritt
Washington Court House, Ohio

1 tube (4 ounces) refrigerated crescent rolls
1 package (3 ounces) cream cheese, softened
1/4 cup sugar
1/4 teaspoon vanilla extract
1 teaspoon butter *or* margarine, melted
Cinnamon-sugar, optional

Unroll crescent roll dough and separate into two rectangles; place on an ungreased baking sheet and press the perforations together. In a small mixing bowl, beat the cream cheese, sugar and vanilla until smooth. Spread over half of each rectangle; fold over opposite half of rectangle and pinch to seal. Brush with butter; sprinkle with cinnamon-sugar if desired. Bake at 350° for 15-20 minutes or until golden brown. **Yield:** 2 servings.

ICE CREAM SANDWICHES

My family loves these as a quick snack. They're so refreshing on a hot summer day.
—Linda Lam, Mt. Sidney, Virginia

1 cup vanilla ice cream, softened
1 tablespoon creamy peanut butter
1/4 teaspoon vanilla extract
4 graham cracker squares

In a bowl, combine the ice cream, peanut butter and vanilla until well mixed. Spread over 2 graham cracker squares. Top with remaining squares. Wrap and freeze until solid, about 1 hour. **Yield:** 2 sandwiches.

Nutritional Analysis: One sandwich (prepared with reduced-fat frozen yogurt, reduced-fat peanut butter and reduced-fat graham crackers) equals 201 calories, 5 g fat (1 g saturated fat), 10 mg cholesterol, 214 mg sodium, 33 g carbohydrate, 1 g fiber, 7 g protein. **Diabetic Exchanges:** 2 starch, 1 fat.

CRANBERRY RICE DESSERT

I make this simple dessert using leftover rice from another meal. I also enjoy it as a snack.
—Georgene Suchomel, Necedah, Wisconsin

1/4 cup dried cranberries
1/4 cup orange juice
2 tablespoons honey
1 tablespoon butter *or* margarine, melted
1/8 teaspoon salt
1/8 teaspoon ground cinnamon
1 cup cooked long grain rice

In a bowl, combine the cranberries, orange juice, honey, butter, salt and cinnamon. Stir in the rice. Transfer to a greased 1-1/2-cup baking dish. Cover and microwave on high for 1-1/2 to 1-3/4 minutes or until heated through. Stir mixture before serving. **Yield:** 2 servings.

Editor's Note: This recipe was tested in an 850-watt microwave.

CHOCOLATE PEANUT BUTTER TREATS

My Aunt Mary developed this recipe when she was a cook at a parochial school that had an abundance of federal surplus peanut butter. It has grown into a family favorite.
—Sandra Cork, Melvin, Michigan

1/2 cup light corn syrup
1/2 cup sugar
3/4 cup peanut butter
1/2 teaspoon vanilla extract
2-1/2 cups crisp rice cereal
1/2 cup miniature marshmallows
1/2 cup peanut butter chips
1/2 cup semisweet chocolate chips

In a small saucepan, combine the corn syrup and sugar. Bring to a boil. Cook and stir for 1 minute. Remove from the heat; stir in peanut butter until melted and blended. Stir in vanilla. Fold in the cereal, marshmallows and chips; stir until blended. Transfer to a greased 8-in. square dish. Cool; cut into squares. **Yield:** 1 dozen.

HOLIDAY MERINGUE DESSERT

(Pictured at right)

This has become our traditional dessert for Christmas dinner and seems appropriate for the season since the meringue shells look like mounds of snow.
—Catherine Morrison, Newport, Pennsylvania

1 egg white
1/8 teaspoon cream of tartar
1/8 teaspoon almond extract
Dash salt
1/3 cup sugar
2 scoops chocolate ice cream
Chocolate sauce
2 tablespoons flaked coconut, toasted
Maraschino cherries

Place egg white in a mixing bowl and let stand at room temperature for 30 minutes. Beat the egg white, cream of tartar, extract and salt on medium speed until soft peaks form. Gradually add sugar, 1 tablespoon at a time, beating on high until very stiff peaks form.

Line a baking sheet with foil or parchment paper. Spoon the egg mixture into two mounds on prepared baking sheet. Using the back of a spoon, build up the edges slightly. Bake at 300° for 35 minutes. Turn oven off; let shells dry in the oven for at least 1 hour with the door closed. To serve, fill shells with ice cream; top with chocolate sauce, coconut and cherries. **Yield:** 2 servings.

GLAZED PEACHES

I acquired this recipe in Alabama, where there are plenty of fresh, juicy peaches to give it fabulous flavor.
—Nancy Koster, Albuquerque, New Mexico

1 tablespoon brown sugar
1 teaspoon butter *or* margarine
3/4 teaspoon water
1/4 teaspoon lemon juice
Dash ground nutmeg
1/2 cup sliced peeled fresh peaches
1/4 teaspoon vanilla extract
Vanilla ice cream *or* pound cake

In a microwave-safe small bowl, combine the brown sugar, butter, water, lemon juice and nutmeg. Microwave, uncovered, on high for 20 seconds; stir. Add the peaches. Microwave 40-50 seconds longer or until the peaches are heated through. Stir in vanilla. Serve over ice cream or cake. **Yield:** 1-2 servings.

Editor's Note: This recipe was tested in an 850-watt microwave.

ORANGE BUNDT CAKE

(Pictured at right)

This recipe was given to me by my mother-in-law, who got it from her mother-in-law.
Although Grandma Tucker has been gone for years now,
her wonderful cake brings back sweet memories.
—Melissa Tucker, Ozark, Arkansas

1/2 cup butter *or* margarine, softened
1 cup sugar
2 eggs
1-1/2 teaspoons grated orange peel
1/2 teaspoon lemon extract
1/2 teaspoon vanilla extract
1/4 teaspoon almond extract
1-1/2 cups all-purpose flour
1-1/2 teaspoons baking powder
1/2 cup milk
GLAZE:
1 cup confectioners' sugar
4 teaspoons orange juice

In a mixing bowl, cream butter and sugar until fluffy; beat in the eggs, orange peel and extracts. Combine flour and baking powder; add to creamed mixture alternately with milk.

Pour into a greased and floured 6-cup fluted tube pan. Bake at 350° for 40-45 minutes or until a toothpick inserted near the center comes out clean. Cool for 10 minutes before removing from pan to a wire rack to cool. For glaze, combine the confectioners' sugar and juice until smooth. Spoon over cake. **Yield:** 6-8 servings.

CARROT CAKE

(Pictured at right)

This simple cake, which is my mother's recipe, stays moist for quite a while.
It was always my favorite at harvesttime when I was a child.
—Muriel Jones, Hythe, Alberta

1 cup all-purpose flour
1/2 cup sugar
1/2 cup packed brown sugar
1 teaspoon baking soda
1 teaspoon ground allspice
1/4 teaspoon salt
1/2 cup vegetable oil
2 eggs
1-1/2 cups finely grated carrots
FROSTING:
2 tablespoons butter *or* margarine, softened
2 ounces cream cheese, softened
1 cup confectioners' sugar
1/2 teaspoon vanilla extract
2 to 4 teaspoons milk
2 tablespoons chopped walnuts, optional

In a mixing bowl, combine the flour, sugars, baking soda, allspice and salt. Add vegetable oil; mix well. (Batter will be stiff.) Add eggs, one at a time, beating well after each addition. Stir in carrots.

Pour into a greased 8-in. square baking dish. Bake at 350° for 35-40 minutes or until a toothpick inserted near the center comes out clean. Cool on a wire rack.

For frosting, in a small mixing bowl, cream butter and cream cheese. Gradually beat in confectioners' sugar and vanilla. Add enough milk to achieve spreading consistency. Spread over cake. Sprinkle with chopped walnuts if desired. Store, covered, in the refrigerator. **Yield:** 6-8 servings.

ORANGE BUNDT CAKE
CARROT CAKE

MAPLE-NUT BAKED APPLES

Now that our children have all married, baked apples are a perfect dessert for the two of us.
—Theresa Stewart, New Oxford, Pennsylvania

2 medium tart apples
2 tablespoons chopped walnuts
2 tablespoons raisins
1/8 teaspoon ground cinnamon
1/4 cup maple syrup, *divided*
2 teaspoons butter *or* margarine

Core apples and peel the top two-thirds. Place in a 1-qt. microwave-safe dish. Combine the walnuts, raisins and cinnamon; press into the center of each apple. Drizzle each with 1 teaspoon maple syrup. Cover and microwave on high for 4-6 minutes or until tender, rotating a half turn twice. In a small microwave-safe dish, combine the butter and remaining syrup. Heat, uncovered, on high for 20-30 seconds or until butter is melted. Pour over apples; serve immediately. **Yield:** 2 servings.

Editor's Note: This recipe was tested in an 850-watt microwave. The apples may also be baked in a conventional oven in a greased 1-1/2-qt. baking dish. Bake, uncovered, at 350° for 30-35 minutes or until tender.

APRICOT CRISP

I like easy desserts that taste like some effort went into them, like this one.
Apricots are a nice change of pace from apples.
—Shirley Heston, Lancaster, Ohio

1 can (8-3/4 ounces) apricot halves, drained
3 tablespoons brown sugar
2 tablespoons all-purpose flour
2 tablespoons quick-cooking oats
1/4 teaspoon ground cinnamon
1/8 teaspoon ground nutmeg
4 teaspoons cold butter *or* margarine
Vanilla ice cream, optional

Arrange apricot halves in a greased 5-in. round baking dish. In a bowl, combine the brown sugar, flour, oats, cinnamon and nutmeg. Cut in butter until mixture is crumbly; sprinkle over top. Bake, uncovered, at 375° for 20 minutes until golden brown. Serve warm with vanilla ice cream if desired. **Yield:** 2 servings.

RASPBERRY-ORANGE PIE

When my six children were little, we had a large raspberry patch.
This recipe was on my "must make" list every summer. It's light and refreshing.
—Sylvia Kunst, Stevens Point, Wisconsin

5 large marshmallows
4-1/2 teaspoons orange juice
1/2 cup whipped topping
1/3 cup fresh raspberries
2 graham cracker tart shells

Place marshmallows and orange juice in a microwave-safe measuring cup. Microwave, uncovered, on high until marshmallows are melted. Cool until thickened, about 10-15 minutes. Place whipped topping in a small bowl; fold in the cooled marshmallow mixture. Gently stir in raspberries. Spoon into tart shells. Refrigerate for 2-3 hours. **Yield:** 2 servings.

Editor's Note: This recipe was tested in an 850-watt microwave.

SWEETHEART DESSERT

(Pictured at right)

Our Test Kitchen home economists dreamed up this luscious heart-shaped dessert that will show your honey how much you care right from the start. Any extra raspberry sauce will taste great on pancakes or waffles the next day.

1 egg white
1/8 teaspoon cream of tartar
1/8 teaspoon salt
1/4 cup sugar
1/8 teaspoon vanilla extract
1 package (10 ounces) frozen raspberries in syrup, thawed
1-1/2 teaspoons cornstarch
1 tablespoon orange juice
1/4 teaspoon almond extract
2 to 3 scoops chocolate ice cream
Fresh raspberries and mint, optional

Place the egg white in a mixing bowl and let stand at room temperature for 30 minutes. Beat the egg white, cream of tartar and salt on medium speed until soft peaks form. Gradually add sugar, 1 tablespoon at a time, beating on high for 3-4 minutes or until very stiff peaks form. Fold in vanilla.

Line a baking pan with foil or parchment paper. Spoon meringue into a mound on prepared pan. Using the back of a spoon, form into a 5-in. heart shape, building up the edges slightly. Bake at 250° for 65 minutes. Turn oven off; open oven door a few inches. Let shell dry in oven for 20 minutes before removing. Cool completely.

In a saucepan, heat raspberries over medium heat. Combine the cornstarch, orange juice and almond extract until smooth; stir into raspberries. Bring to a boil; cook and stir for 2 minutes or until thickened. Remove from the heat; refrigerate until chill.

To serve, place meringue heart on a serving platter. Spoon ice cream into middle; top with raspberry sauce. Garnish with berries and mint if desired. **Yield:** 2 servings (3/4 cup sauce).

BANANA RICE PUDDING

This is an old recipe my mother used. Its "snowy" look makes this a perfect dessert for the winter months.
—Ruth Ann Stelfox, Raymond, Alberta

1 cup hot cooked rice
1/3 cup sugar
1/3 cup heavy whipping cream, whipped
1 large firm banana, sliced
Fresh mint, optional

In a bowl, combine rice and sugar; mix well. Cool completely. Fold in whipped cream and banana. Cover and refrigerate until serving. Spoon into serving dishes; garnish with mint if desired. **Yield:** 2 servings.

CHOCOLATE SNACK CAKE

This moist, delicious cake is so good that icing isn't necessary.
Sometimes, though, my husband puts a scoop of vanilla ice cream
on top with a drizzle of chocolate syrup.
—Debi Peschka, Broken Arrow, Oklahoma

1 cup boiling water
1/4 cup butter *or* margarine
1 egg
1 teaspoon vanilla extract
1 cup all-purpose flour
1 cup sugar
3 tablespoons baking cocoa
1 teaspoon baking powder
1/2 teaspoon baking soda
1/4 teaspoon salt
Confectioners' sugar

In a mixing bowl, beat water and butter until butter is melted. Beat in egg and vanilla. Combine the flour, sugar, cocoa, baking powder, baking soda and salt; add to the egg mixture. Beat for 2 minutes.

Pour into a greased 8-in. square baking dish. Bake at 350° for 25-30 minutes or until a toothpick inserted near the center comes out clean. Cool on a wire rack. Dust with confectioners' sugar. **Yield:** 9 servings.

Editor's Note: Pieces of cake can be wrapped individually and frozen for a quick dessert later.

APPLE BUTTERSCOTCH CRUMB PIE

This cute little pie has a nice butterscotch flavor without being too sweet.
It's a satisfying meal-ender for any season.
—Kathryn Sievers, Bertram, Texas

1/2 cup all-purpose flour
1/8 teaspoon salt
3 tablespoons shortening
4 teaspoons cold water
FILLING:
1 cup sliced peeled tart apples
1/2 teaspoon lemon juice
2 tablespoons all-purpose flour
2 tablespoons sugar
1/4 teaspoon ground cinnamon
1/8 teaspoon salt
TOPPING:
1/2 cup butterscotch chips
1 tablespoon butter *or* margarine
2 tablespoons all-purpose flour

In a bowl, combine the flour and salt; cut in shortening until crumbly. Gradually add water, tossing with a fork until dough forms a ball. Cover and refrigerate for at least 30 minutes. Shape into two balls; roll into two 6-in. circles. Transfer to two 4-1/2-in. pie plates. Trim pastry 1/2 in. beyond edge; flute edges. Set aside.

Place apples in a bowl; sprinkle with the lemon juice, flour, sugar, cinnamon and salt. Toss to combine. Spoon into pastry shell. Bake at 375° for 15 minutes. Remove from the oven.

For topping, melt butterscotch chips and butter in a small saucepan over low heat, stirring constantly. Remove from the heat; stir in flour with a fork until crumbly. Sprinkle over top of apple mixture. Bake 15-20 minutes longer or until apples are tender. **Yield:** 2 servings.

APPLE CRISP FOR TWO

*I like to make this dessert in fall, when the apple crop is fresh and delicious.
I often bake it while we are having dinner so it can be served warm.*
—Emma Crowder, Anaheim, California

2 medium tart apples, peeled and sliced
3 tablespoons water
3 tablespoons graham cracker crumbs
3 tablespoons sugar
1/4 teaspoon ground cinnamon
2 tablespoons cold butter *or* margarine
Whipped topping and additional cinnamon, optional

Place apples in a greased 1-qt. baking dish; pour water over apples. In a bowl, combine the graham cracker crumbs, sugar and cinnamon. Cut in butter until crumbly. Sprinkle over apples. Bake, uncovered, at 350° for 25-30 minutes or until apples are tender. Garnish with whipped topping and cinnamon if desired. **Yield:** 2 servings.

CREAMY CHOCOLATE PUDDING

(Pictured at right)

Here's a recipe that satisfies a sweet tooth without any fuss. This wonderful pudding can be served plain or topped with coconut, nuts or whipped cream for a more elaborate finish.
—Nora Reidy, Montoursville, Pennsylvania

6 tablespoons sugar
1/4 cup baking cocoa
2 tablespoons cornstarch
1-1/2 cups milk
1/2 teaspoon vanilla extract
Whipped topping, optional

In a saucepan, combine the sugar, cocoa and cornstarch. Gradually stir in the milk until smooth. Bring to a boil over low heat, stirring constantly. Cook and stir for 2 minutes or until thickened. Remove from the heat; stir in vanilla. Pour into two serving dishes. Cover and refrigerate until chilled. Garnish with whipped topping if desired. **Yield:** 2 servings.

SWEET CHERRY PIE

After my husband and I had finished picking some wonderful sweet cherries,
he suggested I make a pie. It turned out great. Canned cherries work well, too.
—Juanita Thompson, Grand Rapids, Michigan

1-1/4 cups all-purpose flour
  1/2 teaspoon salt
  1/3 cup shortening
    4 to 5 tablespoons cold water
  1/4 cup sugar
    2 tablespoons cornstarch
    1 can (15 ounces) pitted dark sweet
      cherries
1-1/2 teaspoons lemon juice
Dash almond extract
    1 tablespoon butter *or* margarine

In a bowl, combine flour and salt; cut in shortening until crumbly. Gradually add water, tossing with a fork until a ball forms. Divide dough in half so that one ball is slightly larger than the other. Roll out larger ball to fit a 6-in. pie plate. Transfer pastry to pie plate. Trim pastry even with edge.

For filling, combine sugar with cornstarch in a microwave-safe bowl. Drain cherries and reserve 2 tablespoons juice. Stir in cherries, reserved juice, lemon juice and almond extract. Microwave on high for 2-3 minutes until mixture comes to a boil and is thickened, stirring occasionally. Pour into crust. Dot with butter.

Roll out remaining pastry to fit top of pie. Place over filling. Flute edges. Cut slits in pastry. Bake at 400° for 15 minutes. Reduce heat to 350° and bake 25-30 minutes longer or until golden brown. Cool on a wire rack. **Yield:** 4 servings.

COFFEE MALLOW DESSERT

This is one of my favorite summertime desserts because it's cool,
creamy and soothing on a hot, humid day.
—Helen Davis, Waterbury, Vermont

    8 cream-filled chocolate cookies,
      crushed
    2 tablespoons butter *or* margarine,
      melted
  1/2 cup hot brewed coffee
  16 large marshmallows
  1/2 cup heavy whipping cream
    1 tablespoon confectioners' sugar
  1/2 teaspoon vanilla extract

Combine cookie crumbs and butter; set aside 1 tablespoon for topping. Press remaining crumb mixture onto the bottom and up the sides of two lightly greased 10-oz. custard cups; set aside. Place coffee and eight marshmallows in a blender; cover and process until smooth. Add the remaining marshmallows; cover and process until smooth. Cover and refrigerate in the blender for 2 hours or until cold.

Process again until smooth; transfer to a bowl. In a chilled mixing bowl, beat whipping cream until soft peaks form. Gradually add sugar and vanilla, beating until stiff peaks form. Gently fold into coffee mixture. Spoon into prepared cups; sprinkle with reserved crumbs. Refrigerate for at least 1-2 hours before serving. **Yield:** 2 servings.

OLD-FASHIONED RICE PUDDING

(Pictured at right)

I was fortunate to grow up around fabulous cooks. My mother and grandmother taught me to experiment with recipes, and we tried a lot of variations on this one. When I make this, it brings fond memories to mind.
—Laura German
North Brookfield, Massachusetts

1 cup cooked long grain rice
1 cup milk
5 teaspoons sugar
Dash salt, optional
1/2 teaspoon vanilla extract
Whipped cream, optional

In a saucepan, combine the rice, milk, sugar and salt. Cook, uncovered, over medium heat for 20 minutes or until thickened, stirring often. Remove from the heat; stir in vanilla. Spoon into serving dishes. Serve warm; top with whipped cream if desired. **Yield:** 2 servings.

Nutritional Analysis: One serving (prepared with fat-free milk and calculated without salt or whipped cream) equals 189 calories, trace fat (trace saturated fat), 3 mg cholesterol, 66 mg sodium, 39 g carbohydrate, trace fiber, 7 g protein. **Diabetic Exchanges:** 2 starch, 1/2 fat-free milk.

PEACH DELIGHT

This peaches-and cream-dessert is always refreshing. When peaches aren't in season, I use frozen fruit with great results.
—Laura Pond, Chicago, Illinois

1-3/4 cups sliced peeled fresh *or* frozen peaches, thawed
5 teaspoons sugar, *divided*
1 teaspoon lemon juice
1/2 cup heavy whipping cream, whipped
1/4 to 1/2 teaspoon vanilla extract
2 individual round sponge cakes

In a small bowl, combine the peaches, 3 teaspoons sugar and lemon juice; set aside. Combine whipped cream, vanilla and remaining sugar; fold gently. Cut sponge cakes into small pieces; place in a bowl. Fold in peach mixture and whipped cream. Serve immediately. **Yield:** 2 servings.

PEAR CRUMBLE

*This recipe was originally a pear crumble pie. I shortened it to a crumble when
I was too tight on time to make a pie crust. I've found canned pears
work as well as fresh, making it even easier to prepare.*
—Kezia Sullivan, Sackets Harbor, New York

3 medium pears, peeled, cored and
   sliced
2 teaspoons lemon juice
3 tablespoons sugar
3 tablespoons old-fashioned oats
2 tablespoons all-purpose flour
1/8 teaspoon ground cinnamon
1/8 teaspoon ground ginger
Dash ground nutmeg
1 tablespoon cold butter *or*
   margarine
2 tablespoons chopped nuts

Place pear slices in a greased 1-qt. baking dish. Sprinkle with lemon juice. In a bowl, combine the sugar, oats, flour, cinnamon, ginger and nutmeg. Cut in butter until crumbly; add nuts. Sprinkle over pears. Bake at 350° for 25-30 minutes or until bubbly. **Yield:** 2 servings.

RASPBERRY-FILLED CAKE

*I dug through two boxes of old recipes that had belonged to my husband's grandmother,
looking for golden oldies. This gem is one of them.*
—Teresa Weidemann, Dows, Iowa

1/4 cup butter *or* margarine, softened
1/2 cup sugar
1 egg
1/2 teaspoon vanilla extract
1 cup cake flour
1-1/2 teaspoons baking powder
1/4 teaspoon salt
1/3 cup milk
FILLING:
2 cups fresh raspberries, *divided*
1 tablespoon sugar
2-1/2 teaspoons cornstarch
1 teaspoon lemon juice
1/8 teaspoon vanilla extract
1/4 cup sour cream
1 cup whipped topping
Additional raspberries, optional

In a mixing bowl, cream butter and sugar until fluffy. Beat in egg and vanilla. Combine the flour, baking powder and salt; add to creamed mixture alternately with milk. Pour into a greased and floured 9-in. round baking pan. Bake at 350° for 20-25 minutes or until a toothpick inserted near the center comes out clean. Cool for 5 minutes before removing from the pan to a wire rack to cool completely.

Meanwhile, for filling, heat 1 cup raspberries in microwave for 30 seconds, then mash and measure 1/4 cup juice. Discard seeds. In a small saucepan, combine sugar and cornstarch; gradually add raspberry juice. Bring to a boil; cook and stir for 1 minute or until thickened. Remove from the heat. Stir in lemon juice and vanilla; cool. In a bowl, combine sour cream and whipped topping. Fold in cooled raspberry mixture and remaining berries. Cut cake widthwise in half. Place one layer on a serving plate. Spread with half of the filling. Top with remaining layer and filling. Garnish with additional berries if desired. Store in the refrigerator. **Yield:** 6 servings.

DEEP-DISH BLACKBERRY PIE

I think back to 1942 when I make this dessert. We grew extra large blackberries that year, and Mother canned 400 quarts. She made the best cobbler and jam.
—Dorothy Lilliquist, Brooklyn Center, Minnesota

3 cups fresh *or* frozen blackberries, thawed and drained
1/2 cup sugar
2 tablespoons cornstarch
1 teaspoon lemon juice
1/4 teaspoon ground cinnamon
TOPPING:
3/4 cup all-purpose flour
3 teaspoons sugar, *divided*
1/4 teaspoon salt
3 tablespoons cold butter *or* margarine
1 tablespoon shortening
3 tablespoons cold water
1 egg white, beaten

Place blackberries in a bowl. Combine sugar and cornstarch; sprinkle over berries. Add lemon juice and cinnamon; toss to coat. Spoon into a greased 1-qt. baking dish.

In a bowl, combine the flour, 1 teaspoon sugar and salt. Cut in butter and shortening until mixture resembles coarse crumbs. Add water, tossing with a fork until a ball forms. Roll out pastry; make a lattice crust over filling. Crimp edges. Brush with egg white; sprinkle with remaining sugar. Bake at 375° for 40-45 minutes or until crust is golden brown and filling is bubbly. **Yield:** 2 servings.

Editor's Note: Instead of a lattice crust, pastry can be rolled out to fit top of dish. Cut slits in pastry; place over berries. Trim, seal and flute edges.

PEANUT BUTTER PARFAITS

(Pictured at right)

My husband and I love this dessert. It also makes an elegant finish to a meal when company comes.
—Mildred Sherrer, Bay City, Texas

1/2 cup packed light brown sugar
3 tablespoons milk
2 tablespoons light corn syrup
2 teaspoons butter *or* margarine
2 tablespoons creamy peanut butter
Vanilla ice cream
1/4 cup peanuts

In a saucepan, combine the brown sugar, milk, corn syrup and butter. Cook and stir over medium heat until sugar is dissolved and mixture is smooth, about 4 minutes. Remove from the heat; stir in peanut butter until smooth. Cool to room temperature. Spoon half into two parfait glasses; top with ice cream. Repeat layers. Sprinkle with peanuts. **Yield:** 2 servings.

＊ GENERAL INDEX ＊

This handy index lists every recipe by category, major ingredient and/or cooking method, so you can easily locate recipes to suit your needs.

Refer to this index for a complete alphabetical listing of all the recipes in this book.